A WALK ACROSS
DIRTY WATER
AND STRAIGHT INTO
MURDERER'S
ROW

A MEMOIR BY EUGENE S. ROBINSON

ISBN: 9781627311427

Feral House
1240 W Sims Way #124
Port Townsend WA 98368

www.feralhouse.com
info@feralhouse.com

designed by designSimple

feralhouse.com

Dedication

This book is dedicated to Ermine Kennedy.
The North Star toward which all of my efforts point.

Acknowledgments

I'd like to acknowledge Adam Parfrey, rest in power, whose tireless efforts to get me to write this wore me down, and to Christina Ward who closed the deal by telling me "no one wants to hear about your sex life." Also, the running list of those whose favorable opinions I aspire to own: Grace, Ruby, Lola, Kora and Kasia Robinson.

And because I'm a lunatic: BJJ4LIFE!

Foreword

Lydia Lunch

"WHAT'S LIFE SUPPOSED TO BE ANYWAY? An endurance contest?"
— Valerie Solanas from the play *Up Your Ass*.

There's a lot to fucking hate. Trust me. I know. Look at it this way—an unsuspecting ovum, buried deep within a velvety hidey-hole, is infiltrated by an invisible enemy, one of possibly 40–600 million snakelike invaders swimming inside the vaginal cavity.

The most aggressive marauder worms its filthy head deep enough inside this mysterious labyrinth to crack open the shell of an unsuspecting egg, usually in a vulgar act of misplaced animal passion, thereby stabbing to life a creature that most likely would prefer not to be battered into—yet again—another existence.

Who will forever be condemned out of the bliss of oblivion, after being ripped from a free-floating nine-month-long psychedelic gestation vacation deep within a blessedly onanistic universe. The brutality of this forced expulsion is accompanied by the murderous screams of a flesh-and-blood baby maker who has baptized the little need machine in piss and shit. And to add insult to injury—a hearty slap in the face serves as a merciless message foreshadowing the possible hell of the endless decades of barbarity yet to come. As I've already stated, there's a lot to fucking hate.

"There is so much anger buried deep inside me that if I dump them out onto the world, there won't be any world left. So I chose to turn that anger into strength instead of weakness—I turned that anger into an instrument of creation rather than a weapon of destruction."
— Abhijit Naskar, Mücadele Muhabbet: *Gospel of An Unarmed Soldier*

Even as a sassy and scrappy pre-adolescent scallywag, our hero was smart enough to realize he had to beef up to toughen up because the playground of young boys is a battlefield where any sign of the slightest vulnerability will be beaten out of you—so buck up before you get fucked up, which doesn't mean he didn't face his fair share of ass whuppings before he was big enough to begin to fight back using both fists and words.

After all, the story starts in Brooklyn early 1970s to mid-'80s and if you weren't there, pre-Disneyfication, well, sorry you missed a shitty city that went bankrupt from corporate and political corruption and was told—in not so many words—to DROP DEAD by then-president goofy Gerry Ford.

New York City bore the brunt of having the Bronx and the Lower East Side purposely burned down due to a lack of city services, much to the joy of banks and real estate agents, who with their eye on the prize wanted to be rid of the rent-controlled apartments and the art/scum/immigrant/queer/weirdos who blessed "Beirut on the Hudson" (as I long ago christened it . . .) with a pornucopia of endless possibilities. IF you weren't knifed, shot, bludgeoned, robbed, didn't OD, meet The Son of Sam while making out in a beat-to-shit Chevy Impala, get pushed onto the subway tracks, catch an incurable disease or bleed to death on the sidewalk after being tripped by some jocks from Queens who wanted to engage in the homo-erotic sport of male-to-male battery on the weekend.

There was a lot to fucking hate. There still is. And hate inflames the justifiable rage that burns bright into many an endless night where those of us cursed with the knowledge of generational trauma turn instrumental violence into an art form and bless others with our generosity. And to that end I give you Eugene Robinson.

Harley Flanagan

I HAVE KNOWN EUGENE ROBINSON since the late '70s. I first met him in NYC, which was for the most part a cesspool of drugs, crime, and burnt-out buildings back then—at least my neighborhood was. I was living on the Lower East Side of Manhattan known as ABC Land or Alphabet City. The city was very divided back then, it wasn't gentrified like it is now. You had the very few rich and wealthy who pretty much lived uptown and in nice areas; and then you had the rest of us, who were all living ghetto life to some varying degree, all divided by invisible borders both ethnically and by whatever criminal organizations controlled which areas and streets within the neighborhood. The worse the neighborhood the worse it got. Son of Sam, the blackout etc., were all still fresh in our memories—you could still feel it. It was a filthy place, a city basically run-on crime, corruption and Mafia payoffs. And it all just seemed normal. Prostitution, drugs, crime, and in the middle of it all you had Times Square, which was the welcome mat for all the runaways, thrill-seekers, and fuck-ups who would come from out of town at either Penn Station or Port Authority with all its madness, coming off the buses and trains like fodder waiting to be eaten by the hungry ugly ruthless filthy city. It was a place of complete and total sensory overload. And then you also had the club and music scenes in all the different neighborhoods, along with the art world.

People in other boroughs like Brooklyn, Queens, and even out to Long Island, still called Manhattan "The City." Disco hadn't turned into rap or hip-hop yet, break dancing didn't exist yet, punk rock and new wave were still new things. Punk hadn't turned into "hardcore" yet. There were tons of late-night dance clubs as well as the little punk rock shitholes, never mind all the other madness that was going on. Just thinking back on it makes my head spin.

My first memory of Eugene was at shows at Max's and then at CBGBs, where, in a world of mostly scrawny white hardcore punks, he stood out: Black with a mohawk and in shape, which was not a common thing in a sea of drugged-out punk rock kids. It was a dangerous world we came from. NYC back then was a grimy and violent place, and if you were a punk rocker you were a walking target for the gangs, the cops, and any neighborhood tough guys. So we experienced all sides of the violence, some things best forgotten. He wound up on the West Coast in the early '80s fronting a hardcore band called Whipping Boy, who I saw put on some great shows. And he has never stopped since. Like a machine pushing forward, performing, touring, writing, and being a true freak of nature. He's one of the only people I have known that long that I am still friends with. I could literally count them on one hand. I liked and respected him then, and do now. He is a charming guy and can be very intimidating under the wrong circumstances. Smarter and tougher than most people I have known. An artist, a writer, a Jiu-Jitsu black belt, a father, and a creative force that don't stop. His experiences are unique to say the least, which gives him an edge that cuts deep, deeper than a 007 (the knife of choice for street thugs in the '70s/'80s NYC that was our stomping ground). He is the kind of guy I would want on my side in any conflict, whether verbal or physical. He looks like he could bench-press a truck, but don't write him off as some dumb musclehead. He's an intelligent badass, which can be a real problem. As well as I know him, there are a lot of things detailed in this book I didn't know and I can only imagine will shock, awe, and entertain you. I will take truth over fiction any day. It is way more intense. Eugene is currently the singer for both OXBOW and the Italian supergroup Buñuel, his work appears in *The New York Times*, the *Los Angeles Times*, *GQ*, *Vice*, *MacLife*, *PC Gamer*, the *LA Weekly* and more. A Stanford grad, HarperCollins published his book *FIGHT* which I thoroughly enjoyed. Love you my brother, keep kicking ass! We don't know the future, all we have for sure is now, so own this muthafuka!!! I look forward to the next time we meet, and always do...

These days you can find Eugene on the mats training Jiu-Jitsu, in the gym, on the stage, behind the scenes, or all of the above. And who knows what the fuck else because he is always full of surprises. And if you can't find him, look out, he might be right behind you!

jimi izreal

Leaving a new baby—me—donning a *Black Tail* magazine T-shirt and driving two hours round-trip to meet a random guy was unusual but felt absolutely necessary. He was editor of a new magazine that was all the rage and—inspired—I'd reached out, and he reached back. To thank him and as a show of support, I was going to meet The Man—as he referred to himself on his voicemail message—face to face at the nearest stop to Cleveland his band would make.

In Sandusky, Ohio—known as home to America's oldest roller coasters, a throughway on the Underground Railroad, and the site of the brutal public dragging and lynching of William Taylor—two feet of dreads, aforementioned swag unironically celebrating classic Afro-American pornography—I am the Blackest person in the room, for miles, for about an hour, until Eugene S. Robinson takes the stage. All smiles, hugs, and hail-to-thee backstage, at the microphone, ears taped, bare teeth, and inexplicably pantsless in a pair of faded black draws, he means business, and—judging from the room full of young, white Clampetts, largely focused on his crotch and whatever else Eugene might be selling—business is good. Angry, sensual, hypnotizing, and disturbing: I'd seen hardcore, but this was OXBOW. This performance was a violation, but today, over 20 years later, the violator and the victim are still indiscernible to me. Franz Fanon, the French psychoanalyst who examined the gentle waltz of dysfunction between black people and the white world—what would he say? I asked Eugene. He smiles. "Right?" he said with a chuckle. Often, Eugene's prose is equally as confounding.

Virtually unknown to The Negro World, file Eugene's work, in general, somewhere between Sun Ra for White People and the collected works of Carl Hancock Rux. "Well-spoken," shiny, and articulate, he's art rock's best black friend. Fanon would say Eugene is free-thinking, free-writing, and free-range—unrelentingly talented: stand-up and principled, ready to die but not without a fight. Clearly, one of the Blackest people in the room and, as such, perhaps one of the most dangerous people alive. "Dirty Water," joins a canon of works like Ellison's "Invisible Man," Baldwin's "Another Country" and Rux's "Pagan Operetta" as an earnest dispatch from the front: the DuBoisian Doo-Wop origin story of every Black Man I know.

11

NO ONE WHO EVER GETS a life sentence for just about anything really expects it to last a lifetime. Even if the modifier is "without the possibility of parole." Hope springs eternal but there's always the undiscussed other option. The one where fate is chosen, freely, and the protagonist has about as much interest in escaping as he does of being almost anywhere else at all. Which is to say: not at all. We're here for the long haul. No matter how short it is.

"*They were given the choice between becoming kings or the couriers of kings. In the manner of children, they all wanted to be couriers. As a result, there are only couriers. They gallop through the world shouting to each other messages that, since there are no kings, have become meaningless. Gladly would they put an end to their miserable existence, but they dare not, because of their oaths of service.*"

—*Kafka,* Couriers

"*Sorry for almost beating you to death . . . Do you have any idea how* often *I say that?*"

—*Eugene S. Robinson, Café OTO, London, 2022*

When Wonderland is not so nearly as wonderful as they make it sound.
(Photo by Irma Norman)

A Hebrew Theory
An Intro

JESUS H. CHRIST. Is there anything quite as horrible as being a child? Especially when, during the early life plumbing of memories, you can remember the time *before* the time when you were a child?

This is not just some Shirley MacLaine past life regression. It's very real and undeniable memories of being machine gunned to death. Have I talked about this before? Who talks about this stuff before? Not when Google makes it difficult to conceal the more outré aspects of your character from anyone with a set of eyes and an interest in knowing.

But the reality is this is what I remember and so showing up—had I been a soldier, a criminal, or just in the wrong place at the wrong time?—as a Black infant was a pleasant surprise. I know this because, unlike Chris Rock in his famous speech about how his white audience wouldn't switch places with him BECAUSE he's Black (this was much more to do with well, who would want to be Chris Rock anyway?), I have never wanted to be anything other than what I was. This has been consistent.

I mean I suspect I was Jewish and was machine-gunned because I was Jewish, so, yeah, this would have been a marked improvement.

And taking up residence in the house of my parents—a mother who would eventually become a guidance counselor and a father, a former Air Force intelligence officer who spoke five languages and would later be a professor—in Jamaica, Queens was more than an improvement. It was a dream.

A fact that rolls so heavily against the prevailing orthodoxy that it must be commented on and commented on early. All of whatever media trope you might have regarding life on this planet as a Black person, you need to toss out. Even if you're a Black person. None of it applies here.

I pull into a club in Hengelo. The Netherlands. The club crew sizes us up and move across the room toward us. Sound guys, stage crew, support staff. There are six of us. Four band members, a sound guy and a guy who sells merch.

The lighting guy beelines for me, sidling up with an appraisal that starts like this: "It's terrible this thing in Rwanda, eh?"

As an opening gambit it's risible and I greet it with a hail of largely inappropriate but perfectly placed laughter. He appears confused. Rwanda was terrible but that's got nothing to do with the price of tea in China as my great-grandmother used to say.

I say that I appreciate his attempt to "bro down" but maybe he could just focus on the job at hand. We had been on the road a long time.

"OK. What kind of lights should I use? For your skin?" He wants this to work and his attempt is charming but life on the road is sometimes bereft of charm.

"If you used the Jew bulbs you have back there that should be fine enough for me!"

For the remainder of our time in Hengelo he chooses to not speak to me again. A fact that I find lamentable. AND hilarious.

The point is, and remains: don't bring me that Black bullshit. You want some insight into ME? Ask away. But, presuming you're not Black, well, I'm not your circus animal chirping about a world that's so nearly and clearly foreign to you. You have arms, legs, eyes and ears? Then our struggles are not remarkably different.

That being said, it's very possible to be a deeply complex Black person aside and outside the tropes, and that's where, despite all of the large and sturdy efforts to get you to think otherwise and simplify this issue, just about where we are now.

"I watched your show, and loved it by the way," I leaned into the corner where David Yow was sitting. "But I watched the audience afterward too and they all seemed . . . happy? You had actually made them *happy*."

He crossed his legs.

"And I wondered about that. I mean that's the last thing I want to see an OXBOW audience feeling. I think."

Just two men that's on the mic. (Apologies to Slick Rick.) David Yow and I at The Bottom of the Hill. (Photo by Kasia Robinson)

He paused, like Wizard trying to suss out what to say to Travis Bickle, before Yow finally just sighed and said, "What is WRONG with you Black people?" We both laughed. But, on the occasion of this memoir, I think I am about to tell you precisely what. At the very least you'll be much clearer on what's wrong with ME.

Maybe.

That is to say that it is there, always there, but never where the media, who always gets it wrong thinks it is . . . this experience of Black people. But in Jamaica, Queens in 1962, the neighborhood was all Black middle-class when there was such a thing in great evidence. Politicians, bus drivers, insurance salespeople, business owners. My uncle and aunt who we lived with at the time were part of this thriving group. Civil service workers and my uncle, a former cattle rancher from Texas, owned a clutch of body shops.

It was American bucolic and when we'd leave the house our neighbors would wave. Except for Leonard the Drunk who lived next door and whose dog Bobo once lured me to the fence where I, a three-year-old at the time had been encouraged by Leonard to pet him, and promptly, and with malice aforethought, attacked me while Leonard laughed his ass off.

A few other things also happened that day: I saw my father threaten to kick Leonard's ass but on an almost unrelated sidetrack I remember resolving to kill Bobo. I don't know if this was a strange thought for a three-year-old to be having but I know it's the thought I was having.

Other than that though I was baby sat by the neighbors and we moved to getting our own place out in Ozone Park, by the airport. And even when we did Tony, a gypsy cab driver friend of the family, would take me back to Jamaica where I was cared for by Miss Fay—in the full Southern tradition she was always Miss Fay—a place I stayed until her sullen daughters locked me out of the bathroom and I crapped my pants one day. A day when I was well past crapping my pants as a daily occurrence.

Though I later found out that Miss Fay's daughters were being systematically molested by their piano teacher, I had no way of knowing this then.

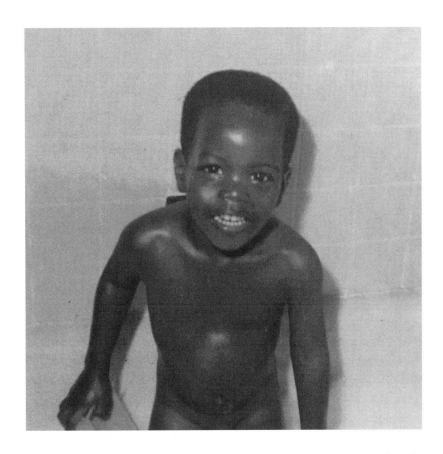

I also knew that the next babysitter, a nice lady named Indi only lasted until my mother had gotten a ride home from a coworker and Indi had asked me "Who's that white man?"

I told my mother what she had said, and she never sent me back again, and my mother's explanation later was concise: "To you 'white' was the color of paper. Or a crayon. You didn't know anything about how it applied to people. And realistically the idea that my son would be defining himself against the rest of the world like this . . . this old . . . country shit? Well Indi was nice enough. Just a little unsophisticated."

All I remember about Indi though was that she was a fan of wrapping her chairs and couches in vinyl seat covers. And TV.

But Ozone Park was where I started to have serious memories. Like fighting with my friend Peaches next door. And some other two neighbor boys where we'd reenact scenes from The Green Hornet

We used Sweetheart soap. A memory later in place when I named an OXBOW song "Sweetheart."

(Bruce Lee's scenes mostly) and Batman. Which meant lots of fighting. Sometimes real, sometimes fun, but never heated.

I remember bedtime stories and baths. Prayers at bedtime. Fantastic Christmas celebrations in the days when you could wrap your trees in fiberglass, what they called Angel Hair, complete with the now-nimbus of cotton candy–looking lights, and Norman Rockwell running to my father on the walk outside when he came home from work.

My pipe-smoking, briefcase-toting father. Years later I would find out, the way you do when you realize the adults surrounding you are much more than just a support network for you, that my father's own story was deeper and darker than any Rockwell original. Or, perhaps, Rockwell was always dark, and we were blinded by both a nostalgia and a desire to keep things . . . simple.

But my father, as the stories would go, was in the Air Force. Where it was discovered that he had had an aptitude for languages. Which got him driven to a Potemkin village of sorts in Texas where he was dropped off and immersed in the languages that he had decided to become proficient at. Given the times, and the coldness of our relations with the Eastern Bloc and the crawling struggle against communism in his case it was Russian, German, Chinese and Japanese.

The fact that this suited him for a career in military intelligence should surprise no one. The fact that the military believed he'd be the most useful kind of asset by being a bass player in a jazz trio? Surprising. Banking on, I guess, a universal disbelief that African American jazzbos would be multilingual, his trio toured West Germany and anywhere in Europe where it might be likely that he could hear anything that might be of any use even if, as he tells it, he spent most of his time being chased at knife point out of gypsy encampments where he had gone to meet girls.

This is the photo that won a citywide contest for Gertz, a department store. This outfit? Undeniably: the shit!

This was not found out until later. Also not found out until much later was that his mother, my grandmother had been kidnapped by a woman who had been having an affair with her father. In the days before the Internet, when people could disappear by moving a block away, so it went that a woman who was wanting a deeper commitment from an already married man, stole his daughter with the understanding put thusly: if you ever want to see your daughter again, please feel free to join us. And then an address.

The machinations of all of this are fuzzy and my now departed grandmother, when asked about it, demurred: "She was the only mother I can remember now."

But it was full-blown Cinderella horror, and eventually having secured the husband, the evil stepmother farmed my grandmother out to a childless white couple during what my grandmother described as "the happiest years of my life." Because while she had been sold as a servant the family fell in love with her, homeschooled her and from the age of four to 13, she was much less the servant she had been sold as, and more the daughter she never was to anyone else.

Then a phone call. The evil stepmother was starting a business and needed "her daughter" back. And the business she was starting? A halfway house for prisoners transitioning back to general society. In all likelihood the least great place for a 13-year-old to be.

"Today they would call it 'rape'." Living in Washington, D.C., and in her 80s, I made the roadie to see her after having not seen her since I was 12. I was in my 40s when I did so and had had . . . questions.

My grandfather, along with his brothers, was a lifelong, committed and organized criminal. Numbers, extortion, loan sharking, stolen goods. Dapper and recalling no one in pictures if not a cross between Cab Calloway and David Niven, it's quite clear that he probably didn't

The artist and intelligence officer formerly known as Eugene Stanley Robinson Sr., but who, in fact, was really always Stanley Eugene Robinson, according to his mother. The father of the son who judges the father. Harshly.

perceive that what he had done was rape, and in the parlance of the day when it was discovered that she was pregnant, he had "done the right thing" by giving his son a last name, an awareness that he was his father and cash as was necessary.

Also, as a product of being part of a crime family, an always standing offer to my father: "You let me know if you need anything. Or if anyone's bothering you." With the implication and the eventual outcome being quite clear.

This, being a product of a rape, framed my father's existence in completely compelling ways. A perpetual sense of being unwanted, along with a desire to want to be wanted, and an aversion to criminality while at the same time having the requisite genetic levels of aggression to make that make sense as a career choice.

His mother denies his characterization and says that she "gave him everything he could have ever wanted." Something his father had failed to do, most significantly when he was at Michigan State on a football scholarship in the days when the scholarship was only good for as long as you could play. So, playing with a raft of guys who later ended up going pro (most notably Willie Wood), he inevitably got injured and when he asked his father for some money to get him through a semester until he was injury-free, he was denied.

So on to the Air Force and a nettlesome relationship to his father that persisted until the man died not too long after I was born.

My grandmother eventually married a man named Sam to escape from the evil stepmother and bore him eight children. I remember Sam from when I was a child.

"I hated him," she told me, neither smiling nor laughing. She ended up having a long career in the U.S. State Department, the education she had been afforded between the horror times standing in her good stead. But I remembered Sam, imperious and baselessly arrogant, and well aware of who I was: the grandchild of rape.

So: fuck Sam.

But as a kid, all of this stuff was occult to me and existed, if at all, on nothing but a genetic level. I remember my father doting on my mother. I remember him taking me out into the snow and later making ice cream from the snow, which I believed was magical. I remember

his taking me to a puppet show in St. Alban's park in Queens where my head had provided a compelling target for some kids in the bleachers using peashooters to target the attending kids, and when I cried out in pain the second time he headed back to the bleachers, and in the scramble to escape, one of the kids fell off the back of the bleachers and an ambulance had to be called.

My father's comment was, "See? That's what you get." A comment I liked almost as much as when he threatened Leonard, the owner of Bobo the dog that bit me, when in a drunken moment he had gotten a little salty with my mother. My father's rage was stolid, and icy, and always 100 percent believable, as it was that day blasting through the accumulated crust of half a dozen whiskey sours, Leonard's drink of choice.

I remember, also, my father listening to a neighbor who had come to him to complain, in a suburban and fatherly way, that his son and I were getting into a few too many scrapes and could he, would he, talk to me about "cooling it" with Tommy? I also remember my father looking at him, having just pulled in from work, and saying, "So it's MY fault that your son is a sissy?"

My Aunt Vi, my rape-y paternal "grandfather," my mother, my maternal grandmother, and my great-grandmother a scant few weeks before I was conceived.

As young as I was I knew that this was not at all what Tommy's father had expected because it was not at all what I expected and I watched as he registered shock, turned on his heel and made his way back up the street, denied by my father who then turned to me and said, "Leave Tommy alone."

Then I remember one day asking where he was and my mother, the only person I knew more formidable than my father, telling me: "He's at our city house."

This is the apartment he moved to after she told him she wanted a divorce.

"He was a really kind of a sweet guy and a good husband," she once told me after I had gotten older. "But he had married the most exciting woman in New York and he was a homebody so . . . "

I don't remember this being especially traumatic. He and I were frequently at loggerheads over . . . stylistic issues. He was an early photography fan and had cameras, maybe something he had picked up in the military, and so we'd argue about photo composition.

"Stand there."

I was wearing another killer outfit. Plaid bowtie, vest, oxblood-colored shoes and navy-blue shorts. He was having me stand by a column (at a church? A museum? Can't remember). I remember thinking that I'd mimic the scenes I had seen in magazines and so I leaned against the column with my right hand raised against it, with my left hand in my pocket. And lest you think this is a bit too precocious it should be remembered here that my modeling career had begun at the age of two when I won a citywide competition for Gertz's department store's beautiful baby contest.

"Stand up straight."

"I don't want to."

He put some steel into it this time: "I SAID 'stand up STRAIGHT'!" Which I did. Under protest. A protest that took the form of a photo ruining dead-eyed non-smile. Naomi Campbell would have been proud.

But I found that I missed him now that he was gone, usually when I was punished for something; punished, though only actually hit twice, if memory serves. But he was soon replaced by my stepfather, a man who I always and still call Doog. Kind of a cross, physically at least,

On Butler Street in Brooklyn. The only neighborhood I ever lived in that was not a "Black" neighborhood. Irma with an "I." Mom on the stairs of our place on Butler Street around 1968. If memory serves, everything in this picture was burnt orange.

between Donald Sutherland and Elliott Gould. Doog was of the age, comfortably Bohemian, fluent in Spanish, had traveled all over South America, and was the son of fairly significant journalists who used to pal around with the F. Scott Fitzgeralds.

He worked at an antipoverty program on the Lower East Side and his fathering style was the exact opposite of autocratic, and weirdly enough this worked much better with me as it usually put the onus of bad decisions right where it belonged: on the bad decision maker.

"I don't think that's such a good idea," he'd say about something that clearly *was* a bad idea. "But maybe it'll work out for you." Yeah, this usually worked. He also came with a son from a previous relationship, and in the '60s, when not tons of people were getting divorced, he also came with another brand differentiator. He was white.

"Brother Louie" came on the radio at one point as we drove along, alone, somewhere. It was the song by Stories with a lyric that ran . . .

She was black as the night
Louie was whiter than white
Danger, danger when you taste brown sugar
Louie fell in love overnight

"You know what this song is about?" I knew he wanted to pull me into a discussion of the racial ramifications of what the song meant but I had learned all I needed to know by watching how he and my mother traversed a world that in 1969 wasn't nearly as ready for interracial romance as it would like to believe it was. In fact, since my father's second wife was also white, I got two barrels of four people, a couple in New York and a couple in Maryland, absolutely not giving a fuck what anyone else thought.

You see, I come from a long line of people who have always felt like celebrities and who perceived themselves sitting outside of class and caste distinctions going as far back as maternal great-grandparents and paternal sharecropping great-grandfathers.

So, people are *looking*? Of course, they're looking. That's what's done in the face of the fabulous.

But in the face of "You know what this song is about?" I just wanted to shut it down. I had seen enough afterschool specials to not be interested in afterschool specials.

"Yeah, I know what it's about." And instead of pushing, which he had never done, he let it drop. Not with any kind of relief but just because we had something better to talk about. We always did.

Mark, my stepbrother who has disappeared, never to be seen again, presumed dead, Doog, my stepfather, the unfortunate and ill-timed dog Sidney, and me on Butler Street. The painting in the background was done by Doog's brother Donny Newton.

The Rape Years

THERE WERE TWIN ENGINES spinning through much of the 1960s I remember. And probably a bunch of stuff before I started remembering. There was the much-publicized chatter about peace and love and a performative appreciation for the benefits of fellowship, and then there's what I like to call reality. A reality that had kitchens in Irish, Italian and Black working-class homes sporting, at the very least, pictures of the dead Kennedys, and I don't mean the band. Though for the vast majority of my life I've lived in Black or minority neighborhoods in Jamaica, Queens, Crown Heights and Flatbush, Brooklyn, I also did for a year live in Cobble Hill before it was well-heeled and when it was majorly Irish and Italian.

In every single Black home I had been in, excepting mine, you could also add in Martin Luther King. The troika of tragedy. All dead. Despite all the peace and love. In our house we had wood prints from Guatemala. And books.

But the Vietnam War was on TV, and not at the movie theaters yet. John Birchers, right wingers, the American Nazi Party, George Wallace, no matter how many laff-track-fueled rose-colored looks back at the decade, tectonically, it sucked.

Maybe not the least of which was because I didn't get out of the decade without experiencing my first burst of real animal hatred for other human beings.

We rented a floor of a house owned curiously enough by historian Lewis Mumford's daughter Allison and her husband Chester. They lived there with Jimmy and Elizabeth, their kids. But these kids never had enough juice to interest me. I was interested in the Deegan brothers. Three Irish kids, one about eight years old, my age, and one older and one younger. All of the middle-class families on the block hated them. They stole, cursed, and you could see despite all of the rebop about race in America we were much more class bound than we're willing to admit. Poor white folks were not welcome.

The thing I am standing in front of? A stereo console. Spreading holiday cheer.

So, my mother had a talk with them when she saw that's where my interests rested.

"Boys," she had gathered them when they waited on the steps to come up and play. "You can come here and play all the time. Whenever you want, you're always welcome. But if *anything* ever goes missing here . . . you can never, EVER come back. Do you understand?" No adult had ever talked to them like this, but my mother had worked at Spofford, which was like a Riker's Island for juvenile offenders in New York, and as fashionable and fabulous as she was, she was still taking no shit, and they got it.

Through them I met everyone. The Italian family with ten kids, all of them slightly developmentally disabled, I suspect from the father beating up the mother, which he used to do even if I was there and most certainly when she was pregnant. And she was always pregnant. I looked to my friends for clues as to how to follow this and they didn't seem especially disturbed so neither was I. It's not how things rolled in *my* house. Besides which I had a crush on their sister Theresa so I was in.

The Irish folks, the Deegans, were darling though. The father was generally aggrieved but their mother was thin and chain-smoked in a kitchen that sported a completely captivating grinning cat clock with a tail that swung back and forth. She always seemed really happy to see me. Partly because she knew that my Mom had thrown her kids no class shade, and in general adults had always liked me. Adults, especially women, people I later knew to identify as crazy, and animals not named Bobo seemed to have a special affinity for me. I have not been able to explain it, and it didn't get any less strange later in life when murderers and mobsters would announce to rooms we were in: "I LOVE this guy!" The guy in question being me.

Maybe it was because I smiled easily and often. In any case my mother was always routinely mystified when I'd go to spend the week-end at my Great-Grandmother's house up in New Rochelle, above The Bronx. Westchester to be exact.

"What are you all doing that you come back fat from only being there four days?" She'd call my Nana, her grandmother, on the phone; "Mother? You have to stop feeding him so much!"

But what she didn't know is that the block that my Nana lived on in Westchester, in a neighborhood full of the Black and Italian maids, butlers, gardeners and drivers for the wealthy in Larchmont, was also filled with Southern women, all of whom would see me out playing in the streets by myself as initially was my habit when I went to Westchester.

"Hey boy . . . what you doing out there?"

I'd smile and say "nothing," as that was usually the case.

"You hungry?"

I never answered "no" to that question. Eggs, bacon, grits, cornbread, by the time I made it back to my Nana's house to eat I had *already* eaten three or four times.

But the Deegans' mom maybe thinking I'd be a mitigating influence on her sons, welcomed me. Their father, largely the cause of them spending so much time out of the house, seemed to be what I would later understand as an alcoholic. But he worked, so his drinking was only *sensed* by me. I just knew that Johnny, Jimmy, and Eddie would leave when he showed up, and we'd go wandering.

When I think now of being a father and the kind of latitude I have given my daughters, and then remember running the streets at eight years old with these cats—catching rides on the outside of city buses rather than pay, who were just wandering into open houses with me if we heard the sounds of a party—I shiver with a certain kind of reflexive fear.

There were bunches of hippie dudes smoking (weed?) and screaming at basketball games, while we poked around because the Deegans thought there might be something to steal or a beer to lift a sip off of. I was there. And it wasn't so much a case of me being fearless as I had seen nothing to be afraid of.

Though there was Gary, because, of course, there was always a Gary. Just enough years older than the smaller kids that he scared their older siblings into silence, and slick enough of an Eddie Haskell that he could, all blond hair and blue eyes of him, snow the parents. The girls steered clear of him though, and the way that he used to call me "Gene," all sing song-y like a song of the day about a girl named "*Jean, Jean, so young and alive*" is largely why today, outside of my family and a few people from college, calling me "Gene" sets me on edge.

I was surrounded by women growing up though, oodles of female cousins and aunts, and then later sisters, so it wasn't that he feminized my name that I found irksome it was his clear intent to needle. And whatever slippery-sloped after that.

One day all of the kids came running. A sparrow had fallen out of a tree. A baby sparrow. I wanted to take it home, nurse it back to health. Gary had a better idea.

"Watch this." And he took a firecracker out of his jacket pocket and put it in the bird's mouth. The bird struggled against it and I struggled against Gary who punched me and then punched at me to keep me off while he lit it and destroyed the bird.

I hated Gary for that. And I had made myself a promise, in a way that I would do over the years with others, that if the opportunity ever afforded itself, I would kill Gary. As it was, I remembered his last name for years with the thought of doing just that, though by the time the Internet was a thing I had already forgotten it. Even if I remembered the prevailing and most true message of all: people were dangerous because they were so reliably unreliable.

And if you think this is me, now, talking, it should be noted that the first time someone tried to kill me I was five. That is, it was 1967, in Westchester, at my Nana's house where the sidewalks were made of gray slate and it couldn't have been more suburban. And in some ways rural.

Or at least that was the sense when the junkman, Mr. Brown, rode through, sitting atop a horse-drawn cart packed to the edges with junk, or the Italian knife sharpener pushed a roll-away with a grinder wheel screwed to it, strolling while screaming, "Bring out your knives."

It was a different time and place and on Crescent Avenue, what had been a nice house on the edge of a field was now a nice house at the base of a highway where my Nana lived with her brother, my uncle Sammy, and me and my mom for a bit after my parents divorced, but before my mother and Doog got married.

It was solid Lil' Rascal-time in a neighborhood where everyone was all living the semi-suburban dream of houses with yards, but among highways, factories and still, deserted fields.

I regularly walked by myself to the Italian grocer with a list I couldn't read. I had a best friend named Louie De Luca. It was the idyll of my young life: Summer was full of Kool-Aid and busy with parties, and winter saw the coal man filling the chute and me meandering down to the basement to toss briquettes into the boiler. It was a house almost never darkened by sorrow. Even in light of the two times I almost burned it down by failing to remember that some kinds of science don't work well at home.

I had a kind of freedom that was almost Huck Finn-esque and I'd often climb through the bushes at the back of the house and wander into my friend Ronnie's place. A house that was almost everything a kid would want and almost everything my house was not: crazily ramshackle, a backyard full of empty refrigerator boxes, old mattresses, and Ronnie's older relatives sitting on the unpainted wooden stairs getting their hair processed, drinking from Mason jars and, if we were on the front porch, screaming at the jumped-up muscle cars to "burn rubber!" as they drove by. And they would.

One July day I wandered in—the doors never seemed to be closed, or if closed, they never seemed to be locked—and the air was sullen. Ronnie and two other cousins of his were there. At age 10 or 11, Ronnie was the oldest, and carried all the muscled bravado of an older brother. And I, an only child at the time, attached to him as such.

"Let's go."

We filed out after him like we were in the Army. It was a mission. I had no idea where we were going, but the fact that we were going was impressive enough. As we crossed their yard, each of the three older boys grabbed a pitchfork, a shovel and a stick. There was nothing left for me to grab, so I walked along between them, my hands swinging at my sides. Excited.

We walked the two blocks over, crossed some unruly shrubbery and stomped through the broken clods of dirt in what had once been a plowed field but now sprouted nothing but dirt and heat. After standing around in the field for a few minutes, I finally spoke.

"What are we going to do now?"

"We're going to kill you." I started to laugh, but the laughter was not returned. There was no mirth on those three faces, and their eyes were steely, like the backs of nail heads.

They grabbed me by the hair and the beating began. I remember watching the shovel and the pitchfork where they lay in the broken dirt. When the beating stopped, they yanked me back upright and Ronnie held me by my hair and said, "But first you got to pray. Pray to God."

I refused. I mouthed words, but the only prayer I'd had occasion to make at that age was a bedtime one. But that's not necessarily why I refused to verbalize a prayer. I refused because that was who I was then, just like that's who I am now. The feelings that you might have expected me to feel—fear, terror—were totally and completely absent in that moment. I felt one thing: anger.

So, I knelt in the dirt and mouthed empty words while they hit me. And then, whether it was because their arms were tired or not, there was a beat, a missed beat, and seeing my house off in the distance, I took my chance and ran. I ran as fast as I could and didn't look back until I got to the hedge break, where I saw my last glimpse of them standing in the field next to the shovel, stick and pitchfork, silent and staring after me.

I never went over to Ronnie's house again, and when everybody at my house asked me how I had gotten so dirty, I answered truthfully: "I fell."

I never saw him, or any of them, again. Despite how, as an adult, I could guess that those kids had their reasons and were probably abused themselves, what I was left with above all else was this aforementioned life lesson: People are shit. Or can be.

It's a fact that has colored my world view ever since, in good stead. It has largely informed all of the weightlifting and martial arts I've done over the years, and honed an extreme sensitivity to changes in the air and the queering of vibes that comes from living among humans. It taught me this as well: Be prepared. And: outnumbered is not always outwitted, so long as you're wise enough to bring a gun to a gun fight.

Good advice under any circumstances. That is, if staying alive is of very much interest to you. And it should be.

Moving out of Cobble Hill and into Crown Heights introduced one other element into the mix, given the age, and the levels of interest: sex. Something at nine that I was totally disinterested in. My preoccupations then? Well, that was the year that I started weightlifting. You see both my father and my stepfather were of the school that all playing fields should be played to full advantage regardless of age or abilities.

Which in my father's case meant that casual invitations to go running with him ended up being Olympic trials where he'd run backward and laugh while asking me why I couldn't keep up. In my stepfather's case it meant pitched battles of Scrabble that had me retiring to the bathroom to sob because I had been outpaced by a word like "ken."

Feeling some sort of sympathy at one point my mother said she offered "Maybe you could let him, you know, win sometimes?" To which my stepfather famously sniffed, "Well, what kind of message would that be sending?"

I mention this not out of rancor. I mention this because I'd have had it no other way and so when I started lifting weights the portfolio was clear to me: The horrible helplessness that was so much a part of childhood needed to stop.

That didn't stop the action on the streets, however, where little girls were drawing cocks and balls on the sidewalk in chalk, losing their virginity in garages at nine, and Louie, the last of the former white residents in a neighborhood now chockfull of Hasidim and Haitians, was clearly luring kids with candy and money for the express purpose of molesting them.

The molestation? Definitely not consensual. The garage action? Who knows? My adult brain now says part of this was probably normal; however, unlike Freud, I believe that in-home molestation was rampant. That the girls were acting out on the streets? Not surprising.

But I was in school at the tony Montessori Academy over in the even tonier Park Slope with the sons and daughters of music producers, lawyers, architects, and professors and yet I don't believe the early sexualization was a class problem. I think it was a problem of the age. A friend later told me that her father justified his multi-year molestation of her that started when she was a child and ended when she was in

college by explaining it away thusly: "Hey! It was the '60s! Everybody was experimenting!"

I'd have killed him just for that, but she was not me and my time would come, as both a perpetrator and perpetrated upon, soon enough.

In that I tell this next part for no one but the girl involved. The school bus ride back to Flatbush, where we had moved after Crown Heights was short, and the irascible bus driver, Mr. Pete—think Popeye the Sailor Man what yam what he yam—indulged all kinds of behavior because I, of all people, loved his rough and tumble, blue collar Navy guy bit. So, the bus ride had become . . . wild.

I was attacked by a guy named Forrest. I broke Forrest's nose. Since I was "defending" myself I had not been punished. But what happened on the bus often stayed on the bus. Like the fact that, for reasons unclear to me, Charmaine used to do a strip tease in the bus aisle, for a period there, every day. And I really liked Charmaine. Not sexy-liked, but like-liked. But one day, beyond the borders of what can be explained, I got tired of the tease part of the strip and requested that she take it all off. "All" being her underwear.

It was a weird request for me to make. Unlike those kids in the garages in Crown Heights I just hadn't been interested. Not at 9. Or

In a burst of later life weirdness the kid standing to my right (and that's me in the fringed leather jacket) is Josh Silver, of Type O Negative. I called a journalist friend in the middle of interviewing him and apologized for the interruption but told him to tell Josh that I said "hello." He did so and then how memory works followed with "Eugene took me to my first rock fight." Which was true. And also the last time his parents let him come over to my house.

even 10. Dominance over other boys? Yes. So, I'm unsure of what was driving this and when she removed her underwear in a rush of fear I, followed by those who had also gathered to watch, screamed, laughed and ran away.

Not something I thought about again until the next day in school when I saw her there with her grim-faced parents and got called to the principal's office. I was never big on lying and, in fact, told the truth, which was: I had ASKED. But I was smart enough to know that while this would be enough to get me off the hook, and it was, it wasn't really what had happened.

While I wasn't like a bank robber who "asked" for the money, an implied threat behind his ask, my strength of character was significant

Me, trying to compensate in light of the fact that I am sporting a pink leisure suit on Easter, my sisters Maya and Pilar struggling with birth order, Keith, the brother of my first girlfriend, and David, who became one of my favorite people ever. (Photo by Irma Norman.)

enough to bend her will to do that which she would not have done but for my urging. It was an expensive private school and her parents did as they should have and removed her from it. That sucked and I suck for having done it.

I hadn't fully considered what happened on the bus until I later found myself tied to a metal pole by the neighborhood bully who was rubbing my chest and tracing a line down to my belt and zipper to the amusement of gathered onlookers. Like most bullies he was afraid, and I had let myself get tied to the pole under the flimsiest of pretexts like "I bet you can't get untied if I tied you." Full-on John Wayne Gacy shit but karma worked in "funny" ways, and I understood it as such.

Eleven-year-old me was saved by a teenager who told the 15-year-old that had tied me to the pole that if he ever caught him doing shit like that again, he'd kill him. I, myself, also made a vow that I would kill him. And unlike the bird-killing Gary, I've managed to know where he is now, because I have kept tabs. Tabs that were in no way lessened when I found out recently that his son was shot to death.

None of that slaked my thirst for revenge. The only thing that came close? Realizing why he had chosen to do what he did. And again, the math came out the same: I had deserved it.

Unbeknownst to me, not only had he been raping a young girl in the neighborhood, a fact not known when she had become a prostitute and a drug addict, but he had been having sex with the older sister of a friend of mine. This friend of mine hadn't started off as a friend. You see he was big, blond haired and blue-eyed.

And he was Black.

And Jewish besides. But we didn't know, and one day when we, me and a group of other neighborhood kids, sat in front of my house on the sidewalk making weapons, he turned the corner and steeped in H. Rap Brown and Black nationalism I started in on a spiel: "Can you imagine they used to use these on us?"

I shook the whips and moved them over in my hands while I talked. My spiel was like a raga and it built in intensity while we watched him and he shot us nervous glances until I screamed, in what seemed the rightest of moments, "LET'S GET HIM!!!"

We chased him from our end of the block to his, whipping him, him stopping to fight, to be whipped again, until he finally fled into his house. With very little discussion we walked back to our houses, off to dinner, and said nothing else about this.

The manner in which he and I later became good friends is now a mystery to me. But we did, never discussing the attack. But apparently his sister told the rapist bully and the rapist bully, in order to continue receiving sexual favors he didn't have to rape her for, set about righting the ship. I deserved that. The fact that he acted out sexually was just him playing to what he knew.

The reality of these events is that it would begin a phase of my life that continues up to these words I am presently writing—a phase where I am rarely unarmed, and also prepared for unarmed combat, is probably a life positive. So, what would I be killing him for?

All of this was solidified and crystallized at 13 when, after four years of lifting weights, well . . . thirteen was a strange age. You see, I was just old enough to see the spread of possible futures rolling out in front of me, but still young enough to completely miss the fact that the future is promised to no one.

I had graduated from being bussed by Mr. Pete to unassisted trips on my local Flatbush, Brooklyn, bus line, to a basic primer on the subway, and subsequent subway riding, in 1975: Don't stand near the edge of the platform when the train is coming in, don't talk to strangers and don't go anywhere with anybody, or as my mother readily admonished, they "might cut off your pee pee." So that and enough money to buy subway tokens was all I had and all I needed for the city to open itself to me, beyond Brooklyn, like something I had been waiting for my whole life.

Which is how it happened that I decided I wanted to see Stanley Kubrick's A Clockwork Orange. In a different story for a different day, I had made the mistake of dragging my parents to a double viewing of A Clockwork Orange and Deliverance, which, if you know the movies, equals about three hours of cinematic depictions of various forms of rape. Men raping women. Men raping men. Not the kinds of films that you want to be watching with your 13-year-old son. The experience was so tense that I decided, as a result of being a big fan of the book, to see at least the one film again, that being, *A Clockwork Orange*.

It was playing at a theater in the far West Village, and I had train fare, a Sunday afternoon off and parents who trusted me. But trust or not, sometimes you gotta do what you gotta do.

"I'm going to the movies."

"OK. Be careful."

And off I went, knowing damn well that if I had said "to the movies in Lower Manhattan," I would have heard a very definable NO. Which was why I didn't mention it.

Got to the train. It was a Sunday and the streets were fairly clear. It was a fall day, and walking the few blocks to the theater, I felt impressively adult. Bought my ticket and felt even more so. Found probably the best seat in the very empty house and scooted in for a tension-free film-viewing experience.

Fifteen or 20 minutes into the movie, people had started to filter in, but ultimately it was never more than about six, or maybe seven. Eating some popcorn, I was enjoying myself. But not so much that I didn't notice a flash from off and to my right. Flash. Then nothing. Then 30 seconds later, another flash. Twenty flashes later, I finally had to look: It was the light from the screen reflecting off the glasses of a guy who was sitting about 20 seats away from me.

I was a city kid, and in city terms this was unqualified bad news. And worse news: Now he's 17 seats away. Then 10. Then six. I didn't want to wait for the inevitable. I had a creep on my hands. I had to get away from the creep.

So, I decided to get as far away from him as possible. I picked the last seat in the top row of the balcony. Knowing what I now know about lunatics, it's very plain to see that this would be construed as nothing but an invitation. Being 13, I didn't figure out my miscalculation until he came and stood right behind me.

I don't know how much time had passed, because I wasn't watching the movie anymore. He stood there for what felt like a long minute before taking a seat nearby so he could watch me. I couldn't relax now. Now I was tuned up, and in my state, I figured the only way to get away was to hide. I went down to the concession stand, stood there for a bit

and thought it through. He'll know I'm nervous and think I left and will hit the streets looking for me. So instead of leaving the theater, I decided to hide in the theater.

Specifically, in the bathroom.

Where I waited just long enough for the colossal badness of this decision to strike me full force, so I decided to bolt. No movie about rape and murder is worth getting raped or murdered over. So, I was out of the bathroom and on the streets and addled from a combination of fear and unfamiliarity. Instead of walking to the subway, I accidentally took a wrong turn and found myself in what I would now recognize as the Meatpacking District, the ramshackle West Side Highway crippled and crumbling across the street.

As I tried to get my bearings, about half a block back I saw him following me and gaining fast. He was about six feet tall. No idea how much he weighed, but he was a grown adult man. His face? Blank but focused. I didn't run since I knew running invites being chased. And, fortunately, in front of me I saw a subway, and I dropped down the stairs only to discover that because it was Sunday there was no one in the booth to buy a token from.

Vincent Rose, whose name I later lifted when I started the SkullGame, the "Yelp for Porno," and me at Shire Village Camp. He was my best friend, totally hilarious and sane enough to never have joined me in threatening people's lives. I did that on my own. Sorry, David A. I was a nut.

I headed up the other side, across the street, and saw him disappear down the stairs I had just gone down. Across the street was another entrance with, I hoped, someone in the booth. And there was, and after buying a token I hit the stairs down to the platform. But it was uptown, and I needed to go downtown. Coming back up, I saw him buying a token and he saw me and now I saw his face was not blank anymore. It was angry.

I slipped down the downtown side and moved down the platform. I figured he could follow me because he was following a blue down jacket with a gray hoodie underneath. Little Gray Riding Hood. I took off the down jacket and bundled it under my arm as a train came in, and I saw him looking in every door and watching who got on the other ones.

Another train came in, and now that there were two trains, I was watching him seethe.

I slipped onto the express train back to Brooklyn and didn't relax until I got into the Prospect Park station, where I put my coat back on and told no one this story. I'd like to say that this was the capstone, the event that framed me for my entry into my teenage years but while scary, this was a singular event and not a sustained reign of terror.

You ever see *The Warriors*, an apocalyptic take on a New York City riven by roving street gangs? This was a fiction while I was at the Montessori Academy. But the Academy only went up to seventh grade. I needed to go to school elsewhere for eighth grade. The elsewhere that was found was a parochial school deeper into Brooklyn.

We had friends who went there, mostly my first girlfriend Lisa (who famously dumped me when I was ten for being "boring") and her brother Keith. They seemed to like it. They never said that they didn't like it.

But the fact that it was a religious school, and we were not a particularly religious family, despite the early life exposure to bed-time prayers, should have been a warning. Failure to heed warnings though? A family specialty.

I mean I'd just spent eight years at the couldn't-be-more-progressive Montessori Academy. Staffed by educators who had studied with Maria Montessori herself and steeped in the British education system, the Montessori Academy was where I cut my wise-guy teeth. So, when my teacher, Mrs. Kumar, wasn't kicking me out of the classroom over ideological differences—I was refusing to stand for the Pledge of Allegiance and, in fact, refusing to Pledge any sort of Allegiance—she was glad to have me air them. Even with this constant battle between open intellectual inquiry and me being a giant pain in the ass, she seemed glad to be a teacher of the time.

From ages six to 13, I not only discussed math, science and languages but also the war in Vietnam, pollution, race relations, sexism, imperialism and a raft of other ideas and notions that largely contributed to me being who I presently am.

And who I had been at Montessori? Well, after seeing *Superfly* with my grandmother and expressing admiration for Superfly, my grandmother, much to my mother's very middle-class chagrin, went out and bought me a crushed blue velour maxi coat, a suit of the same color, a pimp hat with a feather in it, platform shoes and a cane. All of which I insisted on wearing to school.

Not just for one day. Every day. Complete with the fake limp. My mother fought this for a bit but figured, maybe, that public ridicule would slow my roll. In literary terms we might call this foreshadowing, because it did not.

I wore this until it was threadbare and, yeah, I saw the smiles on the teacher's faces, but I also knew these teachers knew nothing about *Superfly*.

So going from Montessori to St. Stephen's couldn't have been more dizzying. From *Superfly* to a school that required uniforms, ties and cleric-taught classes in Latin and religion, I had to . . . adjust.

"Oh myyy God." This had been a common refrain at Montessori, inspired by Sandy Dennis' turn as the put-upon wife in the Neil Simon–scripted movie The Out-of-Towners, in which everything bad that could

On one of those non-Superfly days, 1971, though the railroad engineer's cap that's being sported has never been fully explained. (Photo by Michael Katz)

happen to a couple visiting New York happens. We used it as a punch line, and as punctuation.

"DON'T SAY THAT!" My new classmates froze in horror, and when I asked why, they explained, "You can't use the Lord's name in vain!"

Got it. Outside of that, my friendships flowed fast and easily. Most kids had been at St. Stephen's since they had started school and were happy to have an outsider on the inside. Lesley Pierre, Vonstone, Donna (my girlfriend for a time) and a half-dozen others formed the backbone of my experience there, unmarred by all but two instances.

The first? Being pursued by one of those aforementioned street gangs, specifically the Jolly Stompers, Mike Tyson's gang of record for those taking notes.

It had started casually enough though. I was a funny guy. But comedy is also a sword, and a sword that finds its targets and doesn't hurt if it's successful, and stings like fuck if it's not.

Donna's boyfriend (not the Donna I dated but another) showed up to pick her up one day after school. She exulted in the raw show of power as Brent, since that was his name, and his friends milled about out front waiting for school to let out.

She did a roll call for the gathered girls who watched these teenagers, vests flying their colors, applejack hats, and upside-down golf clubs as walking sticks. She was impressed. Her girlfriends were impressed. My inner monologue went thusly: "FUCK those guys."

I was 13, they were 15, and through a mix of envy and anger I listened to her.

"I know ALL of those guys."

Then my 100-foot leap into total stupidity: "Oh yeah? How much do you cost?"

School photo from the one year I was in parochial school, St. Stephen's, 1975. Where I learned how to tie a tie and dodge street murder.

She burst into tears, her girlfriends shrieked, the bell rang, and they all filed out, she into Brent's arms while her friends detailed that I had called her a "ho." My friends, the remaining guys in the class, while understanding what I had done also understood that in life you're sometimes going to have your ass kicked, so they were going to leave me to it.

I, seeking the better part of valor, hid in the toilet for about an hour until I could no longer hear the Jolly Stompers screaming and raging around the building outside.

Coast being somewhat clear, with a conscience also somewhat clear, I took the very long way home. And at that point I had figured out that I wasn't going out without a fight so stuck a razor blade in my lunchbox, right next to a sharpened screwdriver.

I had already been boxing at the local Boys Club, and inspired by Bruce Lee, taking karate at the church around the corner from where we lived. Though that only lasted until they needed to get paid for teaching.

I asked my mother for money for classes and she said, "Fighting is just for angry people. You don't need to be doing any fighting."

This was a funny idea to me. I didn't choose to be a target for the entire year I went to that goddamned parochial school and yet, of my own doing, I was. Well, I could still stab.

And outside of the classroom was only half the battle. The other half? Largely ideological. It involved a social studies teacher, Mrs. Stubbing, whose pursuit of an aggressively retrograde political philosophy made us natural enemies. She was the first Republican I had ever remembered meeting.

"Remember to bring in your favorite newspaper for a discussion of current events tomorrow," she said one day.

The next day, some classmates brought in the New York Daily News, some the *New York Post*, some the *New York Amsterdam News*. I brought in what I read once a week, the *Village Voice*. We read in silence before the discussion while our teacher cruised the room, checking out what was being read.

"What are you doing reading that rag?" she asked me.

"The Voice?" I said with a laugh, thinking she was joking. "Why is it a rag?"

I expected a punch line. What I got was "If you like reading Commie lies about America, knock yourself out."

I laughed again. Laughed while she glared at me. Laughed because it was ON. In short order, I set about upsetting the apple cart as often as possible. I declared myself an atheist. During free reading, I brought in Mao's *Little Red Book*, which, though virtually unreadable, filled me with endless pleasure to see how much and how thoroughly my teacher hated me for it. Because no matter how much she imagined she hated me, it couldn't have been more than I hated her cloistered take on everything that still forms the basis of our culture wars today.

"For the bicentennial I want you all to pick a person from American history," she informed the class one day. "I want you to come dressed up as that person and read from your biography on whom you've chosen."

She was naturally all about the 200th birthday of America. In a school that was 98 percent racially homogeneous, I guess it made sense for her to have the great-grandsons and great-granddaughters of slaves dress up as Thomas Jefferson, George Washington and Andrew Jackson.

"Who are you going to be, Eugene?"

I hated the assignment. We both suspected she had me checkmated into doing something I was constitutionally opposed to.

"Can I be Karl Marx?" I asked.

The room had grown so quiet you could hear the radiator.

"He's not an American," she said.

"Then I'll be Geronimo."

And I was. From that moment on, had I been academically anything other than a great student, she would have crushed me. Instead, she satisfied herself with ignoring me.

Until, that is, the scores were tallied at the end of the year and revealed that I had the second-best scores of any eighth grader. Which meant I got to give the salutatorian speech at graduation. A graduation to which we had been instructed to wear patternless, dark clothing and to which I wore an oatmeal-colored, unconstructed jacket with a white shirt and a flower-print tie.

During my speech, I looked between my pleased parents, my amused classmates and my teacher. My speech was for me, it was for us, but mostly it was for her and was all about how dreams were big because dreams are meant to be big, and the world was a welcoming place with a plethora of interesting ideas if only we found ourselves OPEN to them.

At the end of the ceremony, my Latin teacher Ms. Reddy, a James Coburn-esque smoker of cigarillos (in the classroom no less), came over to me and wished me luck in all my future endeavors. The social studies teacher, in a deft dance of avoidance, never spoke to me again. A fact largely unmourned by me.

High school, though, lay beyond, and after that, college. I never heard about my nemesis again, but in some small way I hope she found a measure of peace with what was left of her life.

New York's Stuyvesant High School is arguably the best of New York's specialized high schools. Schools that are public but that you have to test into. Anyone can go, providing they can pass the test. A test that's become a lightning rod for present-day discussions about the appropriateness of tests in determining how smart anyone is anyway.

But I studied for it and as far as the people at St. Stephens were concerned, I was their best bet to play in that league. So, they, minus Mrs. Stubbing, were pulling for me. And my parents had the test prep books and were dialed in. Me? Lukewarm. I had wanted to be a marine biologist and there was a school out in Sheepshead Bay that specialized in that, but I was overruled like kids are overruled.

So, I took the test. Killed on the English part but having never seen fractions written using anything other than a horizontal bar, I was baffled to see them written like this: 2/4. So, every math question like that? In the dumper.

Which means I failed the test by five points. There was a special program for the special high school, though, and if you scored within five points of the cut-off, you could prove yourself in summer school.

Stuyvesant High School yearbook. The woman whose signature is to the left of my face died not so long ago. Which I think of whenever I see this picture now.

Having ruined my parents vacation plans I felt a certain amount of guilt, but it was unavoidable, and trucking to Washington Irving HS where they had the summer school put me right smack dab in the middle of Union Square that summer of '76. You see *Taxi Driver* where Jodie Foster first tries to get in De Niro's cab? That was around the corner at Variety Fotoplays, a porno theater of note, and kitty-corner from where I bought my first leather jacket.

But going to math and English classes after wending your way through trans hooker street fights and nodding-out junkies was a comfortably disconnected violence and a nice change-up from the Jolly Stomper fear that had populated my entire school life the year before.

Something else was going on though. The English teacher was not a Stuyvesant teacher. The math teacher was. Barry Glotzer, think Harvey Weinstein with a goatee, had made a determination that I wasn't Stuyvesant material and in whatever kind of horse-trading that made sense at the time, convinced the English teacher to shitcan me, while Glotzer did the same. So, by the summer's end? I had been denied.

But in a Folger's Coffee switch-up moment, what they didn't know was that my stepfather was an award-winning journalist with a steady throughline into the Manhattan Borough President's office. Percy Sutton fired off a missive and next thing I knew I was sitting opposite Vice Principal Murray Kahn.

"You're on probation." He smiled at me. A smile that seemed fairly genuine. The smile that matches the power you bring to it I'd guess. "You maintain at least a 90 average and you're in."

My average for that probation period was 94 out of 100.

Glotzer spotted me in the halls once, registered shock and then contempt. I returned the contempt minus the shock. Later I had Kahn for chemistry and as a point of pride repeated the earlier act and got a 94 in his class.

Stuyvesant was significantly great. Unlike, Stanford, which is where I went after graduating from Stuyvesant, there was real class diversity, though to spell it out like that sounds hopelessly bound to the present day's elitism that plays at caring about such things. The reality though is that if your parents were rich, but YOU were stupid, you didn't get in. And if your parents were poor, but you were smart, you very definitely did. This is a state of affairs unlike any I had ever experienced, and looking back now there was a certain genius to both it and how the social tribal groupings broke down.

The blue-collar cats formed The Crew and flipped out when the Village kids burned a flag during some demonstration. There was a Korean Culture Club, a Chinese Culture Club, a Far East Culture Club, a Japanese Culture Club (the school was majority Asian) and the first person to ever choke me in a violent attack did so on account of me misidentifying him as Chinese.

"I'M FUCKING KOREAN!!!" he screamed after he had leaped across three desks in order to choke me. A choking during which I believe I was laughing.

The Asians who were studious grinds were also different from the ones who disco danced to boom boxes before school started and occasionally got shot in some heavy Chinatown Tong shit.

The summer school I went to was a good and representative mix. I think I may have been the only Black kid there, but I made fast friends with Enrique, a Puerto Rican guy from the South Bronx, and when the first day of school rolled around, we felt on equal footing with the kids who had known each other from their local PS's.

The school itself had just recently turned co-ed; it had originally been an all-male industrial school to which a raft of brilliant alumni had gone—Thelonious Monk, Ben Gazzara and one, or both of the guys from Steely Dan being the first batch that spring to mind—and the teachers, the most famous being Frank McCourt, he of *Angela's Ashes* fame, actually gave a shit.

When they weren't trying to fuck the students. "*Hey . . . it was the '70s! Everyone was experimenting!*" This didn't explain or excuse anything for me but the reality of it was there was no language for this to be corrected then. A scant two years after graduating I almost beat a man to death for having tried to rape a friend of mine—we'll get to this later—but when my high school girlfriend Hewon told me her home room teacher Shulman kept bugging her, we both kind of shrugged.

In fact, this had largely been the attitude to all the sex crimes I had had the misfortune of actually viewing or hearing about. I mean I saw my first rape at ten.

I SAW HIM GET RAPED:
What we see. What we can't unsee.

You know if you own a dog? You have to walk a dog. It's that simple. No one with a backyard wants a dog using it as a toilet and so out on the streets we went. Me. The dog. The walk spreading out in front of us.

This was before Stuyvesant. Before I started weightlifting and carrying a sharpened screwdriver. We lived in Brooklyn. A Brooklyn well before Giuliani and the 1978 Canine Waste Law that required the city's half a million dog owners to actually clean up after their pets. So just me and my malamute. We'd walk down the street on the driver's side of the cars parked from one end of the block to the other. She sniffed tires and would, on occasion, disappear between cars to poop.

The walk was about way more than bowel/bladder maintenance and much more about the contemplative stroll. And the nighttime walks often gave you glimpses into the lives and houses of your neighbors. Through closed windows in the winter and open windows in the summer, it was the smells of dinner cooking or arguments or just domestic noises. Human noises.

But this was the fall and there were still kids rushing in to eat, and adults rushing out to get the kids that needed to eat. The dog and I had already eaten and so in sort of a post-prandial pause we poked down and around the block which, given that I was 11, had become a map of desire, and I lingered longer by the houses of girls on the block that I liked. Hoping for a glimpse.

It was a nice neighborhood in Flatbush. Nothing too outrageous or dangerous happened there. Just human stuff.

But mid-block I catch a glimpse of something. It wasn't so much what I was seeing that had grabbed me. It was the way that what I had only glimpsed was *moving*. It was *undulating* and at the age of 11 I made it out for what it was: someone was fucking someone.

The house housed a slightly older kid named Ernest. He lived there with his family but when you're 11 your world is populated by your peers, so his parents were mysteries to me. But they seemed nice and were always nice to me.

Ernest, three years older than me, was another story. At 14 he had a lot of adult appeal. He was polite, always well dressed, bright and handsome. He fooled all of the adults. But Ernest was mean, so he didn't fool very many of us kids and when someone was scampering over the rooftops and breaking into people's houses through their stained-glass skylights, we were pretty sure it was Ernest.

Just to be clear: his family *also* had money. Ernest just broke bad. And now as I wove my way back to his house I could see in the darkened corner where one brownstone met the one next to it, Ernest's partially naked ass, very definitely rising and falling as he thrust into someone below him.

I couldn't see who and I couldn't hear who. They were being very quiet. But when a car pulled down the street and its lights partially illuminated the corner I could see it was his developmentally disabled younger relative. The six-year-old kid—nephew? brother?—gentle and harmless and well liked in the neighborhood, was now splayed below Ernest.

Ernest was a teenager and I expected he'd have been there with a teenager. I hadn't expected what I should have expected from Ernest. Confused, I hustled home, the dog in tow.

Was this something they did all of the time? Why would they do it? Why outside? Were they having fun? I knew enough to know that his parents didn't know but given all of the attention girls had paid to Ernest did Ernest like boys? Only? Would I be in danger for knowing what I now knew?

I never thought about rape, or consent, or that I was witnessing a crime. There wasn't the language for it back then. Leastways not language that was accessible to an 11-year-old. And while I was not ignorant about sex and sexual activity, I knew it happened usually between people who were not blood-related, but you . . . well, you never really knew what other people did, least of all your neighbors. In a weird co-related crime confession, my friend Mike had told me that his father was having sex with his sister.

He said he had witnessed, on multiple occasions, his father going into his sister's bedroom to do so. When he was asked if his mother knew, and what she thought about it, he shrugged. Very much like it was no big deal.

But also, with a trace of nerves playing around the edge of his mouth. He was the only Filipino guy we knew so at 11 we just assumed the adult world was stranger than we had imagined. But we didn't repeat it. To anyone. Or even to each other again.

Not because we knew it was a crime but because it was sexual and what? You were going to ask adults about this? Not likely.

"How was your walk?" My mother asked from the kitchen while I took the dog's leash off and let her run free.

"OK."

I didn't go to high school in the neighborhood so a few years later I wasn't around much and when I left to college there was soon no more neighborhood to go back to. Everyone had moved away, and into their adult lives. I figured though with the miracle of the tendrils of social media I might find Ernest again. To what end? To whatever end I could find.

And I did. I sent him a friend request. He did not accept it.

Armed & Almost Dangerous

I HATED STUYVESANT THOUGH. And I loved it. Given what I had to do to get there, there was this insane, parental-fueled drive to not be caught left-footed again. So, the pressure to excel was ever-present.

"What the fuck is this? An 88 in math?" My mother threw my report card on the ground. I had had freshly cut scars on my forearms since I imagined a tragedy, an accident of some kind would divert from this moment. So, I cut myself. Deep. And to no avail. But I was overcome with a sudden burst of emotion.

"So. What you're saying is that all of my grades are shit then?" I picked up my report card. There were tears in my eyes but machismo had already wrought an anger response to supplant the sorrow. I went to my room. The thought of killing my parents had crossed my mind more than once. I was an avid reader and if you were reading news, you couldn't miss that going into their teenage years this seemed a reasonable solution for many teenagers.

My mother appeared in the doorway of my room and explained. "I'm sorry," she started. "But life is hard and I remember your father, who I had to convince to get his PhD, because before he had one he was being treated like dirt and I swore that my son would have a different future if I could help it."

At this point my mother and stepfather had had two daughters, as had my father and his second wife. My oldest sister, always an empath, even at five, stood by my desk and held my hand while my mother continued. "Just being as good as everyone else is not ever going to be enough. YOU will have to be BETTER. That's what I would say to you."

And that was in all likelihood enough. Like Lou Reed once sang, I had then and there made a big decision. Instead of being chased to be BETTER. I would make myself unassailably better. Which started with all of the things in my life that were making me comfortable with mediocrity.

So, the mattress was the first to go. It was making me soft. I would sleep on the floor, sans blankets. In the summertime I would wear a winter coat. Inspired by my now-friend at block end who I had whipped home way back when, David being his name, I also started wearing no coats in winter.

I had started smoking pot freshman year of high school. Smoked three times a day, every day, for six months. This was during probation and concluded with my 94-average and being removed from probation. I stopped because I just got tired of hanging around potheads. And I had read that it changed you hormonally, a major concern of mine since part of the NEW REGIME, beyond the scourging of the flesh, was weightlifting. Lots more weightlifting. In what we called the playroom of our three-story brownstone.

For many, weightlifting is a wonderfully uplifting experience. I found a book at the time that captured the way it was for me though. The book was *The Gypsy's Curse* by Harry Crews and it was full of lunatics, cripples and murderers for whom weightlifting was the most normalizing thing that they could have done.

I muttered to imaginary adversaries. I gained weight. I gained strength. Started buying muscle magazines and huffing glandular supplements. Pituitary. Adrenal. Nothing sanctioned by the FDA. Not that I cared about it being sanctioned.

As to the schoolwork, I dug in and dug deep. How deep? After a year of this my mother had grown concerned.

"Why don't you go out with some of your friends?" It was Saturday. Such things were done.

A terse "I've got too much work to do." And it was paying off. My averages were closing in on 100 now. When I got another 88 in geometry I went to the math department and got a tutor. I'd never let anyone drive me with a whip again.

I found a compatriot in homeroom. Piszko, a thickly muscled sax player whose polka band's record was the first record put out by anyone I knew, used to buy *Muscle Magazine*. (My homeroom was full of musicians. One of the first Asian punk rockers, James Seetoo's band Nekron 99 was the second.) We'd pore over *Muscle* before we headed out to class, playing with the lingo and casually referencing our "barnyard door lats" and our "Clarence Bass-esque striations."

My bedroom wall was festooned with signed pics of bodybuilders as my mother started to add the wrong two to the wrong two and came up with a concern that I might be into men. Sexually.

Something that I think any healthy man must consider at precisely this age. As I did sitting in homeroom one day.

"I wonder if I am gay." The thought had announced itself. I still, having just turned 15, wasn't super interested in girls even if I had spent an inordinate amount of time climbing into dumpsters behind 7-11s to fish out old porno mags. But I felt totally comfortable with the gay friends I did have. It just seemed a fair thing to consider and so analytically I went through it. "OK. If I had to have sex with any guy in here, who would it be?"

I looked around the room before my eyes finally rested on a guy we affectionately had started to call "Johnny Karate," and in a flash I relaxed. Imagine a much-more femmed-out John Travolta and you had Karate. What was fundamentally attractive about him were the ways in which he was *womanly*. Had he been sporting a beard and dressed like a lumberjack I'd have guessed differently but I was glad to have gone through this exercise.

It freed me up to work harder. A friend had told me, in that high school game of telephone, "Mary likes you." So, I asked Mary out on a date. We went to see a movie. A Vietnam War movie, *Boys in Company C*. Which sucked. After the movie was over I hustled her back to the

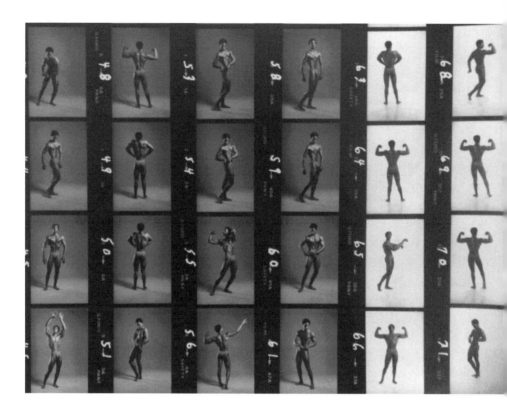

subway, said my goodbyes and headed home to finish a paper on Chiang Kai-shek. There was no second date. Mary was nice enough but had very little to do with sharpening my will in the iron forge of deprivation. This was exactly how I thought about it.

Or to quote Travis Bickle from *Taxi Driver*, a handbook for a handful of us on those same streets caught and captured by Scorsese, "too much had gone on for too long." But the grades were great, more significantly my parents were off of my back about those grades, and I had some breathing room to think. And what I was thinking about at this point was college and began framing a narrative along my interests. Joined the swim team, started writing for student publications, joined the wrestling team for a minute before being forced off of it by my mother who I guessed found this AND the bodybuilding all just a little too...manly? Or blue-collar. Or blue-collar and gay? Then I got involved in student government, which I liked about as much as you can like people who think government is an interesting thing to do.

Tom Caravaglia took some headshots for me back when I was 15. When the session was over he agreed to do a few bodybuilding shots for me as well. This was about eight months before my first competition.

I also maintained a parallel dark track. I started hanging with a junkie. Called himself Paco Chocolate. It was New York in the '70s, and one day making my way from Union Square to Stuyvesant, he adopted me for whatever reason. He was funny as shit, which explained my interest. If you were *funny*? I didn't give a shit if you were a murderer. The Deegan boys were funny as shit. The Haitian guys I hung with in Crown Heights? Riots. And Paco? Funny as fuck, *and* a murderer besides.

Or so he explained to me tracing a jagged scar along his belly where he kept a bottle of some shit, he was constantly offering me sips of. They had tried to stab him with a sharpened stick. He did what he had to do.

We'd get to the school, he'd ask when I was getting out and I'd either come hang with him for lunch or after school. My objective was clear though, even as entertaining as he was.

"Hey man. I need to buy a piece." Guns back then, before the pipeline from the south had been healthily explored, were hard to get in New York. But I figured Paco was closer to being able to get one than I was. I was already buying *Soldier of Fortune* magazine. I was rarely unarmed with some collection of knives. It was sort of the last puzzle piece in my urban pie.

We'd talk, plan and plot. Giving him cash upfront, was a nonstarter. From his end, getting one without cash was probably the same. But I had business that needed to be handled. I wanted, even though two years had passed, to address the wrongs that I felt needed to be righted. Brent the Jolly Stomper and the dude that had tied to me to the pole needed to have their karma leveled.

This was not hyperbole, and from the vantage point of time and experience I can figure out what was happening and what was happening was that the hormonal uptick caused and created by puberty was coalescing into some strange ideas.

The strangest? That I was physically strong enough to stop a train.

Sure, my youth had been full of an addictive attraction to the macho ideation that was part of Hercules cartoons. And Gigantor, whose defining characteristic was being both bigger than big AND stronger than strong. Superman also made the bold claim that he could stop a speeding locomotive so as the trains pulled into the station I frequently had to press my body against the staircase rising behind me, fighting the urge to prove to the world what the power of will looked like.

Was I also reading Nietzsche then? Thanks to Mr. Lipper's philosophy class I was reading Nietzsche, which should come as no surprise to anyone.

I was also getting into scuffles. Typically losing the ones I started, along the same lines—lines of "what the fuck are you looking at?"—and pulling draws on the rest. On the street. Or at swim meets. Or in school. A friend had stabbed himself in the thigh with an inexpertly flipped butterfly knife and was using a cane in the immediate aftermath.

"Hey Chris! LOOK!" I called out to Chris as we piled out of school one day, mimicking his Ahab-like limp.

"That's pretty funny, Eugene," he said while he hobbled over to me and kneed me in the groin. Still laughing, I twisted his head into a bulldog choke and pulled him to the ground before being pulled off of him. We had been friends, which he reminded me of when we were separated and I felt the briefest glimmer of guilt for beating up a guy with a cane, but you know, he struck first.

On meeting him at a reunion years later, I chose not to recall this part of our shared past. Chris had not gone to college but instead made a name for himself in New York building trades. I knew enough about New York building trades to know that this would have been unwise in the extreme and best filed under letting sleeping dogs lie.

But needing money for . . . my plans for whatever, I decided that I needed to either get to working, or start stealing. So putting my swim know-how to use, I applied for and got a summer job as a lifeguard at one of the settlement camps up along the prison rail line in upstate New York.

The camps were a conduit for disadvantaged city kids to spend a summer some place other than the city and it seemed like a good way to get paid. And even more than this, after two years a Spartan, I figured it was also a good way to get laid.

Did this change anything? This changed everything.

Boogie Oogie Ooging 'Til I Just Couldn't Boogie No More

DRUNK DRIVING ALWAYS CONFUSED ME. Not the drinking part. Or even the driving part. But much more so, the fact that people seemed shocked that they went together so well.

I was in Beacon, New York. At a redneck bar called Howie's. This is only important insofar as it was the first scene of me being threatened with physical violence and removed from an establishment on account of the word "nigger." I expected it was for playing the Village People's song "Macho Man" 15 times in a row on a juke box that surprised me by having it there in the first place, but who knows?

I *do* know that I spent a portion of one summer there drinking. Not just me, but me and a bunch of other staffers at the camp for kids, and this is how our evenings unfolded. We would walk to Howie's along a relatively empty country road, drink to excess, and walk back. One night, though, excess was a little *too* excessive and walking loomed as an impossibility. The later crew of staff had showed up, one of whom had a car. A sunburst yellow Ford LTD with a black vinyl roof, if memory serves.

"I can't fit you all in," the driver, a Puerto Rican cat about 27, told us, but we were all thinking the same thing regarding country roads, rednecks and too much drink. "Unless you want to sit on the outside of the car."

This was high-level drunk guy thinking. Which we immediately signed on for on account of? We were high-level drunk.

So, some people sat on the trunk, some people sat on the hood. As the driver calmed those nattering nabobs of negativity who were concerned about the overall *safety* of our solution, I climbed on to the roof of the car.

"Don't worry," I weaved. "I'll keep an eye out for hazards."

"I'm not," the driver responded. "I'll drive slow."

And standing on the roof like the Colossus of Maroussi, arms akimbo, I made a mental note of the difference between how 25 miles per hour feels from a seat and how it feels from the roof of a Ford LTD.

It felt . . . *fast*. And the ground moving by at what felt like some distance now, felt even faster. But even while it was feeling fast I had enough critical distance to note: this is *really* fucking stupid. The thing is, the distance between knowing *and* caring? Miles, years, lifetimes apart.

Like the band the Adolescents once sang, "*trashed beyond belief to show the kids don't want to learn.*"

The world is swirling, the wind is in your face and if it ended here, well what a fine place to end. Fuck it. You're just giving yourself over to fate. Fuck it. Seems like a natural fit to anyone what ever raised a glass over a set of car keys.

We lived. But the Nigger bit? I thought I had only been called a Nigger, to my face, six times. Then I remembered how it all popped off at Howie's. But to understand how we got here, we need to time-shift.

"So me, my uncle, my father and my brother would put on our orange suits and climb in the Cadillac."

The speaker was a roommate of mine, and eventual Best Man, Duane. The audience was a roomful of rapt listeners, listening to him describe just any ol' Tuesday in Portland, Oregon where he hailed from.

"We drive around for a bit with the lights off. Then my uncle, and we let him do it because he was the best at it, would slow down with the lights off and I don't know how he did it . . . he must have just *sensed*

it . . . he'd SUDDENLY flip on the bright lights, stun the raccoon, and knock it unconscious with the car."

He paused. For. Dramatic. Effect.

"Then we'd run out, throw them into our burlap sacks, toss them in the trunk and take them home to roast over the fireplace. Good meat! Good eats!"

There were tears in my eyes. Mostly because when I looked out at the sea of upturned faces, I could see they bought it. Mostly everyone *not* from Portland bought it. And everyone who bought it was white.

So, when people ask me why I don't talk or write more about race, I think about this story and wonder: how would it serve my purposes to try to explain to people, white people specifically, that you don't need orange suits and a Cadillac to catch, cook and consume raccoons?

I get it. I'm a smart guy. Race seems to be a nettlesome problem. Maybe I might have a perspective that others might find useful.

Maybe I'd start off with the fact that I think race, as understood in America, is not about *the state of*, but more *the process of* . . . race. But

Reserving the right to refuse anyone service. It's thus a miracle that we were served. Me, no explanation for my fashion-forward sensibilities, the Leon Brothers (David, hidden) and Rob (glasses), Jaime and our karate black belt. Like the same night we got surrounded and then kicked out of Howie's under threat of bodily harm.

after that all bets are off because America's obsession with race is not about solutions. It's about reifying a standard that no one has any real interest in changing.

So, I don't focus on the macro. I focus on the micro. Or QTAT. Stuff that, specifically, keeps me from making Quick Time Across Town. And interestingly enough Obama told Bruce Springsteen about being called a nigger on their new podcast. But you know, something about those two feels slightly out of time to me. Like they were on vacation and are just now coming back to the scene of some unspecified disaster and sort of forgetting that the rest of us are still here.

Anyway, the first time someone called *me* a nigger I laughed in her face. She was Black as well, which I said. To her face. She didn't drop the "r" either. This was 1972. She was Panamanian and put some spin on it: "You Black Niggers!" We were kids and she was an adult taking umbrage at us doing kid stuff. But we were like the all-Black Bowery Boys, and we just laughed at her. Until she went back in the house and let us be.

The fifth time? It was shouted from a person speeding by. I was in my 20s and laughed at him as well. The strength of his conviction was written all over him driving 55 miles per hour in a 25 miles-per-hour zone and spotting me over 100 yards away and feeling a need to offer commentary on the process of race in America.

Time number four was out in Bay Ridge, Brooklyn where a scant few years later Yusef Hawkins was shot under very similar circumstances. But it was a teenaged me against three *cugines*. Them with broken bottles, a crescent wrench, and a German shepherd. The finer details of the night in question are in my other book, *Fight, Or Everything You Ever Wanted to Know About Ass Kicking But Were Afraid You'd Get Your Ass Kicked for Asking*. But there was very little laughter that night. Not when I was stomping one of the attackers into unconsciousness or later in the hospital when I was getting stitched up, my left ear hanging off of my head.

The looser details? It was the last summer before college. I had gone to see The Clash's *Rude Boy* at a midnight showing. My date had stood me up but I would not be deterred. I also, to get in the mood, listened to one song about 30 times that night as I got ready: the Specials' "Concrete Jungle." Call that more "foreshadowing."

Post-flick I see a fight in the middle of the large avenue that cuts through Bay Ridge. One Black guy, five white guys. I don't know who is doing what but I am armed and in superhero mode. I make my way across the street right as a resolve is being reached. The two older white guys jump in the cab that they had been fighting around. The Black guy jumps in the front seat and one of the teenagers jumps on the hood as the car skids off into a Brooklyn night, falling pretty much at my feet.

"What the fuck are you looking at Nigger?"

I shove my hand in my pocket and then there is a nervous dance of urban fear. But urban fear is always premised on poker. As in, what's in your hand? The hand that's in the pocket of my pants. I knew what I had. But I didn't know what they thought I had.

What I had: brass knuckles.

What they thought I had: a gun.

And feeding off the fear I made the altogether tactical error of laying out my cards too soon not realizing that three guys, already armed with crescent wrenches, a German shepherd and broken bottles would be in no way cowed by the knucks.

A fusillade of broken bottles intended to send me running, something I intuited would be an unwise thing to do at two in the morning on account of that whole running inviting chasing thing. As I turned to cross the street, comfortable with taking the L on this one, a bottle hit me in the side of my head and it was like a warm water balloon burst under my clothes. As I watched the blood spread all over my nice sharkskin blue ska suit, I was filled with a divine rage and since you're never sure what you're going to do in situations like this I am still shocked that I did what I did.

Which was . . . raise both of my fists to the sky and scream a scream that followed my eyes to G-d, and then turned down from the heavens and into the eyes of the attackers and left them only a single way out. Which they took: running off into the theater I had just come from. In a fugue state I stomped the bottle thrower, my leg working like a piston, and the spell was broken only when a man described as his uncle burst through the doors and seeing me standing on his nephew, but by the phones, asked, "You calling THE COPS?!?!"

In this we were bonded and back on Planet Sane. Calling the cops wasn't going to help anyone. I caught a cab home, unsheathed my shotgun from where I had hidden it and made for the car with the intent being to head back to the gas station where the *cugines* worked. Just to . . . "scare them a little." I could hear my mother making her way down the stairs so stowed the gun and answered her questions about my evening as normally as possible to forestall her actually seeing me.

But she wanted to see me and once seeing me it was hospital time where after being summarily left to bleed by the ghetto hospital Doog took me to the private one where an emergency room hack inexpertly sewed my ear back on, permanently making my left ear hole too small. People ask why I started using duct tape on my ears with OXBOW and the answer was always simple though needing more explanation perhaps. But ear plugs never comfortably stayed in after that. The tape held them in.

It was so painful to wash that I showed up for freshman orientation at Stanford University with blood still caked on my face and my left ear sticking out horizontally like a wing. That was time number four.

Nigger Time number three was most notable. I was almost murdered by a mob enforcer, also a *cugine*, in a basement in Ridgewood, Queens. The word itself and everything heaped in, on and around it was really much less of an issue than that I needed to make it out of that basement alive.

But it was my friend Ciccio who got me to go there, and the fact that I was even there was crazy. But this was before time number four. So, more ignorance than arrogance.

"There's a great gym in my neighborhood. You wanna go?"

I had been lifting weights since I was nine years old; by age 16, after multiple viewings of the recently released springboard for Arnold Schwarzenegger, *Pumping Iron*, it had occurred to me that if I was ever going to make my bodybuilding dreams come true, I'd have to make them come true in a place built for it. To wit: a real gym.

I was game, even though the place was 50 minutes by subway from Stuyvesant, where Ciccio and I originally met, and my house. Location was much less of a snag than the neighborhood the gym was in. Ciccio tried to warn me about something I had pretty much been oblivious to so far.

"There are not a lot of Black people in my neighborhood," Ciccio said, almost apologetically. While it was New York during the 1970s and I understood the balkanization of neighborhoods, I never processed New York neighborhoods along the lines of thinking there was anywhere I "shouldn't" go. Which is to say that warnings about possible "racism" didn't yet register with me.

What did register was that I was going to a place that was much less about race and much more about the received secrets of steel and the power to lift it.

If you're familiar with the luxury, fern-fueled gyms of today, this gym wouldn't have made sense to you. It was all cinder blocks and seriously rough trade: Sonny Liston's former sparring partner, ex-cops, former circus strongmen who could bend railroad spikes, and steroid-steeped barbell boys with a jones for juice who had dropped out of high school just so they could do this. Guys who would spit on the floors and walls before squatting four plates, or 405 pounds, for 20 reps. Guys who mixed their orange juice and protein powders with vodka. And me.

I lifted, eventually getting into the rhythm of the gym. Ciccio was long gone by then, abandoned in the wake of my mania for the pig metal we were hoisting and a five-days-a-week lifting schedule. When I walked the six blocks from the subway station to the gym, people recognized me. I had a training partner—two, actually—and when I walked into the gym, the guys were happy to see me.

"Hey, kid! How's it hanging?"

It was a working-class heaven, but beyond that, something else.

"You wanna buy a suit?" A sky-blue Buick had pulled up in front of the gym. A guy I lifted with opened the trunk; when it raised up, the suits hanging from a jury-rigged rack raised up too. The suits were cheap but still too rich for my blood.

At that moment, everything suddenly made sense: the fancy cars, the jewelry, snatches of overheard conversations. This was the modern mob. It's how I got my aforementioned (and first) shotgun. In any case I eventually came to figure out who belonged to which family, knowledge that laid the groundwork for what I would later call "getting way too comfortable." I was a teenager and no matter how much of a badass I thought I was, I was by no means a professional badass.

"You stupid piece of shit! What the fuck is the matter with you?"

The entire room glanced over at the raised platform in the corner. Lester, 6 feet and 2 inches of 255 pound anger was letting loose on Freddy, his training partner. Apparently, a moment of inattention on Freddy's part had caused the 455 pounds Les was bench pressing to slip.

Freddy was terrified. My training partner and I, not so much. We were not connected guys. We were just . . . guys.

"Ladies, ladies, please . . . could you keep it down?" I said, which was the wrong thing to say at exactly the wrong time. But then again, when faced with a steroid-soaked enforcer mid-rant no time was the right time. Lester moved way faster than a man that big had any right to move. He grabbed a 100-pound plate and waved it at me like he was waving a paper plate.

"You shut the fuck up, nigger!" The room froze, because this moment was going to be fraught no matter what, and Lester wasn't about to be stopped, let alone by political correctness. "One more peep out of you . . . even one more peep"—every vein in his neck pulsed—"and I will crack your skull open with this."

The room turned back to me. I was doing everything in my power to not embrace the contrarian I was down to the bone. I was doing the math, and in my calculations, I envisioned myself saying the one thing, and one thing only, that made sense.

"Peep."

Now, I didn't *say* it. I just thought it and then factored in what would happen next.

I definitely knew what would not happen next: The made guys in the room wouldn't stop Lester from coming down on me. Not because I was a civilian, a teenager or Black, but because I wasn't a pragmatist. Which is to say only a jackass or someone with some serious weight behind him would have said anything right then. Sure, they would have stopped Lester from killing me, but I'd never be the same again.

I considered saying "peep" and then running, but I knew I'd never clear the steps out of the concrete bunker of the basement.

So, at 16 and about 160 pounds, I backed the smart play: I said *nothing*. Eventually, Lester's rage subsided and the room's rhythm was reestablished.

My training partner turned to me. "Why didn't you say anything?"

I snorted. "Why didn't *you* say anything?"

"He wasn't talking to me," he soundly reasoned.

Lester and I later became friends, it seemed he bore some vestigial feelings of guilt over his 'roid rage. Sicilian-style, I'm sure he has not forgotten it, but only because he knows I haven't. And it always pays to remember all the reasons someone might want to murder you. Even when he's a friend.

That was time number three.

Time number two? Well, this wasn't time number two but it bears retelling. You see, I used to spend the summers with my father in Maryland when I was a kid and after he left the "city house" and headed back to the Maryland/D.C. area from which he came. It was Kensington, Maryland, and in the ways that people had with kids back then after I got my suitcase in my room, he'd head back to writing (he had started a translation company), and not so much tell me, as suggest "go play."

So, I did. The first kid I made friends with was named David. He picked me and we did some version of Tom Sawyer–type stuff since to me Maryland was the country. I'd see other kids in the neighborhood, but they stayed away from David, and me, when I was with David.

One day we were at his house and his mother was in a sudden panic. "Your father's home!"

We were playing down in his backyard and his mother's panic was shared by David. I made nothing of it until his father's angry face appeared in the upper window screaming something. I couldn't hear what it was. I was a Brooklyn kid, through and through, so I screamed back.

"WHAT?!?!"

But David was ghostly white now and almost whispered, "I gotta go in now."

I left and when questioned about my day I told my father what had happened with my new playmate.

"Well, that's probably because David's father is in the Ku Klux Klan."

"I thought he was the fire chief."

"He's both."

So, while I never played with David again, and no one in that house ever called me a nigger, I was guessing that that's what the father had been screaming.

The rest of my summers there were fairly uneventful. I was a welcome wrinkle to folks who spent all school year together and were generally happy/amused to have the kid with the heavy Brooklyn accent around again. So, time number two really snuck up on me.

"Let's go play some ball." Tommy Smallwood stood up on a slight incline with a basketball under his arm. I stood down below. I think I was having some nature moment like city kids have. Watching lizards or something. He was insistent. He pushed and I pulled back. Tommy had a great sense of humor and I've cut someone with a sense of humor some slack, but our relationship was also fraught.

"Nigger!" And he threw the ball at my head activating a series of events that started with me scrambling up the muddy hill after him, catching him, and then almost killing him. No basketball was played that day.

This was the "So, how is it my fault that your son's a sissy?" day. This still stands as one of the most amazing things I've ever heard a father say to another father, and miles beyond "boys will be boys." And the best punch line was: Tommy and I played together nicely after that. Our fathers never spoke again.

But what I thought was the last time someone called me a nigger was in San Francisco. The San Francisco Giants were playing. People were flooding in; I was walking away through the crowds. I saw him, this white cat, across the street as the light changed.

He was in full-on Eminem mode. Pants sagging, baseball cap at a rakish angle, he bopped across the street, all 5'9", 165 pounds of him, oversized down jacket swirling around his waist. I watched him as we walked toward each other. I smirked while I watched him and when he was about eight feet away . . . "Yo, nigger."

Or maybe he said "nigga;" I don't distinguish and I also, as you may have noticed, don't use "the N-word," though I'm OK with everyone else doing it.

"Yo, nigger."

I didn't stop smirking. I didn't stop walking. I stared at him, silent, and in three feet he was nothing but a memory to me until now. See, I was making quick time across town. I had some place to be.

This is where I would have ended the list but then I remembered Howie's up in Beacon, New York, near Poughkeepsie. And I remember this all because of a photo that just showed up via Facebook. It was me, the woodshop specialist, the music specialist, who happened to be his brother, Vernon, a counselor and a karate blackbelt, and a roly-poly Puerto Rican cat named Jaime.

We would take a table—no one carded 15-year-olds in bars back then—and order some beers and bullshit. Until one night we found our table surrounded by Marines.

"Time to go, Niggers." Which I found to be an interesting turn of phrase since the two specialists were Jews, Jaime was Puerto Rican, and only Vernon and I were Black. But I was not cowed and understood always from boxing and karate that if someone wanted to bring it to you, you should welcome it being brought to you.

I started chuckling and sliding my chair back. Right up until I looked around the table. If you've ever been in a situation like this, what you're looking for is a trigger. A look that says, collectively, we are of one mind and a singular purpose. When I looked around the table I saw our ace in the hole, the karate black belt, staring straight ahead.

I wasn't seeing things the way he saw them. Clearly. As an adult now I can see that he saw himself against five adult males who, with no provocation at all, set upon him, three teenagers and a bespectacled hippie, for a sum total of shit odds.

I was disappointed at our lack of engagement, but I understood almost immediately and continued sliding the chair back, stood, and we left, leaving our half-consumed beers on the table and walked back in silence.

We never spoke of this again but everyone else did. And Howie, who watched silently from behind the bar, lost the camp's business for the duration of that summer and the summer after that.

Instead, we started hanging out at RJ's Lounge, the Black bar in town. The music was better, there were women, and dancing was a thing. I had been to parties before but like the Contours once sang in

"Do You Love Me (Now That I Can Dance?)," I had avoided the dance floor. So, clubbing seemed simple at that point: either drink enough that no one would ask you to dance or learn how to dance.

The Rock, the Spank, the Latin Hustle. People did these dances and I watched while they did them. One of the first rappers ever was there that summer as well. Then calling himself Dollar Bill, he later had a career as Jimmy Spicer. I later had a "career" in Whipping Boy where I stole one of his raps for a song we did called "My Day at the Lake," a paean to macro-dosing acid.

But I watched and, back in my room, would practice alone. No one ever asked in a way that I hadn't been able to beg my way out of, but the night it finally happened, I didn't try to beg my way out and it was great. Barbara was hot, from Queens, and about six years older than me and when I agreed, she made a face followed up with a vocal exclamation that went around the room: "Oooooooohhhh . . . "

I grabbed her hand and we hit the floor and pulled off a reasonable facsimile of the Rock. Enough so that people lost interest in whether or not I could or would, because I had, without much fanfare, joined the ranks of the dancers.

Which is how I spent my nights, routinely. Funny thing though, like Kurt Elling once asserted, sometimes the best things happen when you dance and I understood immediately the social value. *Saying* something stupid was an easy hole to fall into. Dancing stupid? Much harder to do. I mean you can dance badly, but presuming you have a functioning level of rhythm and an appreciation for music? You were in business.

However, my business that summer was lifeguarding and I did a fair-to-middling job of it. The kids seemed to like me, but my bosses were the real ones, cut from a cloth that almost made me feel OK for being only OK at it. Yick was half Chinese and half Puerto Rican, a bad ass martial artist, who had run the program well before I showed up. Jose, his second in command, came from the same South Bronx neighborhood. Both were older than me and both felt like the closest I was ever going to have to older brothers.

I was a ready and open ear for Jose's recent travails with his girlfriend, Antoinette, who also worked there. She had dumped him not too far into the summer and he spent our days at the pool together working through it. The finer points of the he-said-she-said unwinding. But he was 19, she was 16 and what did I know?

I spent a lot of time listening to my mother and my stepfather argue so I had a rough guide regarding what *not* to do, but outside of that? Blank-slating it.

Even more so when I ended up one night gathered around an empty beer bottle and that damnable kissing "game" that started where the bottle stopped spinning. I was game though and the first time someone spun, a 200-pound woman with a beard, it stopped in front of me and the crowd hooted and hollered vocalizing that which they believed was obvious: I couldn't possibly have been happy about this turn of events.

But as I watched her beg off like she hadn't wanted to play and I saw the normative unfolding I got angry. So, what she was fat and had a beard? This was a game and if it was a game we were playing, presumably to have fun, I would play it to have fun and I grabbed her and kissed her deep and long until the crowd subsided, confused, and then silent.

Of course, no good deed goes unpunished, and her spins subsequently seemed to be stopping in front of me way too often. But I was never quite so enthusiastic as the first time and so she graciously retired. Which was not at all what happened with me and Antoinette.

Antoinette was from Harlem, the daughter of a cop, was fit as fuck— think gymnast or sprinter—and one of the hottest women at the camp. I didn't know her side of the story about why she had dumped Jose, but at 15, I was just glad she was there and when her spin landed on me, I knew it was going to be a problem.

"What did you do last night?"

Jose was not that big of a drinker, didn't dance, and was avoiding her post-break up, so he didn't go out much, but how I was going to answer that inevitable question was what I considered the second that bottle stopped spinning. And it set in motion a dilemma that would later be largely part of a very significant Road to Damascus moment.

"Nothing," I answered, and like the chaplain in *Catch-22*, I lied, and it was good. Or at the very least I had scored on two of the three reasons that people had usually lied. I avoided hurting someone, in this instance someone I liked, and I avoided being punished for having hurt him in absentia.

Forgivable the first time but nothing ever ends after the first time, and I met Antoinette again and again. This was the beginning of women who were drawn to authority figures being drawn to me. Credit/blame the bodybuilding. And even more so when she watched me, with a passionate interest, break up a fight one night and when she stepped in to intervene, I lifted her out of the way.

It aroused her, and she spent the rest of our time together trying to generate, or re-generate, the rage she saw in my eyes that one night. None of it was working. In general, I'm a fairly even-tempered guy who flips out only rarely. But she needed to know, and so went for the most obvious hot-ticket item.

"I fooled around with your girlfriend last night." The kid was named Ramon. I say kid but we were the same age. We were almost the same guy. He was my height, my weight, but not as muscled, handsome, and funny. Something 100 times out of 100 I am prone to saying. I called him a liar and then he described what it was like to kiss her, and I understood that he wasn't telling lies.

Moreover, I understood that I was then, and even today, unlikely to be one of those guys that was triggered by this. I congratulated him and understood, on a deeper level, the punch line and then beyond that a certain amount of resolve: I'd be no Jose about this. Ramon had been instructed to report back my reaction. Any reaction. But there was nothing to report. Outside of the fact that I was back at RJ's that night drinking and dancing, ending up at a table with a crowd that included Dawn, the camp's new music director.

She could play the shit out of her guitar and in a place created hand-in-hand with folkie Pete Seeger, was cut from the same sort of folkie cloth. From the vantage point of now it may not have made sense, but Janis Ian, Carly Simon, Carole King, weren't just loved by teenage girls, there was a whole contingent of male admirers whose interest was clearly somatic, and I was among them.

So we drank, danced and someone suggested playing the best/lamest drinking game ever: Truth, Dare, Consequence, Promise or Repeat. Dawn was peppered with questions since she was new, older and still somewhat of a camp celebrity being that she had played shows and was in college.

"Do you believe in extramarital sex?" Someone had asked her.

"You mean PRE-marital?"

"Yes."

"Yes."

The group had dispensed with Dare, Consequence, Promise or Repeat, and it was all just truth now.

"If you had to choose someone to have sex with, who do you think the hottest guys in camp are?"

"Manny." Manny looked like the Marlboro Man, and in fact smoked filterless Gitanes, wore chains, and was a Village People manly kind of man.

"That was guys. Plural."

Then that moment that's part of everyone's highlight reel but just my turn to be high and lighted.

"Eugene."

There was laughter and uproar and I was a good sport and laughed along with the people laughing at me. But I slowed down my drinking and when we got back to camp, the two of us split off from the group and went wandering until our wandering finally found us in a memorial chapel for the war dead where in an excess of thrill we fucked seven times on the gray slate floor.

I don't tell this to say that I'm a stud, as the first two times were rabbit rapid but the length between times extended and at some point we were lit by a flashlight from outside. Mid-fuck haze we neither moved nor protested and the light went away. Whoever carried the light also carried the news back to Antoinette.

But then it was all about that night and when in the morning we wandered out of the chapel, mist and fog rose up against the mountain that loomed near and in the background.

"Am I the first white woman you've ever had sex with?" A question that I thought was weird and never one that I would have thought to ask, but how to answer?

"No." Which was a lie, but the truth was much more involved as she was the first woman I had ever had sex with. Antoinette, in her desire to call forth my anger, as well as genuine 16-year-old panic, had stopped me, multiple times, after I pulled off the Mission Impossible act of opening the condom with one hand, putting it on with one hand, while not breaking off the kissing or offering an opportunity to any kind of second thinking about what we were doing.

Antoinette heard about my night. Which rolled into a second night of fucking with no sleep and drinking, which led to a series of events – and endless jokes about "the crack of Dawn" – that saw me sent to the infirmary with a fever and strep throat. By the time I got out, the folkie was done with me, Antoinette was done with me, and given that the summer was almost over, I was done with me.

Heading back into school, a few weeks after camp I remember feeling...relieved. For? For how my life would change now that fucking would be a normal and everyday part of it.

Yeah: I had yet to smell the coffee and figure out that just because there is food, that doesn't mean you'll get to eat any of it.

The Knives, the Drugs, the Punk Rock of It All

WHILE BOTH MY FATHER and my stepfather were take-no-prisoners competitors, and it seemed, based on the previous account, that my mother was somewhat sympathetic to my plight of being overmatched by adults that were pretty phenomenal in their own right already, it's totally accurate that she is the one I owe the vast majority of this to, since she was by no means any kind of a shrinking violet.

"What's that?" She was teaching me to read, and we were sitting on our living room couch on Butler Street in Cobble Hill. I had paused, so she asked again, this time a little sharper. "What's THAT?"

Well, that, as I stared at it, was a "camul," spelled the way a seven-year-old might.

"What's a 'CAMUL'?" Her eyes lit up with glee and I could feel my skin burn and without a realization that unless I gave it away some other way, she wouldn't be able to tell that I was blushing. Bothered by my casual error and even more bothered that I hadn't caught it before she had.

And we were OFF to the comedy races. "Is a CAMUL like part cat and part mule? What is it EXACTLY?" My mother had always been worried about me being a target for bullies, so lovingly had undertaken

the job herself. So stings about the size of my forehead never hurt and were always processed as comedy. So, was this . . . ridicule or humor? Conflating both has served me in my good stead for the rest of my life, up to and including the streets I lived in when we lived on Butler Street and I had sparked a gang fight in the schoolyard across the street.

Two kids, a little older than me, were playing baseball. Or rather, one kid was pitching the ball and one kid was hitting it. They were project kids and my mom, always a great advocate for the underdog, had taken me over to the projects for their Halloween celebration one year. A trip that lasted right up until a pool ball fight broke out and we both realized that it's one thing to want to help the disadvantaged, it was something else entirely getting your front teeth knocked out trying to do so.

"Get the fuck out of here, stupid!" The hitter, who had been mostly missing, started blaming me for his failures in life. Which made me laugh.

"I said GET THE FUCK OUT OF HERE!" And he hit the fence that my fingers had been laced through. I moved my fingers but made no other motions to leave even in the face of his ridicule which, on a cer-

"Bookies, Nunzios, Menzos too. Packing brown. Shooting goo."
Apologies to The Meatmen. Here we are at the aforementioned Bookies.
A good time was had by all . . . 10 people in attendance.

tain level, I processed as . . . humor? It wasn't until the pitcher spoke up that the energy behind it all had started to build.

"Leave him alone." It was detracting from his win, and it seemed he didn't like bullies any more than I did.

"Fuck you!" And the school bell rang right as the batter threw his bat and the pitcher fired the ball at his head and their friends piled on and the entire schoolyard looked like one of those barroom scenes in wild westerns. I left, my work there being largely done. Besides which, my benefactor may not have come out on top so the time seemed right.

But my mother had built into me a resilience and a hard line that could not be negotiated around. It was this kind of rigor that I brought to how I read when I started reading, and very much part of what was going on when I started writing.

Get it right or go the fuck home.

My stepfather was a journalist at the *New York Post* where he had won the Silurian Award and had a few noteworthy series on antipoverty programs and about Latin gangs in New York. A prisoner of conscience, he quit the *Post* when Murdoch bought it, but he bounced around from *Newsday* to the *Soho Weekly News* and so on after that.

Newspapers were all over the house, and the only fights he and I ever had were over who was going to read *Esquire,* or *Evergreen,* first. But there was a type of news that routinely caught my eye. Crime. Beyond that, the badasses whose pictures were now routinely gracing the paper's pages in 1977: the Ramones. Then the cat who attacked the audience, James Chance. And when the Sex Pistols descended on New York, mostly via the antics, if you can call murder and suicide "antics," of Sid and Nancy, I was in.

David, fellow high school spartan and the guy who I had initially chased and whipped before we became friends, had turned me on to Kiss when I was 13, and though I was steeped in R&B and my deal with dancing had me in love with disco, the emotional palette wasn't enough. Yet guys who carried knives—or looked like they might—and guys who I saw street fighting who were dressed like women but fought like men while looking like the New York Dolls, captured my eyes, ears, attention and interest.

"Here. I got something for you." Doog had been doing salsa reviews forever and was down with Tito Puente, Celia Cruz, Ray Baretto and so on, so he was always bringing home records by the Fania AllStars, but this was not that. This was much more than that. This was Eddie and the Hot Rods and the record was *Teenage Depression*, and as a kid who had already started to exhibit early signs of deep thought and a sobered outlook often confused for depression, I could see how it made sense to him to give the record to me.

The kid on the cover had a gun to his head and the record itself felt badass to me. And the Bowery was only a few stops away from Brooklyn. And a few blocks away from Stuyvesant. I only recall one kid showing up to school in a leather jacket, but he didn't interest me at all. It was instead a friend of mine whose older sister was supposedly friends with Johnny Thunders and Lydia Lunch that finally sanctioned a visit to CBGBs.

But let me lay it out for you if you weren't there in 1978, since you have no idea what 1978 was like. Which is OK, and goes without saying for just about any year before you were born. It's really just a cheesy setup to say: 1978 was a bitch of a year.

Not a COVID bitch of a year but still: junk was king; before there was a name for PTSD, cats were coming back from Vietnam with shit that caused them to lose their fucking minds in whatever manner served those minds. Hippies metastasized into disco cokeheads and murder was on everyone's mind because Son of Sam was shooting people in lovers' lanes. Either because his neighbor's dog told him to OR because they were trying to make snuff films for the tony Long Island set who thought those kinds of things were *kinky*.

CBGBs, the club, not the reconstituted clothing store, was all I had read about, and Yvonne's sister agreed to meet us in front. It was a few blocks over from the men's shelter. So, it was bum central, when bums were mostly men who were committed to a lifestyle of fortified wine and inebriated lassitude, not victims of right- and left-wing policy gone awry. I was 16 and was showing up to see a band I had only read about. The band was called Shrapnel.

Yvonne's sister scanned my get-up (think De Niro from *Taxi Driver*, Vietnam-era field coat, untorn jeans, and construction boots), and had made a decision that it was best to make believe I was invisible. Which was fine. It was way too loud to talk, and I had nothing to talk about anyway. I was in absorb mode and the air, the stink, the sounds, the chatter all needed to be noted.

I was obsessed with Lydia Lunch so that was enough to get me there on the off chance that her sister could pull off an intro. But I was also in desperate need to see Shrapnel. Dave Wyndorf was a weightlifter (it seemed at the time) who dressed up like the WWII comic book tough guy Sgt. Rock, and while it was heavy schtick and concept, because they were from Jersey no one was ever really sure. And this during a time when there was a real stigma to being a "bridge and tunnel" type—no one was going back to Brooklyn or Jersey, G-d forbid, to have sex with you—I felt some sort of affinity based on what I had read.

"OK. Our next song is called 'Hey Little Gook'!" Wyndorf screamed, and if it makes you cringe *now* to hear it, you need to know it almost killed people back then. Lester Bangs or no Lester Bangs, the entire scene courtesy of the swastika-sporting Sid Vicious had weird anti-hippie posturing that played with racism in a way that confused people about how much of it was play.

On my way to the much-vaunted CBs toilet to take a piss later, someone chanted after me "Push push in the bush," the refrain from a popular disco song of the day, and I got it. And courtesy of my mom, I took no umbrage but laughed. It was funny, and it was funny that they thought it was a barb that would sting, and even funnier yet if you considered where that road might have gone: no one here could have beaten me, and no one here was more armed than I was. Courtesy of Brooklyn.

So yeah, I laughed. Not at the "Hey Little Gook" but the disco jab. Mostly because I still dug disco and if I wasn't downtown, I was going to be at Studio 54. Or New York, New York. Or Xenon. Disco dancing. I was skilled enough at this point that I had been waylaid into teaching it at some club-based class for rhythm-challenged college kids and what we'd later call yuppies. Seemed like a good strategy to get laid, especially since I had figured out that getting "laid" required *effort*.

But Shrapnel? Was it satire? Were they serious? Did they mean it? Does it matter?

If you read about them at all you'll see them described as "punk rock." And now with everyone talking about Punk 1.5, this sort of weird bridge between punk rock and hardcore, I think having been there and peeped the vibe, I can comfortably say that what this was, was indubitably hardcore. About which people always asked the aforementioned questions.

The only line that answers that question, I quote almost constantly, and it comes to me by way of the Adolescents, the L.A. band that came along a few years later: "trashed beyond belief to show the *kids don't want to learn*" . . .

Wyndorf stood center stage now, bomb foisted over his head, chewing on a dimestore stogie, and finishing their set—almost an entire set of songs that were paeans to the teenage thrill of traveling to exotic places, meeting different kinds of people and, like the peace posters at the time said, killing them.

And I was in. I have no recollection of ever going out with Yvonne or her sister again but having gone to CBGBs once, I'd return.

Like . . . sitting in the train, going home. Olive-green field jacket now sporting a few buttons that marked me for those with the eyes to know.

A guy sitting across from me who looked like Tony Musante, or the priest from *The Exorcist*, starts talking to me. Pre-AIDS and as pretty as I was, it could have been a *pick-up*. This is no mean boast. Until I was 13 and the weightlifting started kicking in, I was routinely mistaken for a girl. A fact that never really bothered me. I, at this point, now had four sisters and female cousins galore, so it never seemed to be a shameful identification. Or one that made me feel bad. I just wasn't interested in having sex with men, so it paid to make sure. Soon and early.

"Where you going?"

"Home."

"You see any of those bands on your buttons?"

"I only get buttons of bands that I've seen," I say. "Except for the Joy Division one. I haven't seen them yet."

"Let's go to Max's then!" He was about 26. Which means, I thought, that he had money, of course. He could afford to.

"I can't."

"You gotta be home?"

"Nah, man. I just don't have any money to get in or back on the train after I leave," I laugh.

"Fuck THAT. I'll show you how to do it!" And we were off.

Max's Kansas City, up above 14th Street, sidled up by Union Square, was a different deal and vibe entirely. At this point I had been seeing everyone I could. The Rattlers, the Plasmatics, James Chance, Klaus Nomi, Joe "King" Carrasco, the Nylons, Gang of Four, anything Lydia did, Johnny Thunders, Buzz Wayne, Von LMO, Blondie, Talking Heads, Ramones, whoever and whatever had "punk" attached to it.

Or, more specifically, whoever had a flyer with their name attached to it and a look that intrigued. I had long ago stopped telling Yvonne where I was going and what I was doing just because it made it seem like I had a crush on her, which I did, but I was also smart enough to know that she had zero interest in either me or the music. And I was thrilled by both me and the music.

Usually these nights were just cone-of-silence nights. I came alone, spoke to no one, and left alone. This was not sad nor depressing to me, and when asked to report on my doings I always described to my parents, truthfully, that I was having a great time. You see, I didn't have any siblings until I was 10 years old, so my mother had drilled into my head this idea that as an only child you have to entertain yourself. So, I did. I'd see some of the same people at shows and on occasion random people from my high school who I said "hello" to but didn't spend any more time with them in the clubs than I would have in the hallways at school.

But for the first time with this Tony Musante dude I was talking to people. About nothing, but usually the music. Which was all I wanted to talk about anyway. We watched the bands play and pogo'd back when people did such things. That is, a dance that involved just jumping up and down. I had stopped smoking weed but he hipped me to stealing drinks off of the bar. Drinks *and* tips, so I had money to get back home on the train at least.

Then Sid stabbed Nancy, some of the older folks moved off into weird art shit, which I liked, or declared punk was dead and left, leaving a void that would soon be filled by hardcore. But for the newspaper folks, this was all the punctuation that they needed. Punk, for them, was dead. For me, it provided a part of my emotional palette that wasn't filled by anything else. On a Friday night at least.

By which I mean in that interregnum between the stabbing of Nancy and Sid's death and hardcore, I was also digging deep into disco. Yeah, later friends of mine like 11-year-old drummer Harley Flanagan, Claudette, Jack Rabid and Ira, who actually was the one that had hollered "Push Push" at me at CBs and later befriended me when I returned to New York with my hardcore band Whipping Boy, were always there and had never left, but they, apparently, had no interest or aspiration to dance.

Saturdays, now encouraged by my mother who had been thoroughly creeped out by the workaholic robot I had become and now calmed by great grades all the time, I was hitting the discos. The main allure of which was very clearly women, easy availability of drugs, and the possibility that mixing the two might get you in wherever when whatever was happening, was happening.

And that's the thing I had always assumed when seeing the Day of the Locusts throngs assembled outside of Studio 54 pleading to get in, that I was getting in because I had the "look," which, I was guessing, was some version of disco cool. It took me about 20 years to realize, like starting from a suddenly stopped dream, that the only reason they were letting me in was on account of the assumption that I'd be selling drugs.

I was sort of disappointed that it was this and not the cooler, hipper, more fashionable thing, but it also filled in the blank for every single confusing conversation I had had over thumping basslines with strangers who I assumed just wanted a piece of me. I was apparently the worst drug dealer in the world and had no idea why I was being talked to, but liked the recognition even if it confused me.

Something else, a weird sort of quirk: despite my willingness to do drugs, and drink, and try to have sex with people doing the same, I refused to lie. So, when asked by women who went to Columbia if I went to Columbia, I would say that I went to Stuyvesant. They'd ask because at 16 and 17 I looked like I was 14 or 15.

Which narrowed my options. Being handsome and being able to dance meant I had no shortage of dance partners. Being handsome, being able to dance and being 16 meant I spent more time fending off adult men who, pre-AIDS, were living their best and greatest lives and embodying the true spirit of the Village People's "Macho Man" by being "ready to get down with anyone they can."

"Have you ever thought of modeling?" To a large degree the amount and quality of sympathy I have for women comes not just from having four sisters (and later four daughters) and tons of female cousins, but also from being on the business end of men making moves. Later, I decide after a woman friend shows me a letter another male friend had written her trying to talk her into bed, that there are some things we're just better off not knowing, first and foremost: what men say to get laid.

But the model bit was never not lame. Especially since I had been modeling since I was two. Modeling and doing all variety of musical theater. Captain Hook in *Peter Pan*, the Tin Man in *The Wizard of Oz*, textbook photo shoots, and auditions for everything up to and including, most famously, Woody Allen's creepy-now-to-consider flick *Manhattan*.

The not lying bit though: when I met people in the clubs, in the days before cellphones, and they wanted to know where to find you, you'd tell them where you worked. And where I worked was a hoot. It was called "Dennis' Fast & Natural" and it was a fast-health-food eatery on 18th Street and Fifth Avenue. Not far from Max's Kansas City. Which wasn't far from Andy Warhol's *Interview* magazine.

But they had us wear these tight French-cut T-shirts and when the model troll came in one day, I had guessed from the club convo we were both thinking transactionally.

He waited until I got off of work and walked with me toward Union Square. I told him I had modeled and rolled off my résumé. At the time, I couldn't afford to go to Uta Hagen's school to study acting, so a good friend of mine was attending and she'd leave class and pass me her notes. Some version of life under the klieg lights was where I wanted to be and I said so.

"But are you willing to hustle?" I knew "The Hustle" as a dance. I knew "hustle" meant to work hard. So, I said I did.

"Yeah. I'm a hustler!" A statement he could see meant we still understood the term very differently. To say I didn't suspect would be wrong, as at one point he dropped a step behind me and when he caught up, he made sure I could see that he stopped so he could watch me from the back. But like Holden Caulfield in *Catcher in the Rye*, stuff like this was always happening to me. So not a surprise. And if he was willing to aid and abet my fortunes? Whatever.

He started calling me at home. His name was Christopher Hyland and while today he is a CEO of a high-end fabric company, his past was deep and full of work for the Foreign Service, and he is mentioned several times in features on the Irish Peace process, besides being some sort of international bon vivant, fluent in a few languages, and making the claim as he did at the time to being a friend and a habitué of the Warhol crowd.

What he didn't know is that when business was slow, Dennis from Dennis' would have us deliver food, and I had delivered all up and down Fifth Avenue. Into the fashion houses. Out of the fashion houses. Again, places where I was invisible, but places where I had my eyes open, and a lean and hungry look.

Because of my time at Studio 54 I had seen celeb-crazy New Yorkers perform all kinds of acts unspeakable to get from the outer circle to some sort of sweet spot in the inner circle. You'd not be wrong to have guessed that in '78 and '79, Andy Warhol's deal was at the pulsing center of it all.

Journalistically speaking, *Interview* was sort of a soft sell, just like Warhol's latter-day art aesthetic. Its modus operandi was a fly-on-the-wall setup of unlikely interview twosomes. Kind of like the odd pairings you might have found spread across couches during one of Warhol's Studio 54 hangs; the mag kept the upmarket tuned in to downmarket doings, and vice versa.

I was mostly invisible, like a not-so-super-stylish Black teenager would have been, but by virtue of being a competitive teenage bodybuilder and now routinely sporting a work outfit of a sky-blue, tight, French-cut T-shirt emblazoned with the words "Fast & Natural," was a little more visible. The shirts were designed to denote good health and wholesomeness, and to those customers for whom those were fetishistic lures, the shirts provided endless opportunities to double entendre their way through multiple interactions with us.

I'm not saying this is why I always found myself called to deliver food over to *Interview*. I'm just saying that I did. A lot. Like, I always delivered food over to *Interview*. And with a lifelong interest in media, the prospect of going to an office that housed the great man's magazine was only slightly more alluring than heading to any of the fashion houses that used to call me to the set where half-naked models made

This was not Dennis' French-cut shirt but it's exactly what I mean when I talk about French-cut shirts. Emblazoned with the words "Fast" and "Natural."

me for what I was, broke mostly, and therefore of no interest to them: they saw a bridge-and-tunnel kid with a penchant for pushups.

Yeah, Andy's place was the spot, and on the rare occasion I had any dealings with him—handing his order to his assistant or putting it on his desk, some brief chatter and the inevitable lingering for a tip—I always left the encounter shocked at how wildly divergent his cultivated media image was from his actual one. At least as presented to me. Not wan and waif-like at all, Warhol was taller than me at the time and, even with my weightlifting, he was physically much more substantial and imposing, it seemed. Manly is not a word often used to describe him, but it's a word I would have used after meeting him.

These visits left me inevitably and uncharacteristically quiet. None of this Sammy Glick smooth-operator shit that was on display in my first query letter to *Esquire* at the age of eight, or that marked my acceptance of a Gannett Times Mirror scholarship on my way to college. At *Interview* I brought to bear all of the aforementioned watchful intensity and it was noticed by the staff who'd, I'd been told by my manager at Dennis', Howard, said "send the muscle-y one." So noticed, yes, but not for any winks of journalistic promise.

Still, in the full blush of my squandered Basquiat moment—I had no hand-drawn postcards to hand to Warhol, no intimations of my genius then or to come to distinguish myself in his memory—Hyland's entry was well-timed and he played it to his advantage. "Are you willing to hustle?" Indeed.

Bob Colacello, Warhol's right-hand man, was the name he'd drop most often, and as I had seen Colacello in the office, I knew just about how much juice he had. All things considered. And all things considered and from the vantage point of a city that, at the time, knew no boundaries, Hyland extended, by way of Colacello he had said, parties, invites, promises and all manner of chemically inclined sexiness way outside the pay grade of a delivery boy. Though perhaps not of a body-building delivery boy in a French-cut T-shirt. Sex in the city. With a commensurate pay range.

"Now if Andy was having a party, a small party," he worked it as the phone crackled and I sat in the kitchen at my house and listened, "and needed you to show up in your posing trunks, could you do this?"

"Sure." Bodybuilding had made me cocky. "You need a few of us?"

"Just you."

"Oh." This changes the equation. Years later while working as a bouncer for strippers for mobile stripper parties I came to learn this beyond a shadow of a doubt. Also, learned that without a .38 at some of these mobile parties, no one was getting out of there unfucked. "How much is he paying?"

This wasn't going the way he wanted since, in all likelihood, there was no party at all: "Look. Do you have any problem at all fucking?"

"For FREE?"

"Men. For cash!"

And there it was. "Nah. Not doing that."

"Look! If you want to MAKE it in Hollywood, you're going to have to face certain realities. There are lots of handsome guys out there. What would make YOU special?"

"Talent."

"Even people with talent suck dick. Name one who hasn't!"

So, I picked the most straight-arrow one I could think of: "Gary Cooper?"

"HAH!"

And our conversation concluded with some mumbled imprecations about "wising up." To which I thought, "fuck that guy."

Later my mother asked me who that was on the phone and I said "some guy with a radio show that wants to introduce me to Warhol for a show or something."

"Well, be careful."

"Always."

The story would have ended there but for a twist. A year later, a year and about 10 more pounds of muscle, me now weighing in at probably 180 pounds, I happened to spy Hyland over near the Strand where I had been buying some Mickey Spillane books.

There was no need for rancor, and we talked comfortably, mostly about the jobs I had subsequently booked without sucking dick. But the temptation took him and he made another play.

"Look. I'm just going to put this out there, and I can see you have put on some more muscle, and you're probably pretty good with your

Years after the Interview *magazine imbroglio the modeling bit had picked up steam.*
Here, an outtake from a session in San Francisco's Union Square.
(Photo by Merwelene Van Der Merwe)

hands now if you're still boxing," and he shuffled and threw some casual punches in the air. "We could be somewhere 20 minutes from now and I'd pay you $500 to drip hot wax on my body. How's that sound to you?"

I laughed it off. That was not laughing-off money back then but I've never been super motivated by money while simultaneously being SUPER motivated by money. That is, wanted it, but didn't want to work HARD for it. Like most, maybe. So I considered it and the consideration went thusly: could I take him if things started to go south?

Then he made a fatal mistake. "Look . . . I've been lifting weights too . . . feel!" And placing my hand on his bicep I knew right then and there that it'd have been a fight to the very end. Seeing this play on my face he offered one last shot: "You could tie me up while you did it."

Nah. Though later while flipping through the phone book I looked up where he lived. It was around the corner from where we were standing. It, in no way, would have taken 20 minutes to get there. No idea what he had planned that it would have taken 20 minutes to set up before I got there, but the lesson was taken and embraced, solidified by my earlier moment tied to that pole in Flatbush: don't ever give away your edge.

The weird parallel life action that this all implied wasn't lost on me. The punk rock kid, the disco dancer, the high schooler and the bodybuilder, all living under the same roof with the now increasing pressure to next-stage it by picking a college and doing the things that needed to be done to get out of the house where my mother and stepfather's marriage was slow-motion crashing, and into whatever future it seemed to make sense to me to embrace.

During the summers I had traditionally gone to Maryland to spend at least a month with my largely silent father, his second wife and my two sisters. I loved going to Maryland, but Maryland wasn't making me rich, and on the occasion of an argument of some kind, my mother stopped encouraging the trip and my father never insisted. So I rolled over gigs at Dennis' to time at the New York City Jazz Museum, the dance instructing, and at least one more summer as a lifeguard before getting what was, by all measures, a pretty good city job.

Between the first and second year as a lifeguard I continued the summer stunts since there was nothing happening sex-wise at high school. I started hanging out with Antoinette again, who had decided that she "forgave" me for fucking the folk singer but who hadn't forgotten her attraction to rage and difficulty. She'd invite me up to her place in Harlem after her father had gone to work. This is not the Harlem where my mother presently lives, with Hugo Boss stores and Michelin star eateries courtesy of Marcus Samuelsson.

This was Harlem where you could get killed. She had a wonderful brownstone above 110th Street so when I wasn't heading over to the South Bronx to drink Southern Comfort and snort coke with Jose, her erstwhile ex-boyfriend, I was seeing her, still not having figured out how to tell him, while still wary of her desire to get me killed.

I had always timed my exits well before her father's return and this was her in. She started keeping me longer and longer and at that age it took a major act of will to leave. Outside of an instinct of self-preservation. One night she kept me, and the time was melting as fast as my spider sense was tingling. I broke loose and hit the streets, and before I had made it to the end of the block, I was shouldered out of the way by a beat cop in dress blues who had just barreled around the corner like a cop in some action flick. Barreled with blood in his eyes. I knew it was her father because he looked like her and I suddenly understood.

I didn't speak to her again until I had moved to California and it was then that she told me that she had had two kids after dropping out of college. I asked if she had dropped out of college because of the kids.

"No, babe," she laughed. "I got *kicked* out."

"For what?"

"I stabbed a guy with an icepick," she laughed again and explained. He had been flirting with her while she had been breaking up some ice for a party. He was teasing and swatting her and she said that she had told him what she would do if he didn't stop. He didn't believe her and didn't stop. So, "right through his arm!"

"What did he do then?"

"Started screaming like a bitch," she concluded. I still hadn't told Jose and we were friends until the day I figured out that someone had told him. I could hear it in his voice. I was sad but I knew I had it coming. It was fucked, and while I cared that it was fucked, I didn't have the skill set or the fortitude to make it less so, and in that instance? You get what you deserve.

In any case, going back to the camp the next summer after a school year of killing it with grades and working a swim team grift where I would run a "swim-a-thon" deal that both put the most amount of money of any swimmer on the swim team into the school coffers while simultaneously putting the same amount into mine for swimming for six hours straight, I found Jose hadn't returned.

There were new people, and when I gave the initial tour to the camp staffers before the kids showed, one had taken a particular interest in the pool.

"Will it be ready soon?"

"Soon, yes."

"Well, you look like you're ready already." This hung there and after a year of beating back advances from dudes I didn't want to have sex with and having my advances beaten back by women who didn't want to have sex with me, I understood exactly what this was and laughed.

"Always." Joyce was a rarity there in that she actually did not come from the city. She was a local. And even more than a local, her father was the chief warden at Fishkill Correctional Facility. They actually lived on the grounds of the famed House of Pain, Sing Sing Prison, which now stands as a great moment of continued shame for me. Nothing compared to that generated by the poor souls parked there, but for me significant enough.

Coming home from college she had decided on a summer job there and me as her erstwhile boyfriend. But being a boyfriend, nothing I had any inkling of how to do, is not something I had planned on spending the summer doing. Sex? Yes. Boyfriending? No.

So, on my days off, I'd do whatever suited me, and in my case this usually meant lolling around the room I shared with the wood shop counselor. Reading, bullshitting, listening to "new wave" radio—typically in my posing trunks. I was an amateur teenage bodybuilder so hanging around in posing trunks (think modified Speedos) was not as strange as it sounds. OK, maybe it was.

Joyce was insistent we spend our next day off together. Not just together, but at dinner. At her parents' house. Nothing I had agreed to, so I was surprised when she showed up in the middle of the B-52s' "Rock Lobster."

"Let's go." I objected, an argument ensued and finally I hit on an escape clause when asked, for the umpteenth time, why I didn't want to go.

"I don't feel like getting dressed. So, I'll go if I can go the way I am dressed now." Red posing trunks, no shirt, no shoes. "And I don't want to have to talk to anybody. Just like now."

She stormed out and I fell back in bed, victorious, my roommate running after her. They returned together.

"OK. You can go the way you are."

Grousing and resisting still, just with less brio, I stormed out to the car, jumped in. Silent. As we drove through a succession of gates guarded by muscular, angry-looking men with rifles, I'd be lying if I didn't say I was rethinking things. Pulling up in front of a nice Hudson Valley house now, even more.

And then this: "Here, man. Why don't you put these on?" My roommate, who'd been invited to dinner too, handed me some pants.

"HO-HO! YOU DON'T THINK I'LL GO THROUGH WITH IT, EH?" And with that, and without pants, I sprinted to the front door that was opened by none other than the warden. And for me, a rare moment of contrition. "I suppose you're wondering why I'm dressed like this . . . "

"No." He didn't smile. He didn't frown. He just looked at me. As father of four daughters now, I'm dying a little bit inside just writing that.

And, so, in the house I go. The mother, after the initial shock, adjusted quite well. So well that the second part of my ill-formed plan didn't seem that out of place. Which was plopping down on the living room couch and promptly falling asleep. Remember: "I don't want to have to talk to anybody."

By the time dinner rolled around, I woke up to discover that none of what had happened was a dream. It was painfully, uncomfortably real. No matter how hard, now I tried to be charming during dinner. Which concluded without event, leaving us to our own devices.

The car ride back was silent, and after my roommate got out, my girlfriend turned to me and asked the most heartbreaking question ever: "Are you still angry with me?"

And because I wasn't finished being a dick I said, "Being angry is NOT the issue." With that, I left her car and for reasons unknown to me jumped on the hood, walked over the car and headed into the wooded night to find my way back to my room.

"That was fucked up, man." He couldn't look at me, my roommate. And he hasn't really to this day.

The girlfriend? Found through the miracle of the internet some decades later. She's a super successful academic. I'm an apologizing ex.

"What? I don't remember any of that," she emailed.

No idea if she was laughing when she wrote it or if she was even telling the truth. But I had done what I could by way of making amends, and if there was one good thing to come of it, it was this: Having established a baseline for dickishness, I would never sink so low again. But I've also learned to never say never.

The school year unrolled easily enough. But everything else in this trifurcated life was getting weirder and uglier. One night after leaving Studio 54 I heard a scattering, footsteps disappearing off down 54th Street, away from me, revealing a guy who sat on the corner where the building met the street. It was right about where the Jazz Museum used to be, and it used to be 50 yards down from Studio 54.

It was working there where I had met Dizzy Gillespie and Billy Eckstine. Played around on Gene Krupa's drums and now watched a man watch me while we both tried to figure out next moves. Blood pulsed between his fingers where he had been stabbed in the stomach. I had seen the teenagers that had stabbed him run off toward 6th Avenue, but in his state, disco outfit notwithstanding, I was unsure if he'd be able to tell the dandified Black teen from the ones that had stabbed him.

I could see firemen moving through the Studio 54 crowds and if they weren't looking for him they'd find him soon enough. And then a command decision: if they found him, I wasn't going to take a chance on him having the correct kind of recall and so I left him there and did not turn around. Something that was easy enough to do back then.

But then a twist in the school year. I spent the vast majority of my time not going to discos or CBs with a guy who quite comfortably could have been considered, and was by me, my best friend. He was a strange and unlikely best friend for me to have as our interests in life didn't align at all. But he was probably one of the funniest people I had ever met and this was not just more than enough, this was the best of all possible worlds.

So when I wasn't out trying, mostly unsuccessfully, to get laid, we were out walking the city, vision questing, and planning any and all variety of scheme-o-logy.

"I punched Howard Skrill in the face today." Doug was my favorite kind of comedian in that you were never sure how much of it/him was comedy, how much was merely comedic and how much was just leaving you in the dust to figure out yourself.

"What? Why?"

"He called me a 'dancing bear'." Skrill was into the Grateful Dead, and often worse, tie-dyed shirts gaily festooned with dancing bears.

"So, you hit him?"

"I'm no fucking dancing bear." Then: silence. Which was kind of perfection. Almost as perfect as when someone once asked me if I was friends with him and if he was indeed, as some had suggested, retarded.

"Yeah, I'm friends with him, and retarded? You should be so retarded."

We were brothers, and the fact that his mother was a judge and his father a lawyer, and before that his father was a judge and his mother was a lawyer, didn't mean nearly as much as the fact that his father had hired the hottest secretary he could possibly have found, and didn't mind and even encouraged us to hang around his office.

Not that we had any interest in the law. But we did have an interest in hot secretaries who were also funny and cool besides.

"You think your father is fucking her?"

"How the hell would I know?" Which was as good of an answer as any.

As we got closer to the college application process, we had figured out that the disparity in our grades meant that we'd probably not get into our same first choices. Mine was Stanford. His was the University of Michigan. So we hooked up some kind of Tom Sawyer plan.

We'd break into the school late one night and change his grades. It was that simple. So, with rubber gloves, a crowbar, bandannas masking our faces, white-out correction fluid and a whole variety of pens and markers, we set out on our glorious mission.

Since our school day ended at 3 p.m., we figured that the school closed shortly after. Showing up at 9 p.m. seemed a safe bet. But 15th Street was well-lit, and there were still lights on in the building when we arrived, so we cruised by the park, working out the finer points of our excursion into the unknown.

By 11 p.m. things had quieted down. We strolled down 15th and up to a fenced railing where we talked a bit before jumping over into a stairwell that led us down to two doors in what would have been the basement, under the vice principal's office.

"Hold the bag," I whispered, right before jamming the crowbar into the small space between the doors. Then I yanked.

It made more noise than I expected, but rather than scaring me off, it made me dig down even deeper. I yanked again.

"Eugene . . . ?"

"Hold on . . . " I yanked so hard I could see light.

"Eugene . . . ?"

"Gimme a minute . . . "

"EUGENE!" There was an urgency this time, enough that I stopped.

"What?" I hissed. We were almost there.

"I can't do this . . . "

"Come on, we're—"

And he ran. Since he had taken the bag I had to shove the crowbar down one pant leg. When I came up the stairs, leg stiff like a pirate, I saw my friend disappearing into the park. I hobbled up, faster, until I caught up and fell in step next to him, grabbed the bag, pulled the crowbar out of my pant leg and put it in. He was in the grips of a mortal terror.

"I . . . I just . . . "

"It's OK," I told him.

We walked in silence to Union Square, where I took a train back into Brooklyn while he caught one to the Upper West Side.

He got into the University of Michigan, which was my second choice. Really reduced to my last choice since when I had met Michigan alumni at an event designed to lure promising high school seniors to the Midwest, they ignored me, the Black teen, until they found out where I went to high school—a harbinger of undergrad misery if there ever was one, and I had hardened against them.

But he went on to his first choice and by all accounts was happy with it. We see each other infrequently now, but when we do it's very much like old times—minus the breaking and entering. We've never talked about that night again.

During the school year, though, something else of note had happened that was neither part of life at the Olympia, the gym out in Ridgewood or the disco days and nights, or the punk rock shows.

"Hey. You know Hewon, right?"

I knew her and had seen her. She was quiet but noticeable and it was the third time someone had sent feelers my way IN school. The first time, I was in work grind mode and never gave Mary any kind of even shake. The second time it was with the daughter of working-class Italians who, she had warned, would flip if they knew she was dating a Black guy. This also fizzled. I mean stacking up the doings in school with my life outside of school was a struggle that high school routinely lost. I mean despite my mother's dictum of not going anywhere with anyone, after I had started driving and could tool around in my stepfather's orange VW, I was pretty much going anywhere with anybody if there was a possibility of sex at ride's end.

But Hewon's parents, also nuts, were nuts in a way that made obeying them virtually impossible. She could only date someone that they had chosen, and preferably someone from their village back in Korea. So she chose me and I was amenable to being chosen, even if I was very clearly the wrong choice for her and not just because of her parents.

The late '70s were whipping themselves up into an unprecedented mania. It was in the air, in the streets, all over. No one knew or very much suspected that coke was going to cause the problems it later did, and it was comfortably viewed as the status'd drug of choice over the downmarket heroin. But the flights of exhilaration, and grandiosity, that are so much part of a coke high, that and eventual paranoia, changed everything.

And Son of Sam was shooting people. Not for the reasons stated by the papers that stated them, with Jimmy Breslin leading the charge of "crazed lone wolf" shit, but for something deeper and darker. Snuff films were at first an urban "legend" and then a marketing opportunity for enterprising young psychopaths. I had nothing to support this but the gaps in the papers and then their inevitable course corrections up until accused shooter David Berkowitz was caught. But if you had wandered into the Magickal Childe bookstore, or had any kind of offhand interest in the occult, which I had, you could feel it. It being "the crazy."

I wasn't crazy, outside of my belief that I could stop a subway train, which was fueled by puberty, but being fueled by puberty, I was probably not the best first boyfriend for a nice Korean girl to have. But we had a blast and my parents were overjoyed at something/anything that could counter the creeping sense that I'd never be into girls. Read: gay.

Now, point of clarification: my mother was no homophobe. She had just read in some 1960s Dr. Spock treatise that sons raised by strong female figures had tended toward homosexuality. It should also be remembered that homosexuality had initially been spotted as a mental illness for a long time. So it was less that I would have been a homosexual but more that she had *made* me so.

Anyways Hewon was invited over and then after some obligatory face time they tactfully disappeared so I could begin the wholly unflattering attempts to convince someone who hadn't done any fucking before that fucking now made a lot of sense. My goal, in total, was not really sexual congress in this instance. It was mostly not embarrassing myself. So, I imagined I was as laissez-faire as any 17-year-old could have been. But it was a tough job. That is, not pressuring, *and* being faithful, *and* getting to the gym and getting out those college applications, *and* dealing with conversations about the future where the only idea I had was to get as far away from New York as possible.

And wandering through the halls one day I was dreading going to a calculus class. The teacher was a fellow named Fisher. Fisher scared the shit out of the vast majority of the student body. Stooped and beyond irascible, he had earned my love with a stunt that I duly noted and has followed me for years.

One day, apropos of nothing, he asks a girl in the class what two plus two is and she answers, full of adolescent confidence: "Four!"

Which causes Fisher to slam his fists into his desk and send the books and papers there flying.

He turns to her again. Slowly and dripping with no small amount of venom: "I'm going to ask you again . . . what is two plus two?"

This time she answers, red-faced, and slightly less sure: "Four?"

And he repeats the rage bit, coffee cup on his desk flying to the floor. Now he pulls up on her, a foot from her face. "Try. It. Again. WHAT'S TWO PLUS TWO?!?!"

She blurts out, half crying, all terror, "FIVE?!?"

"HAHAHAHAHAHA . . . " Fisher burst into laughter and just as quickly she burst into tears. With a student body of kids whose parents were well placed he may have realized the ramifications of her very bad day in school and tried to clean it up, but I marveled at this like I had marveled at other acts of singular sadism.

I'm not saying I fell in love with Fisher but I made no move to get out of his class since I knew my time would come and I was desperate to know what that would look like. I didn't have to wait long. After a test he began reading out grades, on a scale of 0 to 100, before handing papers back.

I was never a great math student and so was delighted that the math big-brains were taking it in the shorts. Grades of 10 and 37 (out of 100) were being passed out like candy and I was visibly gleeful. He was deducting points if he couldn't read your name. If he didn't like the color pen you had used. And, yeah, I just didn't see it coming.

"And the lowest grade in ALL of my classes . . . " and I'm looking around the room waiting for the punch line, not realizing that I hadn't gotten my paper back yet and so, in all likelihood, WAS the punch line. "Mr. Robinson . . . A ZERO!"

I did the only thing that made sense to me then: "HAHAHAHAHA-HAH . . . " And took my paper. While only briefly surprised, I believe he was pleasantly so. To find someone who could appreciate what a symphony of sadism he had wrought? Must have been priceless.

But these grades had real-world ramifications, and I was in no way prepared for the test I was wandering the halls trying to avoid.

Some hippie woman in a peasant dress wandered out of an empty classroom.

"Hey . . . " She had reddish hair, pulled into long ponytails like the kind later favored by Willie Nelson. "You want to go to Stanford?" She was a college career counselor and the way it worked was this: you got to avoid a class if you were seeing a counselor, so I sat through her presentation, which went thusly: "We're half an hour from the beach, half an hour from San Francisco, and here are some pictures."

After a cursory peek at the *Underground Guide to Colleges* and having figured out that the male-female ratio was not as miserable for my future prospects as where Hewon was going and where she was encouraging me to go, MIT, I was sold. Applications were sent and I had to redirect when everyone at the gym thought I was leaving to go to STAMFORD. As in Connecticut.

"They ain't nothing but fruits and nuts out there," was the refrain that was repeated at both the gym and in my yearbook.

And then this: "If you're going anywhere near San Francisco there are two things you will definitely do." Lorraine and I had met at the Mudd Club. Before I was a bouncer there on occasion—doorman Richard Boch thought it made sense to sometimes trade an entry fee to have some tough punks working the front door with him—I was going there to see people like Klaus Nomi, catch glimpses of David Bowie, and dance "new wave" when I didn't feel like discoing.

Lorraine, who also lived in Brooklyn and had written her number on an old Marlboro package: "You'll get your ear pierced and some tattoos," she said about my impending move to California. She had also told me that her ex-husband lived in California, San Francisco to be exact, and had I ever heard of Biafra? Jello Biafra?

All I knew about the Dead Kennedys at that point was the name and the singles that had blown them up nationally because of, not despite, the band name.

But I had wanted a tattoo my entire life. My grandfather used to read *Moby Dick* to me, the illustrated version, before I could read, and the muscled Pacific Islander Queequeg's bodywork had impressed me. On proclaiming my interest my mother had immediately said "not while you live in this house," but one of my plans upon moving out West involved precisely that. Same with the ear piercing so Lorraine was singing my song.

As the school year was winding down, acceptances rolled in. I had started to compete in bodybuilding shows, so my head, outside of the prom, was as far outside of school time as it could have been. More musicians had popped up in school, and outside of Piszko and James Seetoo from Nekron 99 they all threw shade my way though I'd never seen them at any shows. The single time I saw a guy named Bob, who ridiculed me mercilessly for not knowing anything about harmonics, outside of high school he was with his band, and they were stumbling out of Bleecker Bob's (no relation) famous record store. And they were drunk, taking up a lot of space and singing the words to the Dead Kennedys' "Too Drunk to Fuck."

I said, "Hey Bob."

Bob said, "Whatever."

Which was fine by me. I knew something he didn't know: I was here to stay.

But the prom went off without a hitch, Hewon looked hot as fuck and when she asked what I wanted to do post-prom my answer was predictable. She, however, demurred and we instead went to the promenade made famous by Woody Allen (again) in the poster from *Manhattan* and made out until the sun started to rise.

Later that summer, after almost getting killed in that Bay Ridge street fight, I fought tears in the airport saying goodbye to my mother. She had already kicked my stepfather out. When he told me that they were breaking up I said, "GOOD!" Their fights were long, legendary and frequently involved smashed crockery, fistfighting and the occasional knife play because Mom had clearly had enough.

So we stood in the airport, hugged, the blood still caked on the side of my face and my ear pulsing, and I left to go to California where my seven-year-old sister believed that parrots lived in the trees. Something that sounded good, and believable to me. I mean, what did I know?

California Demons

AFTER THREE OR FOUR bodybuilding competitions, never finishing in the top five, being natural and un-steroided at the time, I was still invested in this as a lifetime calling. So upon landing at San Francisco Airport, the Stanford volunteers who were bundling us toward the buses and noting whose luggage had been lost (mine) told me that when we got to Stanford I could wait, and it'd probably be on the next bus.

"I think I want to get a workout in," I said, trying to hide the bloody side of my head from the chirpy Resident Assistant, *my* chirpy resident assistant, who had taken to calling me the nickname I hated the most since Gary and which I only tolerated/liked from close family members.

"Well, Gene, we had events planned," she smiled, grabbing my arm. Which was way too much closeness for a guy just 30 minutes off the plane from New York.

"I'll join after the gym." And after my workout, which I pulled off with just the sweats in my carry-on and the shirt I had been wearing on the plane, I made my way shirtless back to the dorm.

I was disconcerted by the gym. It wasn't the Olympia. No cinder blocks, no steroids, no guys mixing their protein powder with orange

juice and vodka pre-workout only to pass out mid-workout from mixing protein powder with orange juice and vodka. No *outré* sex stories that involved people blowing loads in their girlfriend's husband's shoes while said husband was at work. No more gun sales or stolen suits. No more cops mixing with Mafiosi mixing with old-style strongmen and Irish and Italian World War II vets.

No more guys like Gary Aprahamian who I saw curl the rear end of a Toyota before he died in his early 20s from a performance-enhanced tumor, or that old sparring partner of Sonny Liston who had murdered a guy who insulted a woman when he punched him through a car window and the guy's throat got cut on the jagged broken glass. He said he tried to stem the flow of blood. By stomping on his neck.

First time driving across country. From the Upper Westside to Denver where I bought my first motorcycle and rode the rest of the way to Stanford. With no gloves. And nothing but a T-shirt on under this leather. Unwise? In the extreme.

And if I sound like I missed all of that, I most certainly did. Because California most certainly made no sense at all to me, and the gym was the first sign that I was heading for . . . a struggle. Everyone was so clean. And coming from a gym where torn and dirty clothing was the staple workout gear, they were...well-dressed in my eyes. Moreover, they were really well-adjusted, so much so that to me it seemed that they were maladjusted.

My hair was uncombed. Like the not-sleeping-on-a-mattress jag, I also stopped combing my hair. Fuck it. A large football player kept staring at me as I worked through heavy sets of bench presses and dumbbell incline presses. His problem? No idea. But I needed to get to my room just in case there was a better bed to choose and meet my roommate.

"JERSEY?"

As I stood there sweating, I think I had just hugged my roommate. Right before he told me he was from "Orange." I assumed he meant Jersey. Apparently, there's an Orange in California too. Orange County. Right in the middle of what I would come to figure out was Reagan Country.

He was a wrestler, into philosophy, with crap taste in music but an expansive worldview that immediately signaled that I had gotten lucky. I mean I liked him and his habit of stroking his beard while running any conversation into dead air, which I fully appreciated for how uncomfortable it seemed to make people feel. I first noticed how uncomfortable it made me, fresh from New York, where conversation is used like it is in prison, like echolocation, better tuned to getting a sense of who is around you, so dead air is like having your radio go down.

But when I noticed a succession of people squirming I knew there was a certain meditative genius to it, and when he passed me a book by Bukowski and another by Alan Watts, I was in. A loose confederacy had started to form, strung along lines of philosophy, politics, sports, music, art and those who got it, separating from the religious fanatics, the repressed, or anyone who thought a frat party sounded like a fun time.

All of the Black men in the dorm were placed physically close to each other and though my roommate was a Jewish guy from SoCal, our across the hall neighbors were the later-to-be-famous Andre K.

Braugher and his roommate who I famously impersonated later on my first trip to jail, Craig. Craig's last name was Spearman but in homage to *M*A*S*H* and a character therein he had decided to have people call him "SpearChucker." It was a laff riot that played out thusly, again and again.

"Hey? Have you seen SpearChucker?"

"You mean CRAIG?" I glared, not caring whether they got it or not. Craig was from the Bronx and I have no idea if this SpearChucker thing was a holdover from then but I do remember reading, before I got to Stanford, that Ivy Leagues like Dartmouth had had a few notable racial incidents. This was enough to cause me to pack the shotgun I was scheming to go and use against the *cugines* that had almost torn my ear off. I had no idea how Stanford was going to play out but it was not going to play out with me huddling in fear of anything, and that Craig would poke this bear unbidden? Seemed like an unforced error to me.

But Andre was from Chicago and showed up at Stanford to be a chemical engineer. Something he stuck to for exactly a month. That was about the same amount of time it took me to abandon the fantasy that I was going to spend my life doing research in swamps for oil companies as a marine biologist. I had shit career counseling but it's because I had been so adamant about being the first Black Jacques Cousteau.

We decided to do a play together around this same time. *The Basic Training of Pavlo Hummel*, a play by the mighty David Rabe. The role I wanted? Hummel's badassed alter ego. The role I got? The much more narrow Sgt. Tower. It was a big role. As big as Braugher's but it required that I use a Southern accent, which was as comical on me as it was on Bronx resident Tony Curtis when he was doing Shakespeare.

"Yonda is da castle of my fadduh," indeed. Two weeks in the director told me to drop my attempt at a Southern accent, which was both curious and dove deep. I mean, my entire life, during the '60s when there was a national cultural obsession with "real" and "natural," conversational norms relaxed and what is commonly understood as "Black English" started to become "authentic" to the Black experience.

I had grown up and watched my mother "code switch" with a kind of wonder. My father didn't at all. He and my stepfather were two of the most don't-give-a-shit men I had ever met. But if my mom could

I'm the one in the leather jacket. Grabbing my crotch.

code switch, I thought I should be able to, as well. I tried once. That is: ONE time, and it felt so stupid to me that I dropped it. Besides which, no one in my large family didn't ever sound anything like that to me. We had made our way from South Carolina up to New York and Chicago back in the late 1800s. We, at home, would casually color that kind of rebop "country."

Failing to do it for a director, who just assumed that I could, lost me the badass role, resulting in the change to the drill sergeant character. Later I remember Braugher claiming that he would never take a role that required him to use an accent that he, hailing from Mississippi before Chicago, could do quite well. Following his career it seems he's largely done that from his first role in *Glory* to his Emmy-winning now.

Though I loved the play I didn't so much love being *in* the play. Mostly because of the feedback loop. I never had the experience of anyone coming backstage and telling any actor that they sucked, and yet some of them must have sucked. Unreliable feedback had me hungering for a more direct feedback loop and the shows that I was continuing to go to had that. Especially now that hardcore had hit in a fairly serious way. People didn't like you, they flipped you off, spit on you and left.

You want the kind of truth that most can't handle? There you go.

Another truth that was hard to handle: with disco dead, a way and a place to go and spend some time with music and women was limited to whenever I could waylay someone into driving. That's if I didn't feel like taking the train—30 minutes Cali time is very different from 30 minutes New York time—and classes were an actual reality, despite the overall country club feel of Stanford. Any sort of fucking was not happening.

Getting to Stanford had been easy for me, as nothing in my life, educationally speaking, had been harder than Stuyvesant. And staying here was even easier. But for many, Stanford, a school that was still billing itself as the "Harvard of the West" when I showed up, was the apotheosis of all of their family's wildest dreams and hopes for their kids. These same kids had spent their time doing little else other than getting here.

Also, who, outside of degenerates like me, was doing much fucking at 18? Even if they wanted to. So, it was like being an adult but being thrust back into some sort of near-twilight high school setup. Example? The first dance, and remember I dig dancing, a woman picks me to slow dance with. She's grabbing my now erect penis. At Studio 54, this would be viewed as an invitation. For at least a kiss. But for a high schooler this was toy time and she pulled her head away from the coming kiss and laughed.

In general, I had grown OK with being laughed at, but being toyed with was something else.

Years later, well after college, she approached me and told me that she used to cry on the phone to her mother over how I had treated her *after* this. A post-failed-kiss comment regarding how much bread she had taken one night at dinner was the cause. But the cause and effect were not connected. I had been watching her deal with her food self-esteem issue for 10 minutes. She picked up the bread. Put it down. Picked it up. Put it down. Tried to get a smaller one and I lost it like I tended to lose it in the face of perceived weakness.

Call it tough love but I screamed out across the dining hall, "JESUS CHRIST . . . take it and EAT it, LISA! An extra pound is not going to kill you!"

I was glad to hear she later decided to become a psychiatrist, and we leveled our misunderstanding into a détente well beyond amends.

"Will you stop your fucking complaining!!!" The speaker was one of my later roommates. I had been complaining about a succession of women who had dumped me. All for the same reason: parental pressure. Though this fact was only shared with me once. Apparently parents didn't believe a man with a mohawk had grand prospects in the early '80s.

Which was reason enough to stick to acting, I guess. Braugher did, but we parted ways over a staging of *Emperor Jones*. He got the role of Jones, which I was OK with. I got the role of Lem, a guy killed by Jones in a fight over a dice game. This excited me. What didn't excite me was the middling attempt by the director to push boundaries. Lem would not be played in any traditional way, I was told. He would be played as a bush.

A bush.

A non-talking bush that mimed the argument and the eventual killing of my character. And you know that while there are no small roles, only small actors, it was somewhere during a feeling and movement drill where we rolled around the floor touching each other and acting like bushes and/or ghosts that I thought "fuck this."

"When the play closes, we're going to take it to Berkeley Rep." There was excitement all around.

"I'm not going. I have a band and shows to do." I was direct.

"It's only a month."

"It's a month I don't have."

A mohawk haircut later, me not being the bush ceased being an issue and someone else was gang-pressed into playing a bush. And Braugher, I figured out later since I have tended to be on the spectrum about stuff like this, had stopped talking to me.

But my roommate was making the claim that my complaining was misplaced because I would come to, in the fullness of time, appreciate that these were the "best years of your life."

"You're around more people your own age than you will ever be again, with almost unlimited free time and very few responsibilities," he had said. Valid points all but still hard to argue with when you are being systematically forced to redefine how you've understood yourself. Which was happening.

After breaking a Stanford varsity deadlift record—I chose to play rugby so that I could work out in the varsity weight room—I injured myself and suffered two concussions playing rugby.

I didn't so much like playing rugby as I enjoyed fighting during rugby games. The concussions came from high-speed collisions and weird stuff had started to happen to my head, and body. I could see staircases spreading out in front of me but sometimes couldn't get my body to make sense of what to do *with* the staircase. Stumbling *down* the stars you might expect but stumbling *up* them?

I also pulled further away from Stanford and spent more time at shows, where the things that were happening wouldn't help anyone's head. The band X for a period of time had wrapped me in its deep embrace. I saw them in New York, D.C., Boston, the Midwest, L.A. and San Francisco. It got weird enough that at one point the entire band looked at me after they had taken the stage with a kind of look that said "What the FUCK are you doing here again?"

Which is what Exene actually said. Under normal circumstances I would have spoken to the band and made myself useful somehow, but I wasn't so much interested in knowing them as I was in figuring out how they did what they did. I'd meet Exene years later but made no mention of this time. In any case, at one of their shows, an overly enthusiastic roadie shoved me off the stage as I pirouetted off the edge, sending me down to the marble floor headfirst.

Everything that had happened before we left for the show that night was blanked and I remember only two things. I remember the look on the roadie's face right before everything went black and I saw regret. And then I remember Sam McBride from the band Fang picking me up off the floor while people stepped on and stumbled over me.

A guy who later ended up being Undersecretary of Defense under George W. Bush, Michael C. Doran, once said about me, "Eugene is like a dog. If you're nice to him, he's yours forever." I don't believe he meant this as a compliment but he *had* been nice to me and so we had maintained a friendship despite his horrid politics, and in the case of Sam McBride it's been true as well. Despite his trial and conviction for murdering his girlfriend, I've maintained a judgment-free friendship with him stemming from that moment of basic human kindness where he kept me from getting my head (further) kicked in.

But this idea that I should be thankful for what it felt like, was to me just something to endure, something that sat with me. Because it's all about perspective, and the reality was that in the context of early 1980s California and the start of the so-called Reagan Revolution, I was going

The Basic Training of Pavlo Hummel *by David Rabe starred me and Andre Braugher. This is the closest I would get to a military uniform. Practicing drills on the roof with our stage rifles, we were later braced by cops who had gotten reports of "Black guys with guns." Since they were questioning us in a theater where we stood with those very same guns, we were confused about their confusion regarding "what y'all are doing here?"*

to school with people for whom Black folks had been traditionally bit players, to say the least.

California with its absence of class diversity meant that my motives and drives were presumed to be frightening, because poor people were, well, frightening. I was as middle-class as many of them but maybe they were right. Or maybe *no one* was making satisfying emotional connections and because I was stuck inside the film of me, I could never see this. Like most teenagers aggrieved is what I felt.

Then this: "You are being invited to a party . . . clothing? Optional."

It had been slipped under my dorm room door.

"Looks like you just got invited to an orgy," my roommate read over my shoulder and laughed.

"Well, I'm not going!"

"Why not?"

*Me in a Sri Chinmoy shirt with freshman roommate and later-to-be
Undersecretary of Defense under George W. Bush.*

He didn't ask, and didn't need to, but hearing my voice in the room clarify why gave it some shape.

"I don't want any guy touching up on me . . . "

"You'll be the biggest guy there." He was now looking at me like he felt sorry for me. "No one you don't want to touch you will touch you."

I reasoned that he was right. The fact that we had this conversation while I was naked and sitting on my bed post-workout was lost on me. But a cursory knock on the door and in burst the chirpy resident assistant. She sat on the bed next to me, either not noticing or caring that I was nude.

"So. Are you going to, you know, the party?" she whispered, even though I was beyond certain my roommate had heard.

"Just decided to, so, yeah."

"OK. I'll see you there!"

And this is a pattern. In the midst of me feeling/being aggrieved about something, something else, usually the most unlikely something else, pops into the picture. Which closely mimics a speech in *The Basic Training of Pavlo Hummel* where Braugher's character Ardell tries to warn Hummel away from suicide because you just don't know what tomorrow will bring.

On the day of the party I wore what we had been instructed to wear: loose-fitting clothing. No leather jacket. No punk rock finery. And headed over, roommate in tow. In getting to the room, stepping in, à la Rick James, the place was festooned with incense, wine and candles. Plus throw pillows, and while there was music playing, I was disappointed to see that everyone was still dressed, leaving me thinking that if I wanted to go to a boring dinner party that's just where I would have gone but I didn't so I wasn't.

Not breaking the happy line of patter I had going with some of the folks who were there, I started taking my clothes off. Just to make it clear, if it hadn't been so before. We had come to a fuck party and fully intended to do what we had come for.

There were bowls of frozen and now thawing fruit, sweets, and with the ice now broken the party had begun in earnest. The chirpy RA had not shown up. And rumors being as rumors are, there were some gate-crashers who I recognized when they made their way in. It was Carter's Secretary of State's daughter and her boyfriend.

I was wrapped up with a former cheerleader from Newport Beach and decided to move on from her to the Secretary of State's daughter who, as my luck would have it, went board-stiff. Not the usual reaction but when I followed her eyes across the room I could see she hadn't thought this through, and seeing her beau wrapped up with the cheerleader I would have been better off staying with threw a monkey wrench into whatever plans any of us had for a long night.

I made my way over to my roommate. "It's about to fucking fall apart," I whispered. "So, we should wrap it up."

I don't know what he thought I meant but what I meant was that going to an orgy and not having an orgasm seemed to make as much sense to me as not going at all. Then the strangeness of it all hit me since most of us hadn't really had an orgasm in a roomful of more than one person before so as I was orgasming I was keenly aware of the fact that the room had slowed and I, along with a woman named Joy, was the floor show.

Which, fundamentally, was fine since the now-aggrieved girlfriend had already grabbed her clothes and fled the room sobbing, and I nodded that we should follow suit. Minus the lack of clothing and the tears. So we did, and as we made our way through a clothing-non-optional party, we could see the full weight of the school law rushing back to whence we came. I guess if the Secretary of State's daughter goes running half-naked through a party crying, people take notice.

I later heard people got in trouble, and I don't recall seeing the cheerleader much after that. The woman I orgasmed with sought me out later, and had I not been so on the spectrum and maybe less in love with the idea that I was alone and suicidal—the shotgun I had brought to protect myself now I often needed protecting from as I sat around my place, post-concussions, putting it into and taking it out of my mouth— we'd have had something going.

But I wasn't and so I didn't. My mother had stopped speaking to me, as I had gotten caught up in her post-divorce imbroglios with my stepfather. But my high school girlfriend was gone; though I had been to visit her at MIT a few times, I found myself with other women and thought it made sense to let her go. Then the others let me go. I found myself living in the only unheated room in a campus trailer in a trailer park that was soon to be condemned, trying to ignore the whispers of my shotgun.

This was far from being "the best time of my life" but I started to work on *The Birth of Tragedy* magazine, a magazine whose title was purposely lifted from the Nietzsche book, and spent most of my time doing that and homework. Until one night there was a knock on the trailer door. I shoved the shotgun back behind the door and opened it, and standing there under the nimbus of trailer light was Steve Ballinger.

Now I had been blabbing about wanting to start a band for a while now. I had played sax in some James Chance ripoff band called Al + The X's, but I was having dreams about this being a very real and necessary next step. Someone had told me about this guitar-playing football player and I had seen him around. In fact, he was the guy who had vibed me out in the weight room.

He was also the guy that we spotted at a party the first time I dropped acid.

The First Time I Dropped Acid: The Dangerous Economics of LSD

IT SHOULD BE SAID FIRST OFF: never *not* take acid when you're hanging with people who have taken acid. Making the mistake of doing this with two friends in Arizona I recall watching them and wondering how long any two people *could* look at a cactus. (Answer: a really fucking long time.)

But they didn't try to kill themselves, or me, so I had figured, given the overall shambles of my life at the point in time where I figured things couldn't get any worse, and never having made the connection between the concussions and the depressions, I made what Lou Reed described as "a big decision" and decided to take some.

An acid-gobbling motorcyclist engineering student and wrestler knew another wrestler who had gotten some liquid acid, and it's over to his room we found our way. I laid out the middling amount of money he wanted and he dropped three drops into my mouth and we hung out and waited.

I was already used to the immediate bark and bite of a coke high, or the gentle crawl of weed. Or the synthetic slip of pills. But after 45 minutes I felt nothing and was vocal about having been robbed. Drugs, on the whole, had disappointed me. I had always expected a lot more than

they ever delivered. I was expecting a Harry Crews *The Gypsy's Curse* moment, when you find the fucking that fits you. Thus far nothing.

"Well, I can give you two more," and he poised the dropper over my opened mouth and squeezed out first one . . . drop . . . then a second one that just sort of hung there until he gave the dropper an authoritative squeeze and two, three, four, five, six, seven. The room grew extremely quiet. Seven hits was going to be a lot, IF it was legit. "Um. I won't charge you for those extras."

And 15 minutes later, I knew it was legit. How so? I'm a Hendrix fan and while I've imagined him in any variety of incarnations I had never seen him in the sky, his mouth struggling against a guitar solo, and yet . . . there he was. And not only him. Just about everything else.

We wandered out to a party. I was wearing a black turtleneck shirt that I had used Wite-Out to mark up with the band name The Circle

Yeah. Guessing it's starting to make sense now.

Jerks. Me and the acid-gobbling biker who was a bona fide genius in addition to being a state wrestling champ. We get there and the vibe is as wrong as can be. Drunks are heedless, and almost everyone is drunk. Acidheads are . . . full of heed, and everything means everything else and on top of this as soon as we get there I lock eyes with a guy who I can tell has done an animal assessment and has marked me as an easy mark. Or at least one out of place.

"WHAT'S HAPPENING MY MAN?" It's the old white-guy-going-ethnic thing that is supposed to . . . cut. "SO . . . *THE CIRCLE JERKS*, EH?" He was about my height, 6' 1.5", and probably about my weight then, 185. But in my Hendrix head I was of two minds. The gentle creature I was more than comfortable being, and the knife-carrying New Yorker with a tendency to overreact at the slightest provocation.

But then and there I was a placid sea of calm. TOO calm, like they say in the movies. He had correctly gleaned that while he thought he had sprung a trap, that he was in all likelihood IN one as me and my acid-gobbling compatriot grinned at him a little too long, our eyes never wavering from his.

He was very drunk but he wasn't very stupid and so he did what guys like that will predictably do. He went a'searching for another victim and he found one.

"HEY! HEY GIRL! COME HERE!" He had called over a girl. A girl I knew instinctively would never have come if I had called, but lulled by the blondness and the blue-eyedness of his appeal she came. "SAY . . . MY FRIEND EUGENE AND I . . . " and he pointed to me and more specifically to my shirt, "WOULD LIKE TO HAVE A CIRCLE JERK ALL OVER YOUR FACE. COOL WITH YOU?"

It was with a mixture of horror and curiosity that I stood there and silently witnessed all of this. I would not participate but the applied semiotician in me would not stop it. She looked at me, having already guessed that, despite not knowing what a circle jerk was, it wasn't something nice, given the fact that it was being pitched by someone who very definitely was not nice.

She excused herself and he wandered off into the night, managing to not be knifed or beaten by us though he very much deserved it. When I later heard he ended up playing baseball for the Houston Astros, I wasn't surprised, so I'd like to take this opportunity to say, fuck you Steve Buechele.

But at one point my acid-tripping friend had zeroed in on some guy, 6'5", about 250 pounds, in the same army field jacket I once had, with a buzz cut.

"Look at that fucking fascist," he groused. After the Buechele incident we were both kind of delayed-reaction edgy.

"Fascist."

"I mean what's his deal anyway?"

"You think he knows he's a fascist?"

"I bet he doesn't."

"I think you need to tell him!" I was now full of a desire for . . . rectitude. And I was all about urging others to do the work.

"I will! FASCIST!" And when the army-jacketed giant turned to see who was talking, the acid gobbler ducked down behind me and I knew two things. I knew that I knew this guy from the weight room. That, and I knew he was the guitar player people had been telling me about that I had been looking for. I didn't talk to him that night as I wasn't much able to hold a very coherent conversation, but a few days later zipping by on my moped in a leather jacket with a ski cap on, in 90-degree heat, I spotted him walking along and waved. He waved back and I kept on going until I realized that that was no way to start a band, U-turned and rode up to him and the woman he was walking with.

"You Steve?"

"Yeah."

"Hey. I'm Eugene. We should talk about this band."

And we did.

"What are you doing?"

I looked at the shotgun behind the door hinge and back into the inner darkness of the trailer. When I found out that they didn't give you lightbulbs, like people in the dorms had, I would only have lightbulbs that I had stolen from some other place on campus. I couldn't afford them otherwise. Since my room was so cold I kept the rest of the trailer hotter than hell in the hopes that it would also warm my room.

Years later I discovered that my room was cold because I had placed my footlocker over the heat register. So, there was that bit of stupidity, which I might have tried to claim as part of my stoic thing but there are no lies here so I won't. And all of my aforementioned habits were actually enough to drive out the university-dictated roommates. Leaving me with a friend who had been grievously injured in a bike accident and couldn't/didn't have the energy to go anywhere else.

"Um. I'm writing," and I stood there expecting and wanting him to turn on his heel and leave me alone. Not because I didn't favor his company but because, well, I was busy. But he stood there and didn't move and then finally broke the silence when he saw I wasn't getting it.

"Come on. Let's hang out!"

Then it dawned on me in a way that I had always been slow to get: this is what friends do, and that's what we were going to be.

Like with Doug a few years earlier, the primary canvas on which our friendship played out involved walking. Like what you do when you're broke, but even more than that, talking. Which is what you do when you have things to do. And we had an excess of things to do.

First off, I needed an explanation of the vibing I was getting in the weight room.

"Hahah . . . that's easy. Most Black guys I played football with were pretty meticulous about their hair," he said. "But you . . . well, I couldn't figure out what you were doing." Which really made a lot of sense. My hair had always been an early-stage indicator of where my head was at, both literally and figuratively.

One of the roommates I had later driven out of the trailer had showed up one night and tried to hustle into his room before The Poisonous Black Toad in the corner room could make him out and put salt in his game. But when I heard a woman's voice it was too late for that. I stumbled into the warmth of the overly hot trailer from a room where you could see your breath in mist.

He had a bottle of champagne tucked under his arm, a dozen red roses, and in tow was one of the more beautiful women I had ever seen in my life. Not beautiful in that bullshit magazine way appreciated by guys who put posters of Ferraris on their bedroom walls but . . . soulful. She was Danish and he was doing the full court press. Once I had made my presence known I went back to my room to sulk.

What was it that Hamlet said: "what would they, had they the motive for cue and passion that I have, do?" In my room I listened and heard him mention he had a bunch of cocaine and a two-inch porterhouse steak and I knew a few things. I knew that if any of this cheeseball shit worked, there was no hope for me. I also knew that this cheeseball shit was probably going to work, even as transparent as it was to me, so there was no hope for me.

I listened through the wall at the strained conversation, could tell he was missing and not hitting but I could also hear her trying. I sat at my desk in front of my typewriter and ran my fingers over my uncombed hair and started fixating on me, the hair, the world.

Very possibly not discernible but I am in hell in this photo, taken in the room of my torturer. A longing, unrequited (first requited, then unrequited, then later requited again) hell with the taker of the photo. (Photo by Nicole Rosenberg)

I knocked on my injured roommate's door. He owned a pair of hair clippers.

"It's time," I said.

"For what?" The accident had damaged his vocal cords so he then and forever would sound like Tom Waits. Or a Mafioso.

"To shave." In total biker life-and-death seriousness I put the period on the sentence. "Everything."

No more questions. He wrapped a towel around my shoulders and oiled up the clippers. The noise and the light in a trailer that had now been lit with candles and red bulbs as my man tried to run up some romance got her attention, and as a break, I could hear her ask him what was going on and I could also hear him dismiss his "crazy roommates."

"I want to see," she said, making her way down the hallway and into the already-too-small bathroom. "What are you doing?"

I looked at her with a look I'd later call the Dracula look, or some version of what anthropologists call "the copulatory gaze," and said simply, "Shaving my head."

Because for me it was now like Caligula in his unraveled response to the death of Drusilla, his sister/lover: holding on to the vanity of hair had gotten me nothing. So, everything would now be possible. With no hair. In a world that made no sense. Part this and part the war footing that motivated De Niro in *Taxi Driver*.

She knew none of this but watched the quiet, earnest ritual while my Lothario roommate tried to tell her that the steak was ready and get her back to the table, and the candles, and the roses and the champagne.

"Can I help?" she asked my injured roommate who was more than happy to go back to bed, and she climbed up onto the back of the toilet, sat, and pulled me between her thighs while she gently and with much professional aplomb finished shaving my head.

My successfully cock-blocked roommate would not forget this and, as luck would have it, sought out and tried to date an ex of mine, since he figured he was owed and what better retribution than to date a woman I had publicly proclaimed my love for. Had I not stumbled along right as he was showing up at her place, and put the rationale behind his sudden interest in her, he might have succeeded, but as things stood this was a noteworthy moment for me for reasons other than the cock-block double.

I took it to mean that causality was a slippery and mysterious cycle of slopes that, like Ardell had tried to tell Pavlo Hummel, no matter how much you might try to predict an outcome nothing was guaranteed.

But Steve was a good traveling companion, and his instinctive desire to shit on anything I said just in the spirit of being contrary was nice

The GOD Issue. With Anton LaVey from the Church of Satan on the cover. See what we did there? (Photo by James Rau)

and totally unlike the California I was still uncomfortable with, where the New York me was viewed as "intense."

"Everything is guaranteed," he said as we ambled along. "Industries have been built on how predictable people and therefore their outcomes are."

And we argued this until we argued something else and as often happened, our positions reversed by the end. He was also now helping me to finish the second edition of *The Birth of Tragedy* magazine. The first edition, the "Sex & Depression" issue, was an unmitigated success in my mind.

You see, I had been embraced by portions of the Stanford community that were interested in outsider art and fashioned themselves painters, artists and poets. So they were excited when I dragged a table and a chair out into Stanford's very central White Plaza and put out the copy-machined pages that I had stapled together that amounted to the very first edition.

I had broken into offices to use their copy machines and I was selling the copies for $1 apiece. I had sold 30 in the first hour and kept up a steady stream of patter with all and sundry while they flipped through the pages. That was Day One.

On Day Two, after many of them had gotten home and actually read through the issue, the tone and the timbre of the subsequent conversations changed. I had a lot of angry customers who complained that they felt like I had rubbed dirt in their eyes.

"Or semen." And I smiled at one particularly gentle soul who I now remember was named Graham. "What did you think you were buying when you bought the 'Sex & Depression' issue?" I was now laughing. In his face and at the small crowd that had gathered. "Poetry about flowers and Sylvia Plath?"

"How about a rebate?" Steve's offer was supposed to be restorative but came across as even more insulting, and off stalked Graham to never speak to me again. In fact, a line had been drawn by the whole coffeehouse crowd and it signaled to Steve and me that we needed to get serious about the band. It's not like we were never not so, but the magazine had taken up time.

We found out that the guy who had run the Stanford Prison Experiment, Philip Zimbardo, had a son who played bass and lived at the fraternity house where we got our acid. Adam had the extra added plus of also being a New Yorker. And for drums we had the guy who first told me about Steve, Dave Nagler. I was never sure if he was a student, older than us by a bit, or really what he was doing at Stanford, but he was alienated as we were, even possibly alienated from us as well, and so we were in business.

One of the hippie Psi Phi co-ops on campus had a basement room where bands could practice for free, and there we went. Playing covers. *They* played. I just listened. Maybe because that's what I had always done in the presence of live music. Or maybe because, despite the stage time I had logged, I was unsure of how this was going to go.

Figuring out it was something that happened when Steve screamed at me one night "SING!"

The basement/rehearsal spot where it all began. Me, Steve Ballinger behind me, drummer number two Dave Owens, and bassist number one Adam Zimbardo.

Steve Ballinger and I at an early Whipping Boy show at Woodside Priory, an all-boys Catholic School. Where, incidentally, I got my first groupie kiss. Not from an all-boy or the priests that looked after them. Closely after them. But from a girl at the invited sister Catholic school that was attending our show. She asked for and I gave her a kiss. The priest chaperones were disinterested in suchlike sleaziness so it exists now as a faded memory of near-felony.

"SING *WHAT*?" I screamed back.

"You're the SINGER. So fucking SING!!!"

And they started a song we all knew, The Monkees' "Stepping Stone," punk-rockized by the Sex Pistols and a band staple since the Teen Idles from D.C. had made it so.

I stepped up to the mic, and though I imagined I was no kind of a stepping stone for the women that had been busy dumping me, I did have some sort of an emotional basis to make this cover feel like more than going through the motions. And like Sinatra once said about being able to tell whether or not you had pulled something off successfully, nobody was laughing.

But in full cart-before-horse fashion and in full consideration of something Steve had that I didn't—a car—we were at as many shows as we could beg, borrow or sneak our way into. And when people asked who the hell we were, we did what you did back then.

"We're in a band."

Six songs does not make a band. A band name is a good start and we were fighting about that. Steeped in the whole Ramones-Zippy the Pinhead thing I thought it made sense to undercut the expected criticism we were going to get for being college kids. So, I pushed hard for The Fucking Idiots.

I thought it rolled off the tongue and played against type. Steve took care of that.

"I'm not spending a minute in a band called 'The Fucking Idiots'," he groused. "That's fucking . . . idiotic."

I was practicing being magnanimous. Or some version of it.

"OK. Gimme a name then . . . "

"Whipping Boy."

And I believe I actually groaned. Any attempt to go antebellum with this gave me douche chills. One of the benefits of having moved through first disco, then punk rock, then new wave, then hardcore, largely with not a lot of people who knew me or were interested in knowing me, was being able to avoid knowing precisely how stupid the people around me were. But with "whipping" in the title we were virtually inviting some sort of discourse on race politics, and why would I want to put myself in the position of that now being MY problem?

"No no . . . in the old days the servants couldn't hit the royal kids so they would designate a friend for him or her. If the royal kid fucked up they'd beat his friend. THAT was a Whipping Boy."

This I liked. I didn't like the way it looked spelled out, or even saying it. I mean there was a certain élan to BLACK FLAG, but I did like this explanation and so I was sold.

"So what band are you in?"

"Whipping Boy." And not once did anyone ever tie this into race. Any more than they would have with the whole "Black guy in punk rock" thing.

Which was already the deal at the shows already. The first big show I saw in California I ran into Bill Graham at the front. I recognized him because of *Apocalypse Now* and here he stood in front of the California Hall at a show with Fear, the Circle Jerks and the Dead Kennedys. Punks had driven up from Los Angeles, and down from Reno and Sacramento. It was packed and I'd have presumed Graham would have been happy. But he was not. Especially at being recognized.

"You going to do more punk shows?" I asked, getting ready to work an angle.

"Nah. Too much of a pain in the ass," he rolled his eyes. Well, it wasn't the Doobie Brothers but things change.

Getting inside, it was a gathering of the shock troops and it was total . . . bedlam. But unlike New York where there were not that many places to be from if you were in the places where stuff was happening, no one knew where anyone was from and there was a geo-pecking order with Los Angeles bands being the Alphas and everyone else, like the Adolescents once sang, "second best."

In the midst of what would not too much later be called a mosh pit, there were hundreds of us on the dance floor and it was a melee. Over the heads of the crowd I spied a guy in a black shirt with a big white swastika in the middle and the rockers emblazoned with the words WHITE POWER over and below it.

He saw me see him. My look was judgment-free. Live and let live, or like a friend of mine, a Georgian who had emigrated right when the world was aswirl with the waves of Soviet Jewry getting the hell out while they could: "People can say whatever they want to me, Eugene. But if they put their hands on me . . . "

Which is right about the time the swastika dude started surfing over crowd top with me as his intended destination. I had always thought West Coast punk rock/hardcore was a little lighter, temperamentally speaking, than New York. I mean it's hard to street fight when you're driving to shows. So, I have gotten accustomed to . . . relaxing.

I still had a push dagger inside my engineer boot—young life lessons stick with you—and it was razor-sharp and kept so by not using it for anything that wasn't business. And this was looking like business.

Given the size of the club there was no need for a circular mosh pit. It was radically random with people bouncing off of each other every which way but I had charted a course that would bring me closer to swastika. I found it always best to deal with problems sooner than later, and as he swam over heads I windmilled through the crowd until we were swinging distance away, and like the butterfly stroke I remember from my days as a swimmer he launched himself over the last row of people between us and as I went to swing for his head, he leaned in and kissed me on the mouth.

Which got from me the only response that made sense. I laughed my ass off and had now officially met Rob Noxious from The Fuck-Ups, a band despised by the folks at *Maximum Rocknroll* for being "reactionary." While I am sure swastikas and songs like "White Boy" about shooting Latino gangbangers in San Francisco's Mission District might rub some the wrong way, I couldn't be made to believe that their "art" was sanction-worthy.

Or put another way and something I've said before: they were always nice to me. "They" in this instance being Noxious and the cult of folks that had formed around him who were responsible for a raft of shitty behavior like bathroom muggings, robberies, fights and all manner of drunken excess. But there was not a single one of these folks, many who later became skinheads when that became a thing, who didn't have an animal understanding of power and violence.

So, when Steve and I started showing up to shows as a duo, me the former competitive bodybuilder and Steve, once voted "strongest hands in Ventura County" on his way to some sort of wrestling championship, well, it just made more sense to be nicer to us than not. Understand that a lot of this . . . punk rock politicking . . . was holdover shit from high school, but when we heard the guys in Crucifix wanted to kick our asses for some reason or another, we went looking for them. We found them at the Elite Club, now the Fillmore in San Francisco, when the ID was finally made, well, yeah. It just made more sense for them to be comfortable competitors (and later friends) rather than for anyone to start swinging.

Besides which, despite my penchant for *liking* to fight, I had realized something. Mostly that I had been on a steady streak, bodybuilding or not, of getting my ass kicked. Kicked out of Howie's. Kicked by the three *cugines*. Punched up at swim meets with the opposing team for G-d knows what reason. Fights during rugby games. The spirit was there but the skill level, well, despite having started boxing at the Boys Club when I was 10 and taking karate and wrestling for a hot minute in high school, just wasn't.

Mostly because being able to fight is not just about knowing how to fight. It's maybe most specifically about *when* to fight. And as for the *when*, my timing was off. However, the optics were always good enough for us to get dismissed as "jocks," a sobriquet that never bothered me much. We started hanging out at KPFA, because we liked radio, Tim Yohannon and Jeff Bales seemed like nice guys, and I had an unrequited thing for Ruth Schwartz.

But the whole Stanford athlete thing seemed hard for them to take. We weren't there to get them to like us though. Neither Steve nor I were that stupid. We were there to figure out the lay of the land and learn what we could.

I don't know what we learned but it was either enough or not enough so that when the entire band was at a Circle Jerks show one time in 1981, we just decided that we should play it. The end product of high-level LSD-fueled thinking.

"We should be playing this show." Stated as writ and it just hung there. Steve and I looked around the room, and he nodded at my flight of fancy.

"We should."

"Fuck it. I'm going to ask them if we can play."

"Let's."

So, we corralled whoever seemed marginally in charge and announced that we wanted to play a few songs before the Circle Jerks came out.

Sizing us up, he folded. Immediately. "If it's OK with Keith it's OK with me."

So, we hemmed up Keith. "Hey man. Let us play three songs before you all play."

Keith looked at us. The Farm, where the show was, was a ramshackle Quonset hut of corrugated tin, and no security that we could see.

"OK. But you can't use our equipment. Ask the Effigies if you can use their stuff."

Tracking down Vic Biondi—who to this day I have a soft spot for because of this—was asked, and considering that they had just played, he was amazingly accommodating, and I don't say it was out of fear. I don't say any of them that said yes acted out of fear. Any one thing didn't seem crazier than any one other thing back then, and since we weren't asking for money, why not?

"NEXT UP . . ." the soundboard cat announced, "THE CIRCLE JERKS!"

And out we came to an audience of people who while we were unsure WHAT they knew, knew beyond a shadow of a doubt that we were NOT the band announced. The realization of which triggered a fusillade of beer bottles and spit while we played the four, minute-long songs that we knew.

Someone not there or part of this milieu would maybe guess that this response was not what was expected but we had no idea what to expect and were really open to just about anything. There I discovered that I much preferred *honest* hate than dishonest love. This realization caused the same sort of reaction that my mother witnessed on the occasion of a Killing Joke show. Despite our brief falling-outs, over time my mother has been my most reliable champion. She came to a Killing Joke show with me out of genuine interest in what had captured my interest so rabidly as a teenager.

Unfortunately, the show was at the Ritz (now Webster Hall), staffed by the kind of *cugines* I both worked out with and occasionally street-scuffled with. One bumped into me on his way to throw someone out. I took umbrage by way of a screw face and he returned.

"You got a problem?"

"Yeah. You bumped into me." Then, to quote Joe Pesci from *Good-fellas*, "bing bang boom," he had hit me. My boxing helped a little as I slipped the punch and his knuckles hit the bony part of my forehead. I ducked, and coming up and out of it, as soon as I swung on him I was pinioned from behind, full-nelson style by one of the other bouncers. When I later bounced myself I noted that we largely bounced in packs, but at 17? Who knew?

They had me aloft, my feet dragging parallel lines behind me as we closed in on the marble stairs they were clearly going to throw me down, when I spotted my mother.

"Wait . . . there's my mother!"

It wasn't like I expected her to rescue me. I just didn't want them to make her see them hurt me. I mean, at least wait until she was gone, but then something magical happened. They looked at her, made a determination that we were indeed related and let me go.

Later my mother made the observation: "You were grinning, you know. And you had this weird light and look on your face that I had never seen before."

THAT's what was happening on stage at the Farm. People hated us, suspected a rip-off was afoot, and in the most direct of ways possible decided to right what seemed to be a sleight-of-hand wrong. All in the face of the reality that no matter how much they hated us, we hated them even more.

Zimbardo was getting punched in the nuts and giving as good as he got while still managing to play a bass that wasn't his. And our new drummer Dave Owens, who had replaced the old drummer Dave Nagler who had managed to get himself fired for thinking the best place to catch up on the news was during practice from a newspaper on his floor tom, ducked and dodged any and all projectiles thrown at his head.

Owens was a transplant from Augsburg, Germany, and part of the band that "sage" journalists had correctly surmised was "half Black," and was as unflappable in the face of chaos as I had ever seen. Steve, however, like the Robert Duvall character in *Apocalypse Now*, had a nimbus of don't-fuck-around around him, and was relatively untouched as he hunched over a guitar that, given his size, seemed like a novelty shop toy.

And me? I was laughing my ass off and grinning like a madman because my calculus was simple: no one in the building was better armed than I was. Beyond that, there was always the truism that had graced my understanding of the world since I was old enough to be able to ball a fist in anger, and that was the fact that, eventually, I had always imagined, I'd have to kill someone. Never accidentally, or unjustifiably, but nonetheless, dead dead dead.

Now I didn't think this was that day, but that was mostly because I was having too much fun and the audience, transmuted by all of the crazy, just decided to . . . come along. The hate and the violence became theater and quickly the "set" was done. Zimbardo was stageside making out with a woman he had just kicked in the chest for punching him in the balls. Steve was being fêted on my other side. Dave was grinning like the devil and I was cornered by two guys I didn't know.

The older impish-looking guy spoke first: "Who ARE you guys?"

"Well, we're," and I paused because I wanted the name to have weight when I spoke it, "Whipping Boy."

"I'm Klaus . . . from the Dead Kennedys."

And the Black cat next to him spoke, half amused, all curious, "And I'm Darren . . . Dead Kennedys too."

My oh-shit moment was now, as I copped to having met a woman who at first I had mis-remembered as Biafra's wife before discovering that I was, in fact, talking to her ex-husband in the shape of Klaus. I went on to explain who we were and what we were doing and Klaus asked if we had a tape and in true *What Makes Sammy Run* fashion I said we had and on the ride back to Stanford, the car was alight with chatter about all the rest of the show and it had been decided that we would record one.

In a scene aswirl with drugs, we had earned an understanding that we were "straight edge," that bit of weirdness from D.C. promulgated by Ian MacKaye from Minor Threat who, rightly, wanted there to be an alternative to punk rock self-abuse. We were athletes and I didn't smoke, and had stopped drinking after the drunken incident in New

Whipping Boy

York where, to save whatever the subway cost in 1979, I climbed onto the tracks and crawled under a stopped train. Only to realize that my drunken ass had been on the right side to begin with, and crawled back all while brandishing a knife because: rats.

I later explained to anyone who asked that it was because alcohol had too much sugar in it and I was competing in bodybuilding shows, but the reality was it "made" me an asshole. And very possibly a dangerous one to boot.

This is why people thought we were straight edge. However, straight edge doesn't and didn't involve gobbling LSD like LSD-gobbling was going out of style. We figured we could do that and still hit the gym. Ian had also done the whole straight edge thing with a twist by making non-fucking a virtue. In literary terms we could call this foreshadowing, since, for some to the manner born, this was never going to work.

The point here though was that we were pretty tuned out to other drugs. The kind you might be on if your father could write scripts and was a noted head guy. Those mooooood drugs.

The first PR photo of Whipping Boy sans the magical disappearing Zimbardo on bass. This appeared in Tim Tonooka's Ripper *magazine in 1982 with photos that may have been taken by him.*

In any case we had set up to record in some fraternity guy's room. Kevin McClain, maybe a Theta Delt. None of that shit meant much to me as what was happening on campus had started to mean not much to me. Stanford had become my job and I dutifully applied myself to going to class and putting in the work at school, and my actual job had me comfortably banking on what I had done in New York by way of food service. And realizing that getting laid on the West Coast was not going to be nearly as easy as it was in New York during the late '70s, I just let them shunt me into the dish room. Perfect place for the antisocial.

Also, my mother's divorce from my stepfather was taking a financial toll, and getting a call one day I was told that I either needed to come back to Brooklyn College, or find another way to pay for Stanford, as the help she was giving me couldn't continue. My father, also going through a divorce, in full-on teachable-moment fashion because he had had to drop out of Michigan State because his football scholarship didn't cover the time he couldn't play on account of injury and his father didn't help him, decided he couldn't help either.

Going over to the administration building to formally drop out, I ran into a woman named Rita Scoren and explained what was going on. She administered the scholarships I already had going. One from the Times Mirror Corp and one for scoring really high on the SAT, so we'd developed a fun sort of friendship, one that let her tell me that if a school likes you enough to let you in, then it also probably likes you enough to keep you going. I had a new plan: with government loans, I could now stay at a school I hated near a city I had come to love because of a scene that was frying my brain. In the good way.

I had ponied up some money from washing dishes and between us we had managed to weasel our way into a recording session. Which was going swimmingly until those other drugs had started to kick in and we watched Zimbardo pack up his bass while muttering something. Something about anxiety. Freaking out. Airplanes. Christmas. And just like that, and before I could get my hands on him, he was gone.

When it came time to can the newspaper-reading drummer, it was easy enough: we just stopped calling him. Hip to this, Zimbardo called as soon as he had come back to California. So then there was the whole band breakup thing, which Steve handled with the kind of aplomb that would have eluded a New York native like me whose preferred MO in the face of emotional difficulty is usefully totally absent, or way too direct and hurtful.

There was a friend, though, who in attempting to form a rockabilly band had tracked down some bass-playing cowboy kid from Montana. Honestly, anyone using chewing tobacco would have been a cowboy to me, but tracking down Sam Smoot was easy. Quiet and soft-spoken when he wasn't, it was an easy sell: "We play hardcore."

And he was in.

California
Über Us

TIM YOHANNON, FROM *Maximum Rocknroll* and radio station KPFA, had an idea. He wanted to put out a compilation of West Coast hardcore bands. Wanted to call it *Not So Quiet On the Western Front*. The Dead Kennedys' record label, Alternative Tentacles, would put it out. It would also feature the first edition of a magazine that many would know/remember as *MRR*.

We said sure, they asked for a tape and lyrics, we submitted a tape and lyrics, and they chose "Human Farm," song and lyrics by Steve that ran "Control yourself, control yourself . . . or we will do it for you." They liked the frat house tape. Given their steadfast weirdness about us being athletes—read: jocks . . . "it's more of a mindset," they tried to explain to us by saying that they weren't talking about *us* so much. Which was just another way of saying that they *were* talking about *us* since we never ever assumed that they were talking about us. We were sure though, and it may have killed them to do so, but they advised we seek out a cat named Tom Mallon to re-record it.

Mallon was a total mensch. Nondescript but there was something in his voice and I had correctly pegged him as an East Coaster, and even months into my still uncomfortable residency in California I found myself gravitating to folks from "back home." He later ended up drumming for and producing American Music Club, but this didn't impress me as much as the rare . . . moment . . . that elevated Tom from just a guy I knew to a guy that was emblematic of something magical about my understanding of the world.

I was walking along Broadway in San Francisco one night. Parked close to the water, I had to walk up the hill; my ultimate destination was the On Broadway, above the Mabuhay—for East Coasters who this means nothing to, think "West Coast CBs." Directly across the street was the straight-up rock and roll venue, the Stone, in front of which I saw Mallon standing. I waved and he spotted me and waved.

It was not that he waved. It was *how* he waved. Like those Japanese maneki cats, it was more a beckon, and so I turned right and started jawing with Tom. What was just supposed to be a how-d'you-do? turned into a three-hour conversation. Noteworthy because San Francisco gets cold as fuck at night.

We talked family, music, business, philosophy, and while not the conversation I was expecting, clearly the conversation I needed. I missed the show at the On Broadway. He managed to make his show at the Stone, but after that, like taking acid with someone, Mallon and I were regulars. I tried to hire him when I could and he returned the favor by returning whatever weird-ass kind of favor I asked of him.

"Tom?"

It was 11:30 at night, and pre-cellphones you just had to ring someone's bell and hope for the best.

"Yeah?" The intercom crackled at his place under the Bay Bridge.

"It's Eugene and . . . " The buzzer kicked into gear and I pushed through the door, liking immensely that he didn't ask me what I wanted.

Getting up to the studio where he lived, I asked what he was doing, and it was what he was always doing as far as I knew, recording, before I asked what I had come for.

"Can I use your shower?"

"The towels are under the sink."

I took a shower. Interrupted his session once more before disappearing into the night and whatever madness I had going on. When he later died from brain cancer I, who in general am not a sentimentalist, felt bad and a true sense of loss.

However, in our first tranche of time together he was recording "Human Farm," and being that it was my first time in a REAL recording studio, I was sponging it all up. Sometime during the session he handed me a record, a seven-inch.

"The Fuck-Ups? They're on this?" I couldn't imagine that the agenda-laden lefties at *MRR* would have let that happen. Despite Bob Noxious' early kiss on my lips, he had felt zero need to curry favor with KPFA folks, or Biafra, so it just seemed strange.

"Nah. They recorded here. You might like it."

I got the sense he just wanted to get it out of there, as with its song "White Boy" it was funnier that I have it than if it sat around his place.

The recording went well, well enough that our next thought made the most amount of sense possible and we decided we needed to make a record ourselves. In 1982 there were not a whole hell of a lot of hardcore records out. Not albums. Seven inches, yeah, but full-length albums? I can count the number of ones I had in my collection and if there were more than 100 I'll eat a bug.

Mallon had agreed to record it, which with us also meant produce it.

The Sound of No Hands Clapping would be what I thought we should call it. This was our version of the Talking Heads' "this ain't no disco." We imagined Alternative Tentacles would release it. Biafra, whose house I had weaseled my way into, asked for the lyrics first and foremost. Glad to give them, flattered even, but his critique rested on a song we had called "Speed Racer" about the joys of one of San Francisco's favorite treats, up there with Rice-a-Roni and cable cars: meth.

"Seems like a tribute to mindless violence," he drawled. Biafra, in total, was a curious proposition. He had hit dead on the money so many times that he confused what anyone in the corporate world would have caught in even the most cursory SWOT analysis. Strengths Weaknesses Opportunities and Threats had worked out so well for him in building a national profile that included a run for San Francisco's Mayor, and notoriety because of the name and truly groundbreaking early records. All of this *without* the requisite paranoia and restless ambition that keeps you staying ahead of the game.

He was also shit at choosing his friends but this is not about that. This is about him having the good taste to walk on by the Whipping Boy record because despite the scourge that meth was/became, I was disinclined to remove it from the record. Which is why we later turned to East Bay Ray, Dead Kennedys' guitarist. Not because we thought he held any more sway with Biafra but because he could tell us all we needed to know about self-releasing.

And he did. It was my very first conversation with him, and my very last, but his contribution was significant, because putting a record out wasn't magic and he had made this clear, and in a conversation of over an hour he told me everything I needed to know.

I don't know what we expected when we released the record, but it was directly in line with what we *thought* should happen: NOTICE. Reviews, given that there wasn't much to review, were positive and forthcoming. And noted well outside of San Francisco, courtesy of the East Coast connection.

A connection that always had the benefit of me not being cocooned in San Francisco as being the center of anything specific, just a place that we lived close to.

"You going to see Black Flag tonight?" Marianne was an East Coaster, and more than that, used to work at an ice cream store in D.C. before she headed out to Stanford. "My friend's the new singer."

I had seen Black Flag play at Irving Plaza back when I was in New York. I had read about them in the *Soho Weekly News* before I had heard a note of music. Chuck Dukowski had on a trucker hat emblazoned with the word REDNECK and they were being quizzed about a song that they did called "White Minority." A song they were being coy about explaining.

So, yeah: catnip for me, and when they hit the stage, while I now had the seven-inch with Dez singing, I was not ready for Dez as a singer. I loved his voice but Bad Brains were playing support that night and besting HR, singer for Bad Brains, was not going to be possible.

But "new" singer?

I was working on the first edition of *The Birth of Tragedy* magazine and I had started putting some skin around the idea of attending as just someone in the audience.

"Yeah. Let's drive together. I'll introduce you and maybe we can get in free."

Which is precisely what we did.

"Hey, Henry . . . ? This is my friend Eugene." Marianne waved him over.

"Hey man," he stuck out his hand, moving a blue pool ball from his right hand to his left as we stood in the entryway to the Mab.

"You looking for a game," I laughed, while he tightened his fist around the pool ball and made to swing it like a punch.

"You never know," which made me laugh more. He reminded me of cats I was friends with in high school. We straight away started talking tour, detoured into weightlifting and how he was keeping in shape on the road . . . yeah, OK, I know: jocks like me *would* ask that. He was shorter than me and I had about 20 pounds on him, but he was East Coast wired and this I dug.

Later during the show, I whipsawed to the front. Shirtless and off-stage and facing a shirtless Rollins onstage, a photographer had caught something essential here and when it came my way via the Internet years later, I thought of nothing but the line from Shakespeare's *Julius Caesar*: "Yond Cassius has a lean and hungry look; He thinks too much: such men are dangerous." In that moment, he was two steps ahead of doing what I was sorely tempted to do. Leaning hard on *Apocalypse Now* metaphor, which was a touchstone for both of us as we later figured out after geeking out over it, this was taking the boat well beyond any reasonable and sane boundaries.

Unbeknownst to him and just about everybody, I had been sitting in my trailer with my shotgun. In my mouth. Aggressively resisting what was feeling like a leveling and wanting nothing more than to vote NO on it all. Now I believe the depression was a product of the concussions I suffered playing rugby, falling off of stages and fighting. But back then, and given the meditations on solitude and despair that were part and parcel of being a 19-year-old, I sat with the gun in my mouth and played it all through. More times than I care to admit now.

Especially when guys like Andre Braugher were screaming at me: "What's your PROBLEM? You're a smart, handsome guy. People would KILL to be you." This, however, had no bearing on me wanting to kill to not be me.

WHIPPING BOY

the sound of no hands clapping

Rollins definitely was not me, and in the middle of the show as I braced against the stage and screamed along with the song "Depression" I had gotten lost. Seeing this or not, I don't know, Rollins stepped on my forearm. Not hard enough to hurt. But enough to get my attention and when I looked up, it was a figurative hand that had been extended. Later, he pointed to some skin with his line "I won't take, I won't break" and in that moment I got it.

After the show I corralled everyone else in the group and interviewed them. But I had just a pen and a wrinkled flyer, so I could tell there was no way for them to know that of the things I wanted to do in life, writing was at the top of the list. I forged ahead, straight into and through all of the weird Southern California cult-y thing Black Flag had going.

Laughing, mostly at me, sometimes with me, I'd print that interview up in the "Sex & Depression" issue that had caused so much upset. And

The only person that could get their hands behind them handcuffed was Andre Braugher. He refused on account of the whole Emperor Jones kerfuffle. So, we found Engseng Ho, nicknamed Harry Ho. I gave him a record for his saving our asses. I even gave it to him wholesale.

when I next met them, they remembered it. Maybe mostly and majorly because the portraiture was accurate. And they seemed sort of like asses because they were not thinking it was going to amount to much. The interview, I mean.

Nonetheless SST, courtesy of always my favorite Beatle, Chuck Dukowski, still advertised with us back when NO ONE was. A total positive.

If for no other reason than that our aspirations at that point were for Whipping Boy to hit the road and with *The Sound of No Hands Clapping* out, a tour seemed sensible/necessary. East Bay Ray had no advice here and none was sought. We just started writing letters to the people who had given us positive reviews and went from there. Occasional phone calls, more when we could organize the reverse-the-charges scam from pay phone to pay phone.

Lyle Hysen in New York was super helpful. Choke from Slapshot, and Al Barile from one of my favorite bands and one of the few to actually have a full-length out, SS Decontrol, were instrumental in New York and Boston, respectively. And then another helpful friend of Marianne's, a guy named Ian MacKaye. Ian for his part had already toured America and could have given us a real sense of what it would be like for a band that no one had heard of to head out and play, but we, us, and everyone who was knuckle-deep in what hardcore was becoming absolutely wouldn't have heard him even if we were listening.

That is, all we were hearing was the Kerouac urge to get OUT. So much so that I took off my Spring quarter at Stanford to organize the tour. To assuage Rita Scoren's concerns, I had re-enrolled for the Fall, but I needed to be ready to hit the road as soon as school was finished at the end of May. We had SHOWS.

These wouldn't be our first shows anymore. We didn't know shit about pacing and endeavored to play as often as possible and if that was every weekend, then so be it. Former Filipino strip clubs run by Ness Aquino in the Tenderloin. Shows in the Mission. Like De Niro in *Taxi Driver,* it was an anytime, anywhere deal.

"You know why I don't book you guys more?" asked Dirk Dirksen, San Francisco's punk rock Don Rickles and impresario who booked anybody who was anybody, and he was explaining to me why he was repelling my increasingly pushy entreaties to play his club, or any club he was booking. Remember I was still very much a New Yorker then, so I was indefatigable and rejection was just a speed bump to me.

"Why?"

"I saw your guitar player here one night and I really didn't like the way he treated his girlfriend. It was like he was some kind of a fascist." I started laughing and looked to see if he was laughing too, since I found the charge laughable. But then again I hadn't spent much time with him and the girl in question. I had spent enough time to know that she had convinced him to check himself into a mental hospital because he had expressed a certain amount of chagrin that during a group sex scene they were in, he complained that everyone was actually having group sex BUT him and he had been frozen out. But fascism?

"You sure it was him?" I asked and realized how ridiculous it sounded once I said it. Steve was never mistaken for anybody else, and outside of Peter Steele who didn't roll in until a few years later, and Four Way from Bad Posture, no one was as big or as tall.

"It was him."

And then something magical happened. I dug down deep and in total life-and-death kind of biker fashion I vowed that as long as there was breath in my body, no one working with me or connected to me would ever do anything shitty. We didn't drink. We didn't smoke. Well, Steve and Dave did. Sam chewed tobacco. We didn't take drugs. Outside of huge amounts of LSD. We didn't steal. Unless it was food that I was steadfastly being denied by the people I washed dishes for, causing me one night to quit in a fit of pique.

"You can't eat here without PAYING!" said my boss.

"The only reason I work here is SO I can eat without paying!"

"Well, YOU. CANNOT."

"Then I QUIT."

"If you quit, you'll NEVER work in food service again," and in this, thankfully, she was correct.

But with money coming in from shows I could eat every now and then, and Dirksen, possibly impressed by the deep earnestness I had brought to bear over fascism, group sex, and the fact that we had never beaten anyone up in any of his clubs, conceded.

"Call me next week."

I did and the shows were copious. Dead Kennedys, Bad Brains, TSOL, GBH, Anti-Nowhere League, Hüsker Dü, Minutemen, Minor Threat, Scream, and more would eventually be added to our dance card, but putting together the first tour we'd play with anyone. Talking to Ian over the phone I said as much, and in a flight of over-enthusiasm I think I may have volunteered that we would even play for free, we were so excited about playing at all.

However, in the burst of enthusiasm of actually getting shows in far-flung locales, we had neglected, like you might do with magical thinking, the hows of getting there. The whys were never in question since Penelope Spheeris' *The Decline of Western Civilization* came out, something she doesn't get nearly enough for credit for; micro-scenes made this as worthy of an adventure as you could have.

Rollins' first show in San Fran was the first time I met him. He impressed me favorably. Which didn't at all stop me from thinking I could have done it better than he did. (Photo by Chester Simpson.)

But we weren't going to ride any rails to get there. Steve's Dad, a former Navy guy who loved me as much as his Mom hated me for being a "bad influence," decided to lend us his *new* Nissan mini-pickup truck with a shell over the back and 8,000 miles on the odometer. We discovered that if we jammed all of the gear in first, there was enough room for two people to sit in the back, next to each other but facing in opposite directions. With their knees bent . . . if they crouched forward. For hours, and hours.

The catch? There was no way to communicate with the drivers of the now-for-certain death trap, but beggars can't be choosers, and so there it was. Getting ducks in a row and trying to arrange accommodations across the country, I called my father. Told him we were going to be in D.C. and we had a show there.

His level of interest/enthusiasm here was . . . soft.

Not so much a fan of pussyfooting I just spelled it out: "So give me the address so we can stay there after the show."

"Ummm . . . well . . . let me ask Carole." I paused to look at the receiver, wedged it back between my cheek and my shoulder and made the universal two-hands-raised sign that said without saying it, "what the fuck?"

He had met Carole at some back-to-school night, as her kids and his kids, my sisters, were classmates. I have no idea how the red shoe diary affair unfolded but it did, and weirdly coincidental to my mother divorcing my stepfather, my father divorced his second wife Myra, as good of a stepmother as I had come to expect from stepparents. Only got out of line once when she accused me of wounding the now-limping family dog, and immediately apologized for it when the vet pegged it as a bee sting. I was bitter enough about this that I've remembered it but I also remembered that she did the right thing by admitting that she had done the wrong thing.

But Carole? Before they had gotten married, she indulged in some sort of kabuki theater when they flew to New York to meet "the son." Like I mattered. Or rather, that my approval mattered. I didn't care though, and took a still-jaundiced view of the doings of adults when it came to matters of relationship comportment. That generation was, by my lights, full of shit. Something Ian and I bonded over when he told me he had had to lecture his parents about smoking weed in front of his younger siblings.

They had tried to buy him off with it being no different than drinking wine, but he wasn't buying and told them to cut it out. No ultimatum, and I always wondered what he would have done had they ignored him, but his strength of character was formidable enough that, at least according to him, they stopped.

My attitude with my sets of parents had always been more laissez-faire. If you live close enough with people long enough you learn way more than they ever give you credit for. Like, in a strange twist, that they were smoking weed and doing coke well after I was. And after stealing their weed for six months, I also knew it was bunk weed.

I had also found my father's porn, disguised as film study books but whatever. My attitude was and remains, who am I to judge? I shrugged through my meeting with Carole and was nice enough but getting her to sign off on him giving me a floor to sleep on? Well . . . OK.

"She says she thinks it's OK."

"OK," I said, sarcasm starting to lace out the end of the letter K sound.

"And no drinking, or drugs, or crazy shit." My father rarely if ever cursed. He also knew that whatever he knew about me, none of it had involved drinking, drugs or crazy "shit." I was a good and dutiful older brother, and while I was no stranger to any of that stuff my understanding of that kind of business was that you kept it *your* business.

With the exception of a punk rock night while I still lived in Brooklyn and had chased down some quaaludes with wine when I got home (never on the subway where I might have to actually fight) to help me "sleep," only to wake up in the morning having to piss and finding my one leg had been slept on wrong and was effectively paralyzed, at least for walking, so to create the reality that nothing was wrong it made sense to me to "act" like I could walk on it. Stepping on it, I'd plunge to the floor, doing a one-legged knee lunge to stand upright, and repeat the step and plunge to the floor, all the way to the bathroom before finally collapsing to my knees and hoisting my penis over the porcelain and pissing that way.

Outside of THAT? The homestead had always been a straight-arrow deal and I resented the implication that it was any other way.

"Have you EVER known me to do any of that 'shit'?" He laughed nervously and played it off on the other side of the line in the room where Carole stood.

"OK. We'll see you then."

"Ooo Kay . . . "

D.C. was "taken" care of and Ian had put us in touch with guys in the Midwest where we could stay and Tesco Vee from the Meatmen and *Touch and Go* magazine had been more than welcoming. *Touch and Go* was a great mag, and though with different ambitions than *The Birth of Tragedy*, neither one of us were dummies and he dug on the "Sex & Depression" issue and I dug on songs he had written like "Tooling for Anus."

Since we had been way more than vocal about the tour, weaseling our way onto local college radio shows to talk about it and getting written up for it before it happened, friends in bands started to ask if they could come. A band called Hamerslag asked. Full of people from other good bands, and people who would go on to other good bands, Hamerslag was a curiosity. With a Dutch woman singer and players who really could play, they were great.

Personality-wise, though, something I had never considered was, well, the rigors of touring would be rough on them. Starting with them touring in a Valiant. No trailer. Jammed into a car with gear on their laps, in the trunk and lashed to the roof. Now move on to fistfights on stage mid-show. Entertaining in short bursts, but when our host in Michigan from the band The Fix asked if he could talk to me, I could smell some wrong coming my way.

Someone had stolen the $1.25 in quarters that he had put aside for laundry. If the malefactor did not confess and return it, we'd all have to leave. I had a talk with the band. I don't remember what I said but I did not scream, or rant. I went icy. Like my Dad. There was no question that this wrong would be made right.

"We took it. We wanted to buy some cigarettes."

"No, peanut butter."

They were arguing over how they spent what they had stolen and I waved my hand before holding it out.

"Give it."

"But it's our gas money."

"That's your problem."

And just like that Hamerslag was off the tour.

They had played only one show, at Bookie's, the leather bar immortalized in "Tooling for Anus." What they missed? All the shows with Minor Threat, playing at a community center basement in Lansing, the Freezer Theater in Detroit, and hanging out in Tesco Vee's backyard with Minor Threat.

"I could even take a guy YOUR size," said Ian in the aforementioned backyard.

We were chopping it up and I missed the give-and-take that seemed emblematic of the East Coast to me. Where everything sounds like an argument, even a fight, but no one gets hurt since the loser is just the one who loses the argument. " . . . IF I was angry enough."

I laughed in his face. "I always hear guys who don't know how to fight say stuff like that," I tried to explain, "since it seems possible. I mean we both have arms and legs and stuff but anger doesn't keep you from getting your ass kicked."

Now he laughed and somehow we got to talking about what now people would call "political correctness" but which he was framing back then as honesty. Specifically in relation to the Minor Threat song "Guilty of Being White."

I'm sorry for something I didn't do

Lynched somebody . . . I don't know who

You blame me for slavery

A hundred years before I was born

Guilty of being white

I tried to explain that interpersonally this created for me a curious division: while the song was catchy as fuck, its message was lunkheaded and poorly placed. I was pretty sure the always present subcurrent of racism, which should not be excluded from any Western field of endeavor, well, that this could have been a theme song for that.

"Well, you don't know what it's like to grow up in D.C. and be the only white guy around sometimes."

"So, it's strange for you to be the only white guy around?" I looked around the party, my eyes widening to make the point, me being the only Black guy there. "For some of us, that's just every day."

He dug in and I refused to relent and so we just started talking about something else and I didn't think about it again until I read that post-Slayer doing a cover of it, he had modulated his position. An amusing turnaround since it was pretty clear that Slayer got it exactly right.

The shows with Minor Threat were easily and quite comfortably epic. I'd never seen a band of peers play that well, and Ian projected force without any sort of really obvious macho ideation. I guess playing foil to Rollins' SOA made this an easy choice, but I suspect it was much less chosen than it was a product of Ian. Passion versus force, if that makes any sense.

To get one of the shows, in the full-blown Little Rascals spirit of just wanting to be involved, I had agreed that Whipping Boy would play for free before I wised up. Post-show I remember, vaguely, bracing Ian for some of the evening's receipts. One hundred dollars. Something I clearly would have forgotten if Ian hadn't mentioned it in a recent documentary about Midwest hardcore where he brought it up and classified it as "fucked."

Which made me laugh and laugh.

Because he was right on all counts, and then like now, I absolutely do not care. The tradition, as it goes, is that if you're willing to give then you should, and if you're not, well, no harm in me asking. I mean, I wasn't threatening him to get it. Besides which if he got ANGRY enough even a guy his size could take me on.

I've had the occasion to speak to him over the years since then. The *most* surprising time was when, after a knock on my dorm room door and an invitation to come in, in stepped Ian and his brother Alec. The *least* surprising was when I was going through D.C. on a book tour for *Fight: Everything You Ever Wanted to Know About Ass Kicking But Were Afraid You'd Get Your Ass Kicked for Asking* and extended him an invitation to show and he said he might. I knew he'd never show but I appreciated the gesture.

"You had a lot of energy out there," Brian Baker, guitarist for Minor Threat, said to me the last show we played with them. He raised his eyebrows and I suspect he was intimating that it was chemically fueled.

"Well, we try to stay in shape and I always try to run before tours." This was a lie. It was this tour that later convinced me that I should start running, since on occasion I was dying on stage, sporting an outfit of leather engineer boots, heavy with sweat jeans, a chain belt, and a flannel shirt. But I had to say something to counter the conclusion that I was coked out of my head. "I'm not coked out of my head if that's what you mean though." Just easier to say than not.

We had one more chance to play with Minor Threat. At the Olympic Auditorium in Los Angeles. Thousands of people were guaranteed to be there. Unfortunately, it fell in the same month as Steve's first wedding. Though the show and the wedding were weeks apart and we volunteered to fly him down, his first wife got on the phone and started calling me a piece of shit for even suggesting it.

My response was horrible, incendiary and totally unhelpful, and put Steve in a position where he could do nothing but not play the show.

"There'll be other Minor Threat shows," he told me by way of reconciliation.

But there were not. I didn't attend his wedding and remained bitter about this non-choice being made a choice for many . . . well, actually, I'm still pissed about it. Before that, though, we had to finish this tour in the pickup truck of death and that involved stops in Boston, New York and D.C., before driving all the way back just the way we had come.

Boston would not be noteworthy until later. D.C., and the show at the Wilson Center, was of note then for no other reason than despite the roadies I had taken to D.C. to see Bad Brains, Black Market Baby, X and so on, the Wilson Center show was the first one that I had been to as a man in a band. Which meant something very different up against the clubby-ness of D.C. But the first bow in D.C. was overshadowed by a family reality that I should have seen coming.

Heading out to Olney where my father and Carole had bought a split-level ranch-style house, I had expected nothing approaching fireworks. One of her two sons was into heavy metal, so was ecstatic at the prospect of a band staying. My sister Gina, a sparkling and ebullient kid who hadn't seen me since her parents divorced, and my younger sister Egan were curious what all the big brother hubbub was all about.

Pulling into their driveway hellos were said all around, and I shoved Dave our drummer to the fore. My father spoke German; I had wanted to test how decent his German was, so I put Dave up to speaking to him in German. My father was surprised but rolled with it. My German at that point wasn't good enough to know if my father's passed muster but Dave said it did. Or he was just being polite.

Later after dinner we sat around the table behind our empty plates and caught up.

"I know you guys arc talking but make sure you clean your stuff up," Carole laughed.

"Oh. Don't worry," I said. "We will." My mother was very desirous of not raising me to be a pig of a man, so I never assumed or believed that this was "women's work."

A few minutes later Carole appeared again. Not laughing this time.

"Don't forget to grab your dishes." This time I looked at her. I hadn't developed the kind of language sophistry where people *suggest* rather than *ask* you to do something, but maybe it was that she hadn't heard me the first time. So I repeated, "No worries. I'll handle it."

We talked more. My father had a film that had gone to Cannes, and it later won the Cine Eagle Award in Germany. Plus he had almost a dozen half-brothers and sisters, some of whom I knew. There was a lot of catching up to do and the rest of the band chimed in when we started talking music, film, art and Germany.

"Hey," Carole again. "Do NOT forget to take your dishes in."

"Hey," I said looking at her with a little steel in my voice. "How about I take them out on the patio and smash them into hundreds of pieces? C'mon . . . we'll do it when we finish." She blushed a hard red but you know, fuck you.

The surprise was when I turned back to the conversation my father looked nothing if not . . . scared? Of? I had no idea but I felt I was well within my rights. Two months later he stopped speaking to me completely. Carole had had the final say. And the say was apparently your son is defrauding us out of $85 a month for a school that he's dropped out of. As an academic, I am sure my father knew the difference between "stopped out" and "dropped out" but he acceded.

This didn't bother me as much as the fact that he used his second wife's bisexuality against her to gain sole custody of my sisters so he didn't have to pay her for their care and upkeep. Then, Carole, in full-on Cinderella fashion, taught them "woman's work" and even had them live in the basement while her sons did not. The next time I would see Gina, gone was the ebullient happy kid I remembered. This, the complete absence of her mother from their lives, and the fact that Olney was redneck central back in the early '80s, had changed her.

This broke my heart, and is as unforgivable as anything that happened to me since I don't perceive that I suffered in absentia. So, fuck him too.

New York that first summer was genius though. We pulled up to A7, parked in front of Tompkins Square, and Bubby rolled up unsteadily on a skateboard that belonged to Vinnie Stigma. Jimmy Gestapo was there and had his deck too. John Watson, the first singer for Agnostic Front, also crowded around, as did Keith, later of Cause for Alarm.

"Who are you guys?"

"We're Whipping Boy."

"YO! It's Whipping Boy!" Now I know how that reads but this was not a holler of recognition. They had no idea who we were but it was a public declaration and an ID. This, with the California license plates, meant the summer had wrinkled again in some way, shape or form, and until we had proven out as assholes, we were some version of family. Especially since the Lower East Side then was a nexus point for junkies, killers, drug dealers, street gangs, Hells Angels and all manner of chaos. Having someone like Steve around, even for a couple of nights, was a total positive.

While the show itself was only partially well attended, the strange thing about New York hardcore was that the action was still in the streets, unless Bad Brains or a big name was playing, and while people would come in and out, there were still more people gathered around our pickup truck than had ever been at the show.

Sam and Dave disappeared to the Upper West Side to a friend's place. Steve and I hung out. Attached at the hip like we were now with

Doug Holland from the band Kraut. We hit the clubs. With Doug as our advance man. Clubs I had struggled to get into before. Doug would whisper a few words, jerk his thumb in our direction and we were in.

I was dying to know what he was saying that was making possible what mere months before had been impossible for me, and all I could catch were whispers like "California" . . . "on tour" . . . whatever.

We got into Danceteria. Harley Flanagan, who I had seen play in The Stimulators at one of the first shows I ever saw, was there on the floor where the old punk rock guard was confronting certain hardcore realities. Like: if you weren't going to be what they were now calling "moshing" and what some journo had named "slam dancing" on the West Coast, you were going to get your ass kicked if you objected to those who were.

It was some measure of delicious watching Flanagan terrorize a crowd of people who had high-handed me months before. I also felt some kind of sorry for them too. But you could see just as well from the back.

At some point before we left back for the West Coast I was asked where we were staying. I said "My Mom's house. In Brooklyn." And I watched them figure this out.

"Yeah, I'm from here," I laughed. "Last show I went to here the only people I remember were Harley, Claudette, Jack Rabid, and Ira here . . . in fact Ira is the one who used to taunt me with 'push push in the bush'." I was laughing now. It was delightful having the opportunity to have an a-ha moment. Ira apologized and explained that back then they got such a raft of shit on the streets he had to return it somehow. I said I didn't care because, as Bubby later ingrained in me, say whatever you want. Just don't put your hands on me.

I told them that I'd be back for Christmas and off we drove, first Whipping Boy tour in the books.

School's in for the Winter

"ALL EUGENE EVER TALKS ABOUT is his . . . band." Jean was anorexic. And in love with complaining. But this was a valuable lesson and offered some much-needed insight into whatever people really meant when they asked, "How was your summer?" They rarely mean "How was your summer?" if you didn't know. They meant, "Ask me about MY summer" and since I had no interest in how the eating-disordered were spending their summers or anything else non-music-related, I effectively severed my social connections to Stanford.

I had been dumped by three women under weirdly similar circumstances that stunk of parental interference in the first two instances. The third I blamed myself for. The Chirpy Resident Assistant, though she hadn't shown up to the orgy she had tipped me off to, started hanging around. Mohawk or not, she didn't care. In fact, she had a string of ex-boyfriends like the one who did things like wander into one of the freshmen's rooms and piss in their garbage can before realizing he was sleep-pissing and fled. Leaving her to clean up the piss.

On top of that I had played rugby with her brother who, in a first, seemed to like me more than he liked his sister and I believe imagined that I was a step in the right non-garbage-can-pissing direction. But since these types of relationships were officially verboten and though we had left my freshman year behind, our doings were still inexplicably covered by a certain amount of secrecy. Or maybe it *was* the mohawk I was now sporting.

In any case, one night in her garage, I spotted a Dan Fogelberg record. I didn't know Fogelberg from Zuckerberg, but he seemed an easy and willing target, all '70s cocaine cool on the cover.

She had been house sitting so I thought, fair game.

"Jesus. Who the fuck LIKES Dan Fogelberg?!?" This is a familiar two-step for anyone who likes music. Getting shade for musical tastes is probably the single best explanation as to why people find themselves open to getting shit online.

But I went in on Fogelberg HARD, and I expected, waited, and wanted some sort of pushback from her so I could admit that I knew nothing about what I was talking about. She said nothing though. Days later when she was dumping me, we stood on the sidewalk at night and she cried that she didn't, couldn't, maintain control of her sense of own self on account of my personality being too strong.

However, all of the LSD had gifted me a kind of through-sight and so I interrupted with a prompt: "You know you don't have to cry to make me feel better about this," I smiled.

And to my surprise she stopped IMMEDIATELY. Something I hadn't expected. But then my thoughts were spinning. Do men really radiate needing tears to accompany their walking papers?

I had gotten out of the shotgun trailer park and was ensconced in an apartment building on the far edge of campus. My roommate with the smashed throat from the trailer now my roommate here. He kept the bedroom in the apartment, and I moved my bed into the living room. I was there only during the week for classes and homework and was at band practice or at shows as often as possible.

Steve had graduated and was teaching at a tony high school where we now rehearsed, so Stanford was a way station, at best. Though, academically, things had started to click this third year. I had dropped the idea that I was going to be a marine biologist and started putting all of that LSD to use when I found myself studying religious philosophy, which would have been my minor if Stanford gave minors.

Moreover, a few professors had taken notice in a way that wasn't wholly negative. Simone Di Piero, Bill Rivers and a linguistics professor had all pulled me aside in one way or another and said something along the lines of "don't know what you're thinking about doing for a living, but you might consider writing."

Di Piero had bought *The Birth of Tragedy* for chrissakes and still stayed in touch with me even after I had gotten a respectable A in his class and moved on.

Truthfully, I hadn't thought about cash because, well, stuff was happening with music. Sam and Dave, Whipping Boy's rhythm section, were ecstatic about a band that had bored me but *had* just gotten signed, the Red Hot Chili Peppers. But I was making more money from shows than I made working in the dish room and that was math I could work with.

At CBGBs. A Bad Brains show. Christmas Eve. You should spy with your little eye, if you're paying attention, Dave Dictor from MDC, and the former Jimmy Gestapo from Murphy's Law. Photographer unknown.

It was these careerist notions that fueled our approach to our second record, *Muru Muru*, a weird pastiche of decidedly non-hardcore music. See, our assumption was that Whipping Boy fans were so because they had signed on to the Whipping Boy journey. That they were not genre-bound.

When we played the songs that we had roughed and now had pulled Klaus Flouride in to produce, his first question to us should have been a heeded notice: "Are you serious?"

Well, yeah.

We were listening to more than just hardcore now. The Birthday Party; we had always listened to Joy Division, and having tickets to their never-to-happen shows in New York was a wound that wouldn't be soothed until I later had the occasion to interview drummer Stephen Morris. Also, Wall of Voodoo and OMD (Orchestral Manoeuvres in the Dark).

Me, naked, in a field. For an ad. Magazines insisted my cock be concealed.
I agreed with the proviso that it needed to say, "Censored by
Cocksuckers." This did not go over well.

If hardcore was a conversation, then it felt like a conversation that made more sense to have live on stage than in the studio. The studio felt like a dreamscape, recording as we were at Harbor Sound in Sausalito, a studio later owned by one of the Talking Heads. Mallon wasn't in attendance, but we felt safe with Klaus and an engineer that helped Steve figure out that there was a difference between a guitar cable and a speaker cable, among other things.

We steered for adventurous and with songs like "My Day at the Lake" and "Myster Magi" it gathered, as coherently as possible, the lack of coherence in our thoughts about the tectonic plates shifting in our heads about music, art, who it's for and what might you say and maybe most importantly who you are saying it to.

There was a story Bart Thurber, later our second guitar player, had about his time being in a Chuck Berry pickup band. One of the side guys asked Chuck what the set list was and Chuck just looked at him. Dead-eyed. And said: "Chuck Berry songs." Striving for Whipping Boy's "Chuck Berry songs" was harder than it seemed. But there were lots of factors involved and having a front-row seat with Klaus and watching him work offered a peek not just into process but also how things worked with the Dead Kennedys.

Right up until the night the tables turned.

"So. You know Lorraine, right?" Klaus peered over his glasses and pushed back from the board during a break in the recording.

She had correctly predicted that I would get my ears pierced and get tattooed as soon as the plane landed in San Fran and she wasn't far off. In the hubbub of our Mudd Club meet I had mistakenly understood that Biafra was her ex-husband, but maybe I just remembered his name versus the less memorable Klaus.

"Yeah!"

"Funny. You knowing my wife."

And while I am sort of on the spectrum in regards to my abilities to always read the reactions of others correctly—hence all of the times I got punched in the face—I sensed . . . that this had gotten away from me. I mean, she had mentioned him as her "EX" husband. He had mentioned her as his WIFE.

"Yeah . . . well . . . ."

"You SLEPT with her didn't you, you little bastard!"

I was flummoxed, and in the middle of a guy who was holding your musical life in your hands expressing dismay at the many crimes of penis, I felt a need to try to . . . save . . . things.

"And you met at the MUDD Club no less!" He was half joking but that meant he was also half NOT joking so I had to try to fix things.

"Hey man . . . the one night she gave me I was totally TERRIBLE in bed," I laughed because it was true. I had been feeling under the weather and so not wanting to blow it, in a move that is unwise from almost every single perspective, I took a bunch of pills. Pills that I assumed were Excedrin and if one Excedrin is what they advised normal people to take, and I was bigger than a normal person, AND I didn't want sniffles to ruin it, maybe I should take FOUR.

I suspected I was in trouble on the way to meet her when all I could hear was a high-pitched whine in my ears but at 17, well, 'no' was not an option of any kind.

The upshot? Nothing to write home about, and while this confession would not have mollified many since I was, indeed, copping to what I had done, the chagrin on my face over the bolloxed performance issues was enough for him to laugh it off.

We finished the record, a record named after an aboriginal greeting that we had been led to understand meant both hello and goodbye, and we made what we thought would be the easy step to have his label release it. Biafra passed on it with a supportive hand wave. This gesture might as well have been repeated all over the place. We had played the songs live so we knew that they worked in a hardcore context but shorn of any antigovernment trappings and 1-2-3-4s . . . no.

I had taken 50 copies up to Rough Trade in a duffel bag strapped to my back while I rode a balky motorcycle. Twenty minutes after record drop-off they called me to come back, 45 minutes on the freeway, to pick up 40 of them.

We were undeterred. If you were smart/crazy you'd understand. If you weren't you wouldn't.

Police Stories

"DON'T FUCK . . . AT LEAST I CAN FUCKING THINK." Yeah, well, good for Ian. Except for, well, fucking doesn't all seem to be such a bad way to spend some time, and while I am sure I don't understand what was going on in D.C. when he wrote the song, I do know I had to recalibrate a few things. Which wasn't a big deal. Out from under the umbrella of disco, drugs and drink, this probably had to be done anyway.

But cruising into the '80s we then had herpes and AIDS to think about so maybe a more measured approach to matters of sexual comportment made some sense.

"Hey . . . you want to go on a date?" The guy asking had a punk rock name totally at odds with his job and vocation. A chemical engineer at Intel, Jake Action was a staple at shows as long as I'd been going to shows in California.

"You asking?"

"Not with ME, man," he quickly clarified. "I know these three girls from Mills. The one I'm digging on won't go out alone with me again, but if you come . . . "

"If I come that's still only two."

"Well, I'm going to bring John Norman." Despite the last name of Norman that seems to suggest an overridingly *normal* set of circumstances, John was anything but, and my love for him harkened back to my love for the Deegan brothers. You see, John was hilarious.

"Hey, Eugene," he drawled, half high-pitch mock and totally high delivery. "What do you say me and you exchange blows? You hit me and then I hit you. Actually, let me punch you first and . . . "

"Nah, John," but I was already laughing because he was playing with both the premise of "blows" as in punches and the other kind, and just as quickly he'd pivot: "Know anybody you hate?" And that's just the way he constructed that sentence and because it always struck me as curious, I mention it here.

"Know anybody you hate?"

"Fuck YES!"

"Let me know when they go on vacation," he nodded smiling. "And I'll cut you in a third."

You see, John was a thief. Unrepentant. If you went to a show at the Elite Club in San Fran, now the Fillmore, and your car was broken into that night? Chances were very good that it was John, with a spark plug connected to a shoelace smashing car windows all up and down Geary stealing car stereos when those were the things that people stole.

Thanksgiving dinners, insofar as anyone really cooked, seemed to sometimes happen at Jake's house, and would at some point involve the ritual unfolding of product and John announcing, in the case of a camera I was lusting after but too broke to buy, "Just don't use it around Bascom Avenue."

True or not, it was hilarious just the same. Unless it was your camera and you lived on Bascom Avenue.

I was the third for my first triple date/double blind date and since the proof of the pudding is always in the tasting, my enthusiasm was held in abeyance until I actually got to see what the women looked like. Jake was bald and 40, the Action last name notwithstanding. John was a wiry redhead who, despite being the scion of some Silicon Valley bigwig, the fact that the bigwig had abandoned his wife and him, their son, played on him, and he'd taken to the streets.

Showing up at the expensive all-girls school we met them on the other side of some glass-enclosed gazebo. I could see them notice Jake first, and then John, and then a studied look of "Oh God, is this what we have to do to spend a Friday night out on the town?" Which made me want to abandon ship then and there. But one of the women was my type, says the guy who professes and really believes he has no type. Comely and smart, she looked at me and we looked at each other through the gazebo.

But her look attracted the notice of the other two. While I was less interested in them, I could see their enthusiasm for a possibly cool Friday night had been renewed. I don't know what constituted a good date back then, or now, or ever, really, but in the car as we tooled over the Bay Bridge to San Francisco I was enjoying talking to them and so maybe that was enough.

I did notice that the woman I liked kept deferring to another before I asked and found out that they were sisters and I knew at that point that there was no way that the older sister was going to let this happen. The younger sister seemed to know it too or at least deferred enough times that I just tapped out: older sister it would be. I'm nothing if not a pragmatist.

We get to the club, Jake is buying drinks but I'm not drinking and keep fleeing the table to fling myself into the pit. I want to say that TSOL was playing but the historical record does not back this up as far as I can find. The conversation is comfortable, even in staccato bursts, and the night felt like a success.

Even more so as we made our way down Broadway to where Jake's car had been parked. Jake and John rushed ahead to meet the women. I strolled. Because suddenly the street didn't smell right. There had been a paddy wagon in front of the club and cops had been harassing people so it was already tense, but then popping up over the hill two police cars came careening down the middle of the street, lights and sirens blazing.

"Um . . . Jake?"

Nothing! They could see the women across the street on the corner, waiting, and enthusiasm had won out.

"John?"

At this point I could see cops, Starsky and Hutch-style sliding across the hoods of their cruisers, nightsticks drawn, making for the corner where Jake and John were now chatting with the women.

I stayed standing in front of a video arcade and watched the cops nightstick them down to the asphalt, a blur of black stick and screams. Two Latino guys screamed at the cops and pointed to me, "THERE'S ANOTHER ONE!!!" Which got from me a look and a shrug that said nothing but "REALLY? You're going to SNITCH me out?!?"

Considering this was all nonverbal semaphores it was clear that they got it. Score one for the Black punk rocker as Jake and John were cuffed, thrown into the police car and taken away to the North Beach station.

I followed up with the women, had no answers but got them a ride back to Oakland while I cadged a ride off of Howard, roadie and drum tech extraordinaire for Los Olvidados. His Chevy Chevelle set in steel and chrome my lifelong love of the car.

But over the intervening days during which Jake had bailed out and John remained, the story unfolded. That night John had robbed the paddy wagon. Stole Maglite flashlights and cop hats. To add to the stolen ones he had on him already. Well, that plus the crank he had on him (the earlier iteration of meth). While Jake the Intel engineer correctly claimed to have nothing to do with it and was released, he could not convince them to release his "adopted son."

No. John they walked out to the parking garage to an I-beam with a mattress around it and handcuffed him there where they beat him. He said he pissed blood for three days afterward. He also said he needed my help to enact some street justice/revenge on the offending cop.

"I found out where he lives, man." John, always easy with a smile, was now not smiling. "I need you to drive the car and we'll . . . " He lifted up a blanket in the back seat of his car and uncovered what looked like an Uzi. Now there's a reason he asked me. It's seemed to me in tribal groupings people cohere to certain phenotypes, and just like I went through that distinct period where I was attracting women who had a thing for authority figures, in this grouping my propensity and interest in "exchanging blows" was known and identified as a group positive.

When two carloads of cholos—think Latino *cugines*—had seen the movie *1984* about dystopic punks running riot, they decided to go kick some punk rock ass and found Butch from Santa Cruz, on his lonesome, up the hill from where Jack and John got braced by the cops. Hearing this I hollered at Mark Dagger, a known holy terror in San Francisco and guy who to the manner seemed born if the manner was extreme violence.

As we turned the corner and saw Butch backed against the wall by four cholos trying to work up the nerve to jump—Butch was a two-fisted badass himself so that was the only reason he was still standing—Dagger begged off.

"Where you going?"

"To get help!"

Whatever. I headed up the hill, a knife in each hand and closed the distance.

"Bro, bro, everything's cool! Everything's cool!" I should have thanked Butch for this as the number imbalance had me enraged. One on one they wouldn't have done this. It took four and that violated my sense of fair play and there was blood in my eyes. I murdered no one that night and cooler heads prevailed, but this thing with John and the Uzi?

"Nah, bro." I just had a hard time understanding that the punishment fit the crime. Also, I did not relish the idea of murdering a guy in front of his family, and if you were going out there JUST to "scare him," as John suggested, it seemed a misapplication of the performing arts.

But for the first time some of these kids had felt like Negroes, in how they were treated by cops. Though, if truth be told, cops had been complete non-factors in my life before leaving New York. In pre-Giuliani New York, no matter what you were doing, you were unlikely to find cops who were interested in checking you for whatever reason.

I lived through and witnessed two massive power outages, Son of Sam murders, street gangs, and cops being a factor in any of this? Not really.

Coming to California? A total wake-up call.

Starting with my roommate coming by Steve's trailer and interrupting an interview we had been doing, his face stricken. He pulled me outside. Apparently, the cops had just surrounded our trailer with guns drawn. They were looking for me. They were asking about my shotgun. None of these things seemed to be good on the face of it.

I sent Steve to run interference, moved out of my room, put a large padlock on the now empty room, and hid out in the dank basement where we rehearsed until it was either time to leave on Whipping Boy's second tour or sanity returned.

Steve had found out that they were looking for me on account of two charges having to do with a *moped* violation. The same moped I had ridden up on Steve the first time we met, I spent a few years cruising around campus on this. At one point a cop named Hopgood had pulled me over.

"What?" This was my first response. I'd never been stopped by a NY cop in my life.

"You drove between those bollards." Hopgood, an older Black guy, was trying to son me through this interaction and I bristled.

"The assumption here is that those roadblocks are to block anything they can. As you can see my moped, a modified bike really, fits quite comfortably *between* those bollards. And the space between the four bollards I just drove through is approximately eight feet. So, what are we talking here?"

"You're not supposed to go between them," he was not listening. And for sure not caring.

"If they felt that way then there would have been a chain."

"You'll have the opportunity to explain it to the judge."

"How much is the ticket?" Now I was angry.

"Eighty-five dollars. Name please." Eighty-five dollars would mean not eating for a week of the next month. Or cadging food off of people who had meal programs and could provide food.

"Name? Craig Spearman. My friends call me 'Spearchucker'." Don't know how I got there but there I was and I figured when they came back to him on this he'd cover for me. We didn't like each other very much but he was from The Bronx. And yeah: fuck the police.

But he didn't. While he later dropped out of Stanford, he did so to become a cop. So back then he just fingered me. Of course, because they thought I was him at the time they pulled up on him *in* class, guns drawn, so I understand it might have been a skosh upsetting, but, in any case, the game was up, and it was me they were looking for.

Including bursting into Steve's trailer at 5 in the morning and checking under his bedclothes as they thought I might be there. I was, but was hiding under his *roommate's* bed. And then finally: "I know you guys are going off on tour," one cop said to Steve. "But if you're stopped for a traffic violation in Michigan or someplace and they check the system, he'll have to deal with it then. Or in September when you all come back. So better now."

Steve brought me the news and some food and so we made a decision that Public Moped Enemy Number One would turn himself in the next day. Which would have been a welcome relief. I didn't mind spending my days napping on a dirty foam sound baffle, reading, masturbating and voiding my bowels and bladder into pots and pans. But I did miss the sun.

Next day I wandered over to the police station. "You wanted to speak to me?"

"Ah. Mr. Robinson." They got the paperwork out and I could see despite Craig's protestations that he had not fingered me for it, the paperwork given out in the photo lineup indicated he had done precisely that. Which wasn't hard. Black guys with mohawks and leather jackets were not a Stanford staple. They walked me out to the police cruiser and Officer Del Bandy, all Adam-12, blond hair and blue eyes of him, asked me, almost nicely: "We don't have to put the cuffs on, do we?"

And I shook my head like that was the most ridiculous thing in the world.

"You're clean too, right?" He had not frisked me and understood underneath it all I was still just a "good ol' Stanford kid."

"Yeah." See, I figured I'd get to keep my own clothes while in jail. If that was the case, I also knew I might need my knife. So, though in general I hate to lie, here it seemed to make sense.

But driving into the basement of the courthouse, the lights dimming as the sun gets blocked by all of the concrete, much less of it was making sense, and loading me into lockup an overweight cop had started in on me right away.

"Hey. Who does your hair?"

I laughed. "Your dietician?" He did not laugh. But he wasn't angry. He just seemed like he didn't know what a dietician was. Or he did and wouldn't be stopped. So for the next 20 minutes of intake he must have asked 15 more times and while I laughed at first, by time 15 I understood it was being done for one reason and one reason only: to make it clear, Stanford boy, where exactly you now found yourself.

Being put in a security cell was the next stage.

"Strip." They gathered at the door of the padded cell.

I had just written an article on the constitutionality of strip searches and was about to argue my point but we were in the no-play zone and all of the weirdness of cop-Black person interplay I think hinged on unspoken issues of sexuality. If there's another explanation for why they were all looking at my cock I'd like to hear it, but this is where we were now.

"I thought you said he was clean." And one of the cops like pulling a rabbit out of a hat pulled out my knife. The city cops throwing shade at the campus cops, all while I stood still and naked at the cell's far end. Bandy started to pull out his nightstick and come toward me. I stepped forward and raised my fists. Slowly. The message here: this is not reflexively defensive. This is planned and no one here is going down without a fight.

I don't remember thinking I was smiling here. I remember feeling the feeling that I was trying to get Anton LaVey, the head of the Church of Satan, to identify: a wildness and willingness to murder or be murdered in the process. It's not anger exactly, but a bloodlust. Whatever was on my face, the city cops pulled Bandy back.

"It's OK." Bandy looked at me, betrayed. Fuck Bandy.

They tossed me some lime-green coveralls. With a broken zipper in front. They took my underwear so I was almost naked despite the coveralls, and I had figured out that this is how they use jail rape as a tool of control. But I was put in a cell with a bunch of other men. One guy had tried to murder another commuter on his way to work in the midst of some vehicular dispute. A few guys in for drugs, stealing. The happiest guy I ever saw in jail? The forger. He had his own cell and when people identified him as a forger it was with an air of respect. But he smiled and smiled, and I liked him immediately.

"What did they get you for?"

I guess the question was inevitable. Saying "a moped traffic violation" was not.

"They think I'm crazy." And as I stood there, largely with my cock almost hanging out, festooned with tattoos and sporting a mohawk when the only other Black guy sporting one was 3,000 miles away and in a band called the Plasmatics, I guess they bought it.

Jail memories: the food was terrible. Like beyond terrible. And I consumed every bit of it. Waiting in the stairwell before court they called my name and I gathered the ends of my coveralls around me and strode in.

"You realize this is all ridiculous, don't you?" The judge peered over his glasses at me.

"YES! I feel exactly that way!" This is what I said before I realized he was talking about MY part in it and not the charges brought against me.

"You have been charged with False Impersonation and False Information to a Police Officer, how do you plead?"

"Well, it seems like you can either impersonate someone or NOT impersonate someone, but FALSELY impersonating someone I believe is impossible."

"Soundly reasoned. We'll toss that charge."

I was on a roll.

"Being that I am, not in fact, a man nicknamed 'Spearchucker,' I would guess my plea to the second charge would be No Contest!"

"Hmmm . . . " He had had it. "You realize with a plea of 'No Contest' we'll have to see you back here in a few months and you'll have to . . . "

I interrupted him with a hand wave, "Guilty."

"Duly noted. We'll credit you with the day spent in jail and you're free to go. Try to stay out of trouble for the next 18 months and this will just be a memory, Mr. Robinson."

Back in the stairwell lockup, the others cheered. "You got off EASY!" And, in general, there was an air of celebration while the fat cop got his last digs in. The gates locked behind me and Steve was waiting for me on the other side.

"Let's go."

I told him what happened as we drove to where the van was parked and ready for tour. I also told him that the process had also both demystified jail for me in a way that I suspected was not helpful while cementing for me the reality that this was nothing I ever wanted to do again. The lack of control was galling, and the food was shit, and Whipping Boy's second tour wouldn't wait.

Bigger, Longer, More Dysfunctional

IF THE FIRST TOUR was a gimme, in the sense that we made no money and knew we wouldn't before we left to play to small audiences when we weren't playing with Minor Threat, *and* were jammed inside a death mobile to do it, then the second tour was designed to improve on all of that. A reach that really wasn't that far at all. Seven shows to now almost 30. A Brobdingnagian increase made possible by the fact that the national landscape for hardcore had totally changed and not just because Black Flag, the Circle Jerks, Dead Kennedys and so on were crisscrossing the country. The whole zeitgeist had just . . . changed. The scene was developing sinews and vascular systems to support people who were opting out of whatever the whole *other* program had been.

Pre-internet, the touring master list was written on loose-leaf paper, torn from a notebook. Addresses of where we were going, names of the people we were staying with, who was paying us and how much, and phone numbers for all of the above. We proudly displayed it on the front dashboard of our 1965 Ford Econoline Supervan I bought. Right under a Space Shuttle refrigerator magnet. The van had been owned by a coffee distributor, smelled like coffee and had a spotlight on top that

would shine for three seconds of brilliant glory before it burned out every fuse in the van. So: used only once.

Seeing Minor Threat the year before with a van that actually made sense to tour in, Steve, always handy with tools, kitted out our van with a loft, blue shag carpeting, insulation, and speakers. I added an El Tech cassette player that, we noticed, played faster the faster you drove and slower the slower you drove.

We also had come up in the world. One of Steve's students, Amy Keim, had signed on to be a roadie. She had been one of only a few punk rock students at the pricey private school he taught at and she had had it with California, the Silicon Valley-Stepford vibe of Menlo Park, and wanted out one way or another.

*In Menlo Park. Toward the end. But pre-*Muru Muru*. Photographer Matt Etheridge who, if memory serves, is the only one to ever photograph me skateboarding.*

"She's going to carry gear, right?" Leave it to the singer to find yet another way out of having to carry gear. Steve assured me that she would. And sell merch, and whatever other tour-managing stuff we needed.

Cruising across the Bonneville Salt Flats in Utah, Steve took note of the Space Shuttle magnet and with an "oh cool" lifted it off of the dashboard. The master list took flight and blew out of the window.

"What was that?"

"That was the tour master list," I said. Not especially perturbed.

"Do we have copies?"

I was doing about 80 miles an hour now. "Nope!" I loved driving and I loved speeding.

"How are we going to find out how to get to the shows?" Steve asked, panic now creeping into his voice.

"Ah, man," I said, "we'll figure it out."

"STOP THE VAN!"

And I did. Steve realized that was pointless. "HEAD BACK!"

I flipped a bitch, got us to where we could see the list lifting in the highway breezes off in the salt flats. Steve jumped out and gave chase. Dave jumped out and did the same. Strangely, as Type A as I usually am, I just sat and watched. Sam, Amy and I watched.

Every time Steve closed in on the list, a gust of wind whipped it up and away. It was Little Rascals-esque and while Sam quietly chewed tobacco, occasionally spitting in a 7-11 cup, and Amy scribbled in her diary, I watched. And sort of chortled. Not because it was funny as much as it was like G-d was talking out there in the whitewashed flats and I was yielding to fate and circumstance so it was a full-bodied whatever.

You see, no one thinks when they start a band that they're starting on a lifetime journey. I mean whose luck holds out that long? Making this a way station and a chapter and when Steve finally got the list I said, "They got it."

Making their way back to the van, Dave climbed in, and Steve rode shotgun, grousing about how ridiculous it was that we had only one list and he was going to make copies. Copy machines cost money back then. That's how that was. I saved 75 cents by not making copies. But Steve would do it by hand, hand everyone one of them, and we pulled into Salt Lake City just in time to get the word that the show had been canceled because the community center that was sponsoring it had been flooded during the previous night's rains.

We played with a lot of bands that tour. I'm just going to name some of the ones that I remember and please excuse if my memory is not as on the money as I might imagine.

The Clit Boys, Kilslug, The Accused, Corrosion of Conformity, The Zero Boys, Scream, JFA, Sacred Order, Die Kreuzen, Negative Approach, L7, Legal Weapon, Crucifix, Social Unrest, Girl Trouble, Rights of the Accused, Dayglo Abortions, the Stretchmarks, and more.

Of course, the lifetime playlist also included, notably, Bad Brains, Dead Kennedys, Fear, Circle Jerks, GBH, Anti-Nowhere League, Hüsker Dü, Minutemen, the Damned, the Meatmen, Minor Threat, MDC, and D.O.A. but this is not about lifetime. This is about seeing whatever we saw that kept us in pocket long enough so that the knee bone connected to the leg bone that connected to the ankle bone and kept us moving long enough to be sitting here writing this with both a historical take and an ahistorical take about being submerged in a cultural change premised on fuck you.

Because pre-MTV and the leveling of youth culture, if you rolled into small towns in a rusted-out, sky-blue van with a tattooed and mohawked Black guy driving, and Steve who now had a mohawk as well, as did our roadie, rainbow-dyed if memory serves, you didn't know what the fuck was going on.

"Look at that faggot! Let's get him!" We were at some truck stop in let's say Nebraska, and I stood at the pump while two country boys, fixated on Steve's mohawked head, followed him into the convenience store.

"Watch the gas," I told Sam and Dave, and grabbed what we used to call "the tour guide," a mini-cudgel, and I followed them while they looked for Steve. Who they found turning a corner, right into all 6'5" of him.

And . . . they just kept on walking.

Steve, oblivious, looked at me, tour guide jammed in my fist with a face that suggested a reason for it, and asked, "What the fuck are you doing?"

"Those guys were scheming to kick your ass."

We both turned and looked at them as they hustled out to their car. This would be the last tour that I would ever do without a gun on me. While I didn't need the cudgel then, I would need the gun later.

One of the "fun" things about the Supervan was that the gas gauge was screwy. You had to keep track of the mileage, a habit I continue to this day, just to be sure you were never caught short. But inevitably you were always caught short. Pulling into the Midwest we were caught short and as I had refused to get gas at the most recent convenient stop—I was a bear about driving and liked to stop for nothing—it was on me to walk this one out.

Call it karma for the salt flats incident. I grabbed the gas can and started out. Steve, having a sense that he'd be better off with a living singer versus a dead one, volunteered to come with while the others sat on the van apron or in short lawn chairs we had requisitioned from somewhere.

We talked and walked and finally got to the dirt edge of a gas station when another van started bearing down on us. Too fast for their own good and definitely too fast for ours. Hanging out the passenger window as it spun around us kicking up gravel, it felt like when Captain Willard finally gets upriver and finds Dennis Hopper's American photographer.

"WOOOOOOO HOOOOOOOO!!!" He had long raggedy hair, was about 10 years older than us and was beating the side of the van. I switched the gas can to my left hand and tightened my right hand around the handle of a hunting knife I had hidden in the small of my back.

"WHIPPING BOY!!!!!!!"

I loosened my grip on the knife.

"YEAH!!!!"

"We're DOG BREATH! And we're here to RESCUE YOU!" Turns out some lifers, roadies for MDC and damned near every band from Austin, had been beating it back home after a tour and saw our van stranded. We had zero punk rock stickers on it; preferring to hide in plain sight, we had U.S. Marines stickers, but they saw Amy's mohawked head and figured we had to be someone worth saving.

They had a bass and drums and their deal at this point was simple: they'd give us a ride back to the van IF they could open for us tonight. No money need change hands.

"Deal."

We show up at the venue, tell the club owner the deal and he did not care, at all. They set up a drum kit and a bass rig and turn in a show worthy of Flipper. I remember lines about Mount Saint Helens, and virgins. I remember them repeatedly announcing themselves as Dog Breath, and just as soon as they had started, they ended, drinking up all of the beers meant for a band that didn't drink beer—us—and all of us thought it worked out so well that a decision wasn't so much made as just relaxed into: we'd have them do more shows. I mean, the price was right.

Eventually, they went on their way back down South. I think this had to do with them not being able to make it into Canada, but in the end, they were off into a future of raising hell on the road. We all said we couldn't imagine being their age and doing the same thing. As it is now, only one of us who said that *is* still doing it, and that's me. I'd tell myself now what I said then to explain the last four decades: why not?

Canada was funny though. A weird combination of comfortable politesse and extreme violence. Right before we had gotten to the show in a basement of a hotel in Saskatchewan, some kid had been killed and left by the railroad tracks. Apparently murdered for sporting punk rock finery. By the time we got to Winnipeg we had recalibrated. Negroes were First Nations people, and were liked as much as Negroes were south of the Canadian border.

"Look at that Black bastard with that beauteous white queen!" Steve was forever being shanghaied into whatever cause the local Canadians felt like needed a white guy with some muscle behind them. Not knowing that Steve is the same guy that almost murdered some fraternity guys for singing "Dixie."

Steve looked across the street and took the time to note to the drunk Canadian that the beauteous white queen was a 250-pound prostitute and the Black bastard appeared to be her pimp/boyfriend who, as it turns out, was not Black at all. This was Winnipeg, and the show and the guarantee that we got for playing it were noteworthy enough that we treated ourselves to Chinese food that night versus our regular cuisine of government cheese and peanut butter sandwiches.

Heading back out to the van after the show, we started the all-night drive so we could hit Minneapolis the next day where we had both an all-ages matinee to play and a 21-and-over show. The van started and popped into a steamed explosion when one of the radiator hoses burst. On the one hand, better in town than on the highway. On the other hand, after the show no stores were open, and this would play havoc with our schedule.

Driving around we had figured that finding an open auto parts store was unlikely. Finding older vans about the same make and model? Much more likely. Steve slid under one and came out with a hose that we discovered did not fit. Now trying to make a right out of a wrong, we went back to replace it at the same time the owner came out of the building it was parked next to. We kept walking until he pulled off into the Winnipeg night.

Drag.

I mean, we truly felt bad. It was going to happen to him for sure if the hose had fit, but knowing the hose didn't fit and the driver was going to get two blocks and be fucked? Yeah, sort of a drag. Also, given where we had parked and were still parked, it wouldn't take too much detective work to make the necessary connections, so we pushed the van as far away as we could and got a replacement hose first thing the next morning.

We eventually made it to Minneapolis, but the all-ages show at Goofy's was fucked. We got ready for the over-21 show. The ex-pro-wrestler and the 300-pound biker who were running it when we pulled up didn't seem too bothered though. But when Steve came back from the bar, *he* was. The biker had just told him a story about fucking his girlfriend while holding her head underwater in the bathtub and watching what her anus did when he did this. The pro wrestler thought it was a hoot. Steve read it for what it was.

"We're dealing with psychopaths."

"Let's put Amy at the door with the clicker." We had heard that shady shit happened at this club, and on account of the biker-wrestler muscle, they got away with it . . . most of the time. Amy didn't take any

shit and armed with a clicker, we'd have an accurate read of how many paying customers came through the door so that our money was right.

And at the end of the evening it was. You could see that it was killing the ex-pro to have to pay it.

After the shows, I was jawing with someone and Steve was busting my balls for not helping load out when he did one of the most amazing things I had ever seen. Dismissing him with the claim that I was "handling the business," Steve, in a fit of rage while standing at the top of the stairs at Goofy's, hoisted a full-size bass cabinet over his head and walked down the stairs, grousing all of the way about me "doing business." The biker and ex-pro wrestler watched this from the top of the stairs, and decided to pay in full. They could make up for what they lost later.

At Goofy's in Minneapolis. Shorts, unwashed. Photographer unknown.

Whipping Boy members, from left, Eugene Robinson, Dave Owens, Steve Ballinger and Sam Smoot

Why were we in a bathtub? Unknown. What is known:
Steve's coat of many colors STILL makes me happy.

Which, as luck would have it for them, was the next day. We had just enough time to do one last matinee at Goofy's before we headed out to Kansas City and if the headlining band for that night, Legal Weapon from Los Angeles, didn't mind, no prob. They didn't mind and so the show was on. I am guessing they agreed since we had a few shows scheduled together and it's just nicer and easier being nice and easy.

We warned them about the ex-pro-wrestler cat and his hefty bouncer. Advised them to put someone at the door to count bodies. They looked at us with a look that said, "We're from L.A. and your advice, while well-intentioned, is clearly for people we call LOSERS."

OK.

The show was great, we watched them play, since it seemed only right. Post-show as we rushed to load out, all while saying our good-byes, we heard the ex-pro mid-fuck start to explain to Legal Weapon that too many people had snuck in, that something had gotten broken, that the numbers were inaccurate, something/anything would tally out the same way: Legal Weapon was getting fucked. We watched and he watched us watching. He paid us exactly what he should have but his look was a dare that said "And?"

I guess if I was Ian, I would have said something, but I'm not Ian and I HAD said something. They just chose to ignore what it was I had said. Too bad, too sad. We had to go.

The next show, in Kansas City, had us headlining and Legal Weapon playing support. The show was cool and when I say cool, I mean lots of people (80 or so) who were into it, and the money wasn't funny. There was a pool party afterward and everyone was in a good headspace. Someone from Legal Weapon came over and started talking about how cool the shows had been, and then the logical breakdown, which was leading to a touch I hadn't seen coming.

"We figure since you lost your matinee and we did you a favor and let you on our show the next day . . . "

"Yeah," I said.

"Well, because we got ripped off for our fee, that maybe you could kick us something now?"

"We told you those guys were crooks."

"Yeah. But. You know . . . we let you on our show."

We had gotten paid what the promoter said we would. In the spirit of keeping things light and happy, though, I guess I should yield? Sam, Dave, Steve, and Amy were less hard-line than me, but communicated the generalized need for concessions.

"I can give you $20," I said.

"We were thinking $50," they said. "For gas."

"How about $40. I mean we gotta buy gas too."

And the deal was done. The pool party was in full swing and everyone was having a blast but my relationship to cash is complicated and I brooded about this for the rest of our time there. On the one hand, there's this distinct *public* aversion to cash that was punk rock fashionable. On the other hand, some people on the scene were sporting leather goods worth hundreds. Since everything had collapsed for me regarding familial support, I'd been keenly aware of the fact that money is not at all funny and what you can't save for today you'll not have to spend tomorrow.

But then a wrinkle. While Sam and I had no romantic relationships with anyone, Dave's girlfriend was scheduled to meet us in Chicago and Steve was married. Calling back home during one break, a few things happened.

The first? Someone other than Steve's wife answered their phone. A phone that was only in their bedroom. The second? A set of parents at Steve's school were wondering why if touring with Whipping Boy was a sanctioned school trip, why was Amy the only one on it?

The school had called Steve's wife, she panicked and claimed ignorance. Which panicked Amy's parents and the expensive school administrators. Had Amy been kidnapped? Was this the product of an affair? With a 17-year-old student? Why doesn't his wife know? And beyond this, and at my prodding since I had never been a fan of his erstwhile wife: why were dudes answering the phone in his bedroom at midnight?

We stayed with Jay Yuenger of Rights of the Accused (and later White Zombie), and I promptly fell in an unexpressed love with his girlfriend. Steve also decided that if he wanted the tour to end very much how it had begun—with him being married and employed—that Amy had to go, and his wife had to join us.

This was a source of some concern to me since the last time she and I had spoken it was her telling me exactly the kind of piece of shit she thought I was and me advising her to kiss my ass. So, not a prognosis for a happy family on the road. But after the phone call with the dude named Brian, apparently, Steve was miserable and that had to be dealt with.

Amy took it well enough since she had partially created the situation with her inexpert falsehood to her now totally panicked parents. She later spun a tale about hitchhiking to New York with another punk kid and having to fight off horny truckers with her pocketknife. I'm an easy audience so, sure, why not? However, if I had also been told that her parents had wired her cash so she could take a bus there I'd have believed that too.

Having Steve's wife with us was . . . rough. Halfway through the tour we had been burnished into a touring unit. Which means all manner of unacceptable behaviors had become comfortably acceptable. We heard from Barry Henssler from the Necros that Henry had refused to wash the clothes he wore on the Black Flag tour that we, apparently, were right behind. Always competitive, I thought I could do better than that AND save money in the process. I'd wear the same clothes that I refused to wash and would jettison the rest. I liked a neat van and outside of smelling like gas and car exhaust I didn't think I smelled bad.

I kept on believing this right up until I woke up one morning to Steve screaming.

"COME HERE!" We were staying at a place with a washer and dryer and Steve had stolen my clothes and thrown them in the washing machine. The water was black and had consumed all of the available extra soap he had thrown in. "You see THAT?" he admonished.

"Whatever, man. You ruined my experiment."

"What experiment?!?!?" Steve was genuinely confused. This harkened back to my love of the Stoics though, and fuck all of you who believed the fiction that clean clothes were somehow a NECESSITY.

Also this: he had taken the boxer briefs he had given me and had systematically sewed the dick holes shut.

"What the fuck?!? What did you do with my underwear?!?!" Now it was my turn for the confusion.

"First of all, it's MY underwear and . . . "

" . . . Not after you GAVE it to me . . . "

" . . . .AND I am sick of your dick flopping around on stage!"

This was a summertime tour, and while I had slowed on the aspirational bodybuilding I was fine being shirtless and as the tour wore on, pantsless. Pants were just a drag, soaking wet as they were when I left the stage. The oversized boxers worked for me. The cock didn't work for Steve.

Now if he had just done it and not said anything about it, I probably would have been fine. But he said something about it and now had me fixated on it. I felt like I was suffocating on stage now.

Steve and I were the only two people who could talk to each other the way we talked to each other, though. Everyone else buckled or got afraid and backed down but Steve understood, as did I, that this wasn't about the ability to beat the other person to death but more to WIN the argument through the careful application of intelligence, wit, craft, and fortitude.

Defaulting to violence would be the same as losing—born, as it would have been, out of a frustration at not being able to win any other way. But the cock conversation had gotten out of control and at some point, in the backstage of some venue in Boston that was also apparently a kitchen, it came the closest to ending up in blows. The future math was simple though, and I knew it. Once we started fighting the ability to continue on would be severely compromised. So whatever we were arguing about would have to mean more than what we were doing.

And while I like my cock, more than almost everything else in my life at that point, I didn't love it enough to die on the hill of having it flop around during our stage show. Though my point remained unanswered: why do you give a shit what my cock does when we're playing?

"It's an unpleasant distraction."

"I'm disturbed that you notice at all." I, at this point, was now lightening the mood and laughing.

"Well, you Black guys have a different outlook on things and..."

I was enflamed again. Though this was supposed to have been a compliment, if you're not getting laid, the size of your penis is largely immaterial. At least in any positive sense. And whether it was the straight edge dictum of no fucking OR that no one really wants to get with a guy who refuses to wash his clothes, I was focused now on the racial ramifications of our stage show and the argument continued until it was showtime and ended with Steve declaring that if my cock got too distracting, he'd leave the stage.

Which is precisely what it took to win that argument.

So Nice They Named it Twice

WHILE IT WOULD HAVE been nice to have played CBGBs just to say you had played CBGBs, we didn't this tour. (That would come eventually.) This tour we played at Great Gildersleeves with an L.A. band called Channel 3. We had a few shows with them and they had been heavily inspired by bands like Agent Orange, plus Steve was from Camarillo and so officially a SoCal guy so it sort of felt like family. Those were the pluses.

The minuses? No one really went to Gildersleeves.

Or maybe it was the space math and though the 100 people or so who showed would have felt like a crowd at CBs, at the larger Gilder-sleeves it felt underattended. But the pay was right and when the show was done we ended up hanging out at CBs anyway. Or I did. Sam and Dave headed back to their friend's place, Dave with his girlfriend, and Steve took off as well, his wife now with him.

Meaning I had the run of the city AND the Whipping Boy van. I also had the Whipping Boy van with all of the equipment fitted under the van's loft so no matter where I was, I was going to be sleeping in it. Because of an unfortunate set of circumstances all having to do with the hurly-burly of my mother's divorce from my stepfather, I wasn't going home, but sleeping in the van in the summer wasn't bad, and it's where I had slept the entire tour anyway.

I don't remember who was playing that night at CBs but I went in. I don't remember the owner, Hilly, even charging me anymore, and worked my way to the dance floor. The circular mosh pit always seemed a distinctly New York turn of events. CBs in the end was smallish, so it was just a more economical use of space to circle around like that. It changed the dance style though. Low to the ground and twisting at the hip while punching the air in front of you just seemed to be the template.

California style? Upright and more the way you might imagine things to look if you were shoving your way through a crowd.

Anyways, I tripped. Managed to not fall but it felt like my engineer boot, that now had nails digging into my heel because it was so worn, had caught something on the floor. The second time around I tripped again, and this time thought "that's weird." In general I've not been what anyone would have called clumsy.

Going around a third time I kept my eyes on the floor and saw some stoner dude stick his foot out. I grabbed the lapel of his denim vest and jammed a finger in his face by way of warning, right as a guy who I had seen on the stage while the band played launched himself over the crowd fist-first and connected with the stoner dude's face. It was pretty clear that stoner dude was no longer conscious, and the puncher proceeded to drag him out of the club.

You hear people say something "happened so fast" and then something fast happens and you're left wondering if it happened at all. But it happened and the puncher came back in, took his spot on the stage and later, when introducing himself to me, let me know his name was Raybeez. I was tired from having already played that night so was thankful for the fist assist, but more importantly my eyes were opening to a new New York zeitgeist.

Gone were the days when the now-older punk rockers would hope they could get to the oasis of the club in one piece. Ray was my height, skinheaded, and wore what went well beyond a fashion statement back then: a big chain for a belt with a lock on the end with which you could have made any variety of points about keeping the party polite.

I guess Hilly just thought it made sense to make him a bouncer instead of trying to bounce him out, and he was by no means the toughest. Even the seemingly not tough guys like Jimmy Gestapo, who was always known as sort of a "fun-loving" guy, used to sleep with an axe and had a temper to justify it and a father from whom it came.

The *Village Voice* once described them . . . us . . . as "shock troops" and I am sure people reading that thought of someone like Stephen Ielpi, singer for the False Prophets, who I used to see on the D Train when I was in high school. Tall, with a Hitler mustache and a monkey skull on a walking stick, Brooklyn had never seen anything like him before. Like an Italian Screamin' Jay Hawkins. Ielpi was, in actual fact, a pretty easygoing cat. Nothing beyond a look that shocked.

Not so much the case with the people I gravitated toward and who likewise gravitated toward me, all of whom seemed to reach the same point in their lives at the same time and were quite comfortable with that place being "enough is enough."

Later, before rounding up the rest of Whipping Boy, and heading back on the road, Vinnie Stigma asked me the question that New York was always asking me in my head: "When you coming back?"

"As soon as this tour is over." But yeah, first: the tour must be over.

Which it would be soon enough. And not just the tour but this iteration of the band as well. Sam and Dave were breaking down. Dave at one point tried to jump out of the van while I was driving, and remember, I was never of the mind to stop while I was driving, much less slow down. In the instance of his attempted "escape," in all likelihood to see his girlfriend who spent the summer shadowing the tour but strangely enough not seeing any shows, he had had it.

I sped up though, and the van buckled with the passenger door now swinging and by my lights he almost lost his leg, a turn of events that made sense to even me at that point: one-legged drummers didn't drum in any hardcore bands that I knew of. So I took an exit, let him off on the street, and made plans to get him later. Later, he said he contemplated not coming back at all, but figured he'd never see his drums again.

"You figured right," I said. Since what undergirded all of this, as Ian had so sagely guessed about Whipping Boy, was getting PAID for our ART. You cancel those shows, you've robbed me, and I'd have done

anything in that sense to make up for the shortfall. Including selling everything he owned that I could get my hands on.

I remember reading a book by Mafioso Sammy "the Bull" Gravano and in it he used a phrase that stuck with me—he described having a frenzy for felony. Like an animal, he calculated that every day he was lucky enough to wake up was a day in which none of his meals were promised. His earning, in a Mafia sense, was completely panic-fueled.

When your songs are 30 seconds long, your set list looks like this.
(Photo by Lynn Beldner)

This marked my mindset. I had to have enough cash to make it back to New York for the remainder of the tour to make sense of my summer and repair whatever was going on with my mother at that point. It was that or live for the remainder of the summer in the van.

Which meant simply: the shows HAD to be played.

Of course, sleeping on floors and sitting up in a van for weeks had started to break Sam too. One night, in an impassioned plea to rent a cheap motel, a move I was opposing, he plaintively wailed, "I just want to sleep in a real bed tonight."

And in a high-pitched sing-song voice I mimicked him, "*I just want to sleep in a real bed tonight . . .*" It was a shitty thing to say but I can see myself saying it 100 times out of 100. " . . . You fucking baby." That too.

I hadn't seen it coming and hadn't thought it through. Steve had already graduated from college and was into his adult life and was enjoying how his life was unfolding. At least short-term style. But Sam and Dave were a year or two younger than me; for them, this is not how they saw the twilight of their college careers playing out.

Sitting outside of the Crystal Pistol in Oklahoma, a guy dressed up like a Nazi pulled up next to us in a tan-colored Volkswagen Karmann Ghia. He rolled down his passenger window, stuck his booted foot out of the window, lit a cigarette and turned on his music. War marches and Hitler speeches.

I started giggling. Then I started laughing.

"What are you laughing at?" Steve was sitting in the back with his wife by the loft. It didn't matter so much that she was Jewish. I mean, you don't have to be Jewish to think that this shit was stupid. But it suddenly just struck me as some kind of deeply dark and comical play of confusion. I mean, this was our audience. In Oklahoma?

I looked at the Nazi and he looked at me and then leaned over and turned the music up. I headed into the club. The show? A blur. Outside of this incident, all I remember was a swimming hole we stopped off at the next day. Which was notable because the fish in it would bite you.

Then Dallas. Dallas, Ian's "no fucking" dictum aside, was the only place on the entire tour where I came even remotely close to being able to convince someone to have sex with me. She was a beauty, so much so that I thought it was some sort of trick or trap. When I told the band that I was going off to sleep at her house, and catch a quick shower, they all did exactly what I would have done were the positions reversed: cock-blocked me like they invented cock-blocking.

They didn't know how they would find me the next day, no one wanted to drive the van, we desperately needed to get on the road to get to the next show for some reason, and after about the fourth fusillade of helpless fuckery I relented. I told her "next time," and of course, I never saw her again. The fact that I remember it now? Yes: I have not gotten over it. Much like the last Minor Threat show we missed, my sense was that this was something I'd never get again. Sex, well, yes, sure. But not with this woman, who was funny and smart enough to have made staying with her make sense.

OR, alternatively, smart and funny enough to lure me to my demise because of the death cult she ran in her basement. I mean, it was Dallas after all. So, who knows?

We made it back to California. Dropped Steve off at the apartment he and his wife kept in Menlo Park. Sam and Dave disappeared as soon as they physically could. I headed back to NYC, changed but ready for whatever.

"If I go to the toilet in my pants," I said to my mother, standing in front of the house in Brooklyn, "I would have needed help with that."

I had come back to Brooklyn to fix things with my mother. The scissure was ridiculous. When I left for Stanford, I made the moves to take everything I needed with me. Blankets, warm clothes. California was, despite one of my kid sisters thinking it was warm enough to sport trees full of parrots, cold in the wintertime. But she had taken Mom ownership of my things and said she would send them.

Flash to sometime later and in a phone conversation I mentioned that I had talked to my now-departed stepfather. It stuck in her craw, and by the end of the conversation this: "If you're so friendly with him, have HIM send you that stuff!"

That was the end of the conversation. Not just then. For months after. Eighteen months. Take two people whose family coat of arms could be emblazoned with the legend "What the FUCK Is that SUP-

POSED to Mean?!?" and you understand. This was rock meeting hard place, so 18 months of nothing.

A few weeks before when the tour took us to New York, I showed up as we left to head back west and loaded my stored stuff in the Whipping Boy van. The greeting was curt from both sides but as I disappeared into the van innards with a brief wave, I heard her say, not very loud at all, "Well, let me know if you come back," and I understood that for what it was, and knew that if I wanted to repair things this was the invitation to be accepted. Or not, if I didn't.

"I will."

So, there we were a few more weeks later, standing on a sidewalk in Brooklyn talking about poop.

"But I don't need help with that now," I said working toward a point. "We're going to have to reframe our relationship now if it is going to be successful." All of the LSD had helped me move big-picture-style, past the weeds and well into the forest. I was already paying for Stanford myself. Hadn't asked for anything from her, my father, or my stepfather, and so, in my mind, we were coming to this meeting as equals regardless of how we had started out.

"Well, I'm STILL your mother!" She said it without raising her voice. More to forestall any hippie-fueled idea that I would start calling her by her first name or something like that.

"Oh yes. But this is the start of the whole son going from a boy to a man thing, right?"

"Right."

"OK."

"OK."

And just like that I was back. I had shown up with one bag, came from the airport and had planned to move over to the Lower East Side where I could sleep somewhere if things went badly. Things going well meant I could leave my bag there and head out. I wouldn't mention the fact that the sole reason I was standing there then was because my now ex-stepfather had introduced me to some criminal named Billy B., who traded in stolen airline tickets, and so I had flown for $50 as one Mr. John Howard.

Rolling up to a show at 2+2 at Houston and Second, huzzahs were all around. Everyone knew I said I was coming back but everyone says everything and not everyone delivers. But I sure as fuck wasn't going to hang out in California, in my van, for what remained of the summer, and having supped at scenes all over America, New York still felt most like home to me. So, there I was.

But never as a New Yorker, since that was not how all but a few had come to know me. Always as a Californian. And even stranger, as a straight edge guy for no other reason than I didn't smoke or drink. People just assumed and never asked about anything else so it was me as super-ego in a full-on Freudian sense. By which I mean, people were always circumspect around me about drugs, yet I found the fact that everyone around me was high on drugs I didn't take to be weirdly comforting.

Having to spend the summer with a bunch of other acidheads would have been a drag is what I am saying. But the wild emporium of what was being huffed that summer made for the kind of unpredictability that tends to make summers great.

Back then, all of the hardcore kids who lived in Brooklyn and along what used to be the D Train line that ran along Flatbush Avenue figured out if you weren't staying at Vinnie Stigma's apartment on Mott Street, which was as close as anyone had ever lived to CBs, or over on Rivington with Robbie Cryptcrasher and Linda, which was the nearest place other than Jack Rabid's to 2+2, that if you coordinated the times, you could actually meet on the train.

Bubby, the former ambulance driver, Soviet Georgian Jew and brown belt in judo, was there; so was Pete Guy who lived three blocks away from me on Hawthorne. I had never thought about the concept of "strength in numbers" since it was rare for me to get hassled now. The number of Black guys with mohawks, tattoos, muscles and giant chain-linked chains for belts, in a city of 10 million people, was probably like four. The cat from the Plasmatics, Dmitri from Shok, Pete and me. And Dmitri never sported a mohawk. I was generally given a wide berth, enough that I had been blithely unaware of what kind of visual impact was being made.

I realized it when Pete, whose father most famously sung for the '50s doo-wop band The Coasters, swung by my house and we made our way to the Prospect Park subway station one night.

"YO! PUNK ROCKS OUTTA BROOKLYN!" A scream had come from a porch of a house on Midwood Street, and without missing a beat Pete swept up a discarded 40-ounce bottle of beer, flung it at the porch, and to the tune of it shattering glass all over the place offered his response.

"YO!!! WE'LL BURN YOUR FUCKING HOUSE DOWN!"

Silence.

And as we stood on the platform and Bubby stuck his head out of the last car, also known as the car where trouble dwells, we were complete. Pete looked like the Marine he later became—when faced with either four years in prison for selling stolen goods or four years in the Marines, he took the Marines. The judge favored '50s doo-wop and so gave him this choice, which fit Pete better than anyone knew. But he was about 6'2", 190 pounds, a Black guy with a buzz cut, also not super popular then. Bubby was about 200 pounds and bowling-ball thick with the shoulders and arms of someone who had been doing judo since he was five years old. Which he had.

But on the train together we were focused, excited, and because of that, we were all pretty much terrifying.

Years earlier, I remember walking up to the legs of some guys about my own age who had propped their legs up on the standing pole, blocking the pathway. This was during that period when I was getting my ass kicked a lot and this was sort of the reason why: I walked up to their legs, though it was clear I could have walked around, and said "Excuse me."

They stared straight ahead. So I repeated myself because, you know, maybe they hadn't heard.

"Excuse me. I need to get by?" And still with the straight-ahead staring and a fork in the road that emerged in clearly drawn terms: I stomp on their legs to get by and reap whatever comes out of that, stand there until they cut to the chase, OR walk around.

They stared straight ahead and I looked at them. They were afraid, but resolute. On account of their numbers and who knows what else. I fingered the Camillus hunting knife I had strapped under my coat and thought it all through. Was I going to stab someone for being impolite?

No New Yorker reading this even believes this is a question without the answer "yes" attached to it, but I didn't.

Which means I had to walk around. Something I deserved because it was an unforced error. I could have gone around; them being rude should have nothing to do with it. But it stuck with me. After this encounter, one night as Pete and Bubby and I were barreling from the last car to the first where it would drop us off closer to the exit, I watched some people pull their legs back to let us pass.

Bubby, for whatever reason, was moshing through the subway car, Frankenstein-stomping his feet as he went. Pete strolled behind in his wake and I lost my mind. Those who hadn't pulled their legs back, whose feet and legs even partially blocked the path, I stomped on. Their feet, their legs. And when they looked up like they hadn't seen me, even though they most certainly had, I, eyeballing them, said loudly and clearly, "EXCUSE ME!"

And then, "SORRY, SORRY, SORRY FOR THE INTRUSION!" In my voice I could hear the tremolo of a certain kind of a madness and knew as sure as I was breathing that this was a close-to-the-edge embrace of the kind of chaos I, again, wanted to know if Anton LaVey had experienced. Not out of control, exactly, but so deadly in control that the fact that I was a bully and an asshole, in this instance, was miraged in the swirl of desire for fucking shit up.

This didn't just happen on the subway. When driving with Bubby one night in the copper-colored woodie station wagon that he had pulled from some shityard out by Brighton Beach (his stints in jail were mostly all for car theft) he was telling me that he was an anarchist and he didn't care. He would do whatever he felt like at any given moment.

"Bullshit," I said. "That's a ridiculous way to live." The car was full of Brooklyn skinheads and on the BQE. I have no memory at all of where we were going.

"WATCH!" And when an anarchist says this, nothing good is going to happen, but what happened is he sped up and plowed into the car in front of him. It wasn't traffic. It was just him. The guy slammed on his brakes and jumped out. We jumped out too but unclear what the mission was.

"WHAT?" The guy was Hasidic but Bubby's Jewishness didn't inter-fere with his anarchism, and taking one look at us, the guy apologized with a hasty "Sorry!" and got in his car and drove off.

Bubby was quiet for a few minutes as we drove away before punctu-ating the moment with, "I'm a fucking anarchist."

The summer, or what remained of it, was thick with shows. And what had preceded shows as well. Hilly, the owner of CBs, was striking while the iron was hot, and everyone was there all the time. Bands from Boston, D.C., the Midwest. One night before the Whipping Boy tour was over and while the rest of the band was doing normal non-hardcore things, I pulled the van up outside of CBs.

No idea who was playing but I had an idea of how fucking hot it was inside in the summer, where if they didn't clean the toilets there was no way were they air-conditioning the place. I had stripped off my shirt and having no place to leave my jacket where I thought it wouldn't get stolen, I moshed with it.

At one point during a break between songs I felt a tap on my shoul-der. It was a girl I knew. She was from Jersey and had a car and we hadn't really ever had occasion to do a little more than bullshit since it's not like we were on the train together, but she was friends with the guys in Channel 3 and knew some other people from Cali so we became some version of associates.

"Gimme your jacket."

It wasn't computing for me what I was being asked for. It wasn't cold so it didn't make sense to me that she wanted my jacket. But I agreed since it was a drag to be holding it. After the show we rolled out front and she handed me my jacket. I thanked her, and went to throw it into the van. I was among friends but I still understood the temptation to redistribute wealth, and all of our gear was snugged tight under the loft, leaving the main floor free. But you could still see where the amps and guitars had been wedged in. Which meant: I now had to stay with the van. Which was OK. I had seen who I wanted to see and needed to be about picking folks up so we could head out.

But she stood there with me and we chatted comfortably while I did math in my head. For large portions of my life up to this point and for a few years after I was kind of on the spectrum about the science of attraction. I didn't understand why people who wanted to be friends with me had wanted that, and I sure as shit didn't have a sense of why people who seemed to want to have sex with me, wanted to.

This is why disco made so much sense. Everything was so big and over the top that I never had to guess. The lack of subtlety helped.

"Oh, this van is so cool," she said, and sitting down she scooched in and I crawled in behind her and shut the doors. I don't know what I was thinking, or thinking of doing, but it didn't seem like there was much thinking needed, despite Ian's dictums that thinking would have been a preferred way to proceed.

However, I was suddenly aware of the fact that I was about to fuck in front of CBs, and people, them knowing I wasn't doing the kind of drugs that would require privacy, would know precisely what I was doing, and I became uncharacteristically modest.

"Let's drive." And I drove over to 9th and 4th and we had some version of sex. I say "some version" since, given how little I was fucking back then, I can't remember much about it, but I liked her and it was fun enough to do again despite Bubby asking me why I had done it in the first place. There was still this weird Puritanism that infected the scene and I never knew how to answer it since to me this encounter had been a total good and positive.

She called me later from the Chelsea Hotel where she was tripping her ass off after dropping acid with Ad-Rock (who most people would know later for his time in the Beastie Boys) at a house party nearby. I don't remember much of what she said and I don't know if I understood it but with acidheads it's all about frequencies and we were on the same one.

But there were no cellphones, and weeks seemed like years during that New York summer; neither one of us can remember what had happened. What I think happened? I think she ended up with one of the guys from Channel 3, and me? Well...

What had happened for *sure* was later that summer when I got back to CBs I met JT, a runaway from D.C. whose story was as unbelievable as it was, sort of, believable. Her claim of being a perpetual delinquent who had left home fleeing an abusive father who was also in the Mafia? Well, OK. Her first port of call was Minneapolis where she hung out with Prince and Morris Day, a little less so. But she certainly had the look and this was maybe almost more believable than not.

The fact that she was 15? Yeah, that didn't work for me. I was 19 and had always liked women older than me. I mean, it was the power metric. Older women had cars, apartments, and actually *liked* fucking. Klaus' wife was 20-some-odd years older than me. So much that when I saw her later that same summer walking down Flatbush Avenue near the edge of Park Slope where she lived, with a cane, I did a head-snapping double take.

"You see someone you know?" Bubby asked, weaving the station wagon in and out of traffic.

"Um . . . " Would I deny her like Peter denied Christ? "Naaahhh . . . " Yeah: coward.

But a 15-year-old? Well, it had already been settled anyway. She had chosen me and for the remainder of the summer that was what it was going to be. Aside from her age, she was an interesting choice for me as she was unlike anyone I had ever dated before or since.

"What's the matter?" I'm not an eggshell-walker, and if it seems like someone is trying to communicate something with baleful silences, I'd just really rather get to getting it over with than delaying anything.

"Nothing."

And then a little bit later, after 10 more minutes of sighing and baleful glaring: "There's *nothing* the matter?"

"What's the matter is people keep asking me what's the fucking matter!!!"

Stunts like this even a few weeks earlier would have invited the pull of an exit cord, but for some reason, and I'll paraphrase the line a prostitute friend once used to explain why she did the job when she didn't need the cash: I guess I wanted to learn what it was like to be with a woman who was a pain in the ass. No other way to explain it.

She had also become fast friends with Lisa from AntiWarfare. Partially because of Lisa's unrequited interest in Sab from Iron Cross, a D.C. skinhead band, and JT's somewhat tenuous connection to them as a result of hailing from D.C. But mostly because Lisa didn't have a boyfriend that could be stolen away, so JT was a safe choice.

Lisa had also decided to become a junkie that summer. So, there was that. At the crossroads of depression and what we would later discover was gender dysphoria, Lisa was committed. Went over to Avenue B to cop and sort of disappeared one night.

"Lisa's gone," JT said. Bubby and I were posted up on the hood of his station wagon.

"Where'd she go?" I asked. I liked Lisa but I didn't like drama and realized too late that these two went together.

"Over to Avenue B," JT was getting exercised. "We need to go find her."

Hanging out that summer was a perfect storm of doing nothing and everything all at once. Bubby was glad to drive. The car was packed with a few of us, one of whom was a dealer named Shorty that everyone figured would know the lay of the land when it came to places she might have gone to shoot up.

JT was cold and then did the most gangster thing I could have imagined at that age in a car full of men: she took her shirt off and changed into another. It was funny watching everyone trying to act like it wasn't happening, most of all me since, without a steady place to stay, we were going out largely in theory and I hadn't been able to fuck her yet, much less see her naked. It was high school style. Holding hands. Kissing. And I was well past being comfortable with high school style but getting her back to Brooklyn was proving to be a chore.

Bubby stopped in front of a street of bombed-out ex-tenements. Shorty said "that one" and we all looked at the dark and crumbled innards with much more than a sense of great foreboding.

The only existing photo of me and JT.

"Someone's got to go in and get her." JT stared into the broken brick- and garbage-strewn remnants of failure.

"Well, maybe she'll just come out," I offered in the breathy quiet of the car. Bubby said nothing.

"OK! If YOU are not going to go I WILL," and then there was this whole performative dance where JT acted like she was going to do just that. I don't think that she would have. But she might have. And if she did and I didn't, I had guessed, probably correctly, that we were done.

"Nah, nah," I sighed. "I'll go."

I crunched across the brick. I was still wearing the engineer boots worn thin and the nails from the heels were digging into my heels. But on a landscape of broken glass, rusty nails and such, I imagined I would be OK. More so now that I picked up a brick.

Stray dogs, rats, junkies, freaks, lunatics abounded. Or I imagined they did as I ducked into the overhang of a collapsed second floor and called her name.

Nothing. Then I called and nothing again. I thought or maybe even spoke out loud, "She's the one who wants to die. Not ME," and made my way back to the car where Lisa was already standing. She had been in the fully functional building across the street. She had loaded up a syringe but at the last second got so scared she spazzed its innards all over her arm instead of in it. I'd have been angry if I hadn't been so relieved to be free of man-duty shit.

We pulled back to 2+2. Lisa stayed in the car. JT wandered off with Linda, and Bubby and I headed into the club to watch whoever there was to watch. Sitting on the stairwell inside where the music was still loud but quiet enough to talk bullshit.

Lisa ran in, wild-eyed.

"Shorty just tried to RAPE ME!"

We responded. Slowly. "What?"

"Fucking Shorty just tried to RAPE me! I was taking a nap on the front seat." (Bubby was the drummer of the band Lisa played in and he let her crash in his car.) "And he rolled over on top of me and tried to fuck me."

"Noooo . . . " Bubby said he couldn't believe it.

"What?!?!?" Lisa had been back 30 minutes, 30 drama-free-minutes, then this. Though truth be told, I had a large amount of sympathy for her in this case and while she railed at the other guys for not backing her up, I thought it through and I had come to a conclusion.

"Out of all of the things she could have said when she came in here tonight," I had waved Pete over. He was hoping to catch a ride back to Brooklyn and had come in on the tail end of this. " . . . Why would she say that if it wasn't true?"

Everyone got quiet until Bubby said, "Let's go talk to him," and so we followed him out to the car and asked if anyone had seen Shorty. Shorty was savvy and street-smart at the very least and didn't stick around.

We went looking for him. Went to Tompkins Square Park where we had heard he had raped this junkie chick that used to hang out with the one-eyed cowboy everyone called Spacely. He wasn't there. We went over to CBs, and someone said he had headed back. The whole time the mood in car had grown darker as the certainty had grown that he had done exactly what he had been accused of.

By the time we found him, we were missiles. The car screeched up on the curb and to his small credit he didn't run.

"What's up?"

"Hey man," Bubby was the spirit of diplomacy. "Lisa said you tried to rape her back there . . . "

"She's a lying bitch," Shorty snorted, and that was precisely what it took for me and Pete to lose our minds and turn into pistons of angry action. It was a fusillade of punches that drove him to the ground, and despite the dictum regarding not kicking people when they're down that's precisely what I did. Stomped, more specifically.

Bubby held us off. He needed . . . clarity. And he placed himself between us and Shorty. "What the fuck happened, Shorty?"

"She's," through ragged breathing now, " . . . fucking telling you lies . . . "

And again: we beat him, and the rhythm of the beating was picking up speed and the taste in my mouth was the taste of death and the desire to will this man off of the planet.

Bubby waved us off and said in the best good cop to our bad cops, "Just tell us what happened."

"OK, OK." The math he had done was simple: he wasn't being beaten as long as he talked. "She was sleeping in the front seat and I wanted to smoke a cigarette and so I leaned over to use the cigarette lighter and fell on top of her."

"She said you had your dick out."

"Yeah," he said, "it fell out." We all had owned penises for the entirety of our lives and the proposition that they had ever "fallen" out at any given point not aided was preposterous enough to be comical and we responded in kind, a welcome break for him I am sure.

"It FELL out?!?!" I laughed, but here he made a fatal error that those who know me better have figured out, and that's that just because I am laughing, there's no guarantee that anything good is going to happen.

Indeed, it did not. Now that we were in the last act, it became clear we were going to kill him. Bubby couldn't hold both me and Pete off and we were spinning into a frenzy. Right up until we heard the sound of metal on metal and a voice from above.

"Oye . . ."

The Puerto Rican drug dealer in the apartment right above where Shorty now laid bloody and unconscious was very desirous of us not making his block hot. Or hotter. And dead dudes, even in New York of the '80s, still had to be hauled off of the streets.

He tapped his pistol against the window frame.

"Leave him alone now."

I looked at the open door of the station wagon where we had left our big chains and baseball bats and calculated how this was going to play out. Even if we made it to wherever, not having a gun put us at a disadvantage even if stopping seemed almost impossible. However, getting shot over Shorty didn't make much sense either.

So we turned to leave and screamed at his crumpled body, "Next time we see you, we're going to kill you."

We drove back to the club, Lisa piled out to find JT and retell what had happened, and the night unfolded without further incident.

The summer didn't, though. Trips to Jersey Boardwalk with Lisa and JT and Lisa's sometimes crush Paul, former roadie for Rush and eventually the father to Lisa's kid, ended up with me and Paul running from fight to fight up and down the boardwalk. Anytime there was any distance between us, the *cugines* would start in on JT and Lisa, who would promptly tell them to fuck off. They'd get hit, come to us, and we'd have to hit back. It was exhausting, and after a few hours of running up and down the boardwalk fighting all and sundry, Paul and I called a truce and pushed to head back to more civilized climes. It wasn't the fighting that was exhausting. It was the running.

The summer was nearing an end and I had some stark choices to make. I had taken JT out to Brooklyn to meet my Mom, so there was that, but she was weirded out at the prospect of fucking in a place where my mother might hear us. The van was back in California so that was out, and all of the various nooks and crannies where I might have actually been cool fucking someone didn't appeal to her sense of "adventure."

"Maybe you should come back to California with me." I wasn't convinced this was the right choice or even a good one, but it was an ABC deal. I had to Always Be Closing and since this was as close as I had gotten for a while it had to be where it made the most sense to go.

"Are you asking me?" She didn't do coy well, so this was spoken like a challenge.

"Yeah. Come on back." We negotiated how it would play out. I was scheduled to be a boarder in an on-campus fraternity that was chronically under-full. She could live there with me. It'd be fine.

Billy B. got us two more stolen plane tickets and back we flew. To San Francisco Airport, into a bus, and then we walked to the parking lot where my van was parked.

"Here we are!" I hadn't seen the van for weeks and recalling Eric B.'s commentary on his Rolls, I found I had missed it the way one misses a lover.

"*Where* we are?" I don't know why I hadn't seen this coming, but I hadn't. "I'm not sleeping in THAT."

"It's fine," I said. "I mean, it's not so cold with two people sleeping here." I raised my eyebrows in what I now know that anthropologists call "the copulatory gaze."

"If you think I'm going to have sex with you in THAT, you're crazy." I hadn't realized how lucky I had been with my other van conquest. Chalk one up for the genius of nice Jewish girls from Jersey.

"OK."

I scrambled and found a friend on campus. We could stay on his floor. However, vacating so we could fuck on said floor was a no-go. Steve was close by in a one-bedroom apartment in Menlo Park where he was still teaching, having weathered the "kidnapping teacher" debacle.

His wife was no happier about having us stay. At first. After meeting JT, however, it was clear that those two would be fast friends because his wife, after all, actually had a social network. You know . . . of people, and parties and suchlike things.

I was solitary in my habits and when I wasn't running around the Lower East Side was prone to be found reading or writing. But school started in three weeks and we just had to hold on until it did.

One night there was a party at the party spot that had come to be called The Flat. The place was above a liquor store in Menlo Park, on the Peninsula south of San Francisco, where a succession of band cats lived and it was always good for a party. I was just never good for a party. But Steve talked me into going. He wanted company as his wife and JT would be running around.

I sat bored, mostly not drinking or smoking at a table of Brits in some band called The Five Pliers. They were about nothing, their chatter was driving me out of my mind and I was counting the minutes until I could leave.

"So, who's this then?" They nodded over to where JT was dancing around. Usually, I'd say absolutely nothing but I didn't view this as an opportunity to learn and therefore keep my mouth shut, but instead I sought to forestall what seemed to me to be loose talk.

"She's my GIRLFRIEND," I said and instantaneously regretted it because the look that shot between them was full of weighty measure.

"Oh."

And then me, in my head: "Oh fuck."

It took a few days for it all to play out and when it did it was Steve's voice on the phone at my friend's house whose floor we had been sleeping on until she had decamped for some place with a real bed.

"JT is fucking Vincent." Steve was angry. I was not.

"Who's Vincent?"

A woman once screamed at me as I left her apartment late one night that the "big SECRET of EUGENE ROBINSON is that while everyone thinks you're this wild and crazy guy, you're one of the MOST CON-TROLLED PEOPLE I KNOW!!!" I wasn't sure if I was supposed to be insulted by this but by my lights, I was so close to being in that place where the bottom falls out that I would gamble with nothing that might make the bottom fall out. Even as I was doing that a lot of the time.

"The fucking hairdresser!" And this is where I learned the whole "gay friend" dodge. As long as the man has a penis you open yourself up to having this conversation, and no one needs to have this conversation much more than once.

"OK."

"What are you going to do?" Steve knew me pretty well, but I think he had gotten carried away with the fiction of me being this wild and crazy guy that woman spoke of. He had even imagined that like in the Gilgamesh epic, a retelling of our history as friends, that I was Enkidu. The wild man of the steppes.

"Me?" It seemed sensible. "Nothing."

The future will have its way with us, and while Steve was out of school and I had also been seriously dismissed by a succession of girl-friends, I needed some measure of stability to finish my last year at Stanford. This had to happen, I figured.

But my "nothing" didn't fill the dramatic quotient for all who presumed themselves involved so they juiced it up in retelling.

"Eugene said he's going to KILL Vincent! And he's looking for him." This was what had been passed around and what was easily believed. Though it still had nothing to do with my now-dead relationship.

So, Steve's wife called. "JT wants to talk to you." I had started to move into my place that was now ready and open for business. I had found an old vial of what had been liquid LSD before making the move. I added some water to it and figured it was pretty much dead. Or at the very least it would add a nice little buzz to my day, so I had consumed all of it.

That is: ALL OF IT.

While it did indeed add some buzz to my day there was nothing *little* about this buzz. In any case when Steve's wife called it all made sense in the way that everything makes sense on psychedelics.

"Sure. Put her on."

She handed off the phone. I sat on the windowsill.

"I want my fucking shit." She was nervous, I could hear. But bluffing her way through it was part of a skillset that had gotten her this far.

"Sure. I got your clothes around here somewhere."

"I don't care about those so much," she continued. "I care more about the makeup."

Oh. The makeup. That had been my one concession to dramatic gesture and I had thrown all of it out in the field next to where my new place was. Partially to have some sort of response that felt "appropriate" and partly because in my head state I couldn't find places for it. I also didn't know how expensive makeup was.

"I threw that out in the field."

"You fucking asshole."

I hung up the phone. This had been her usual stunt. She'd hang up on me and I wouldn't call back and she'd call me back telling me I am supposed to call back and I asked where'd you see that and she said, that's what the man was supposed to do! I mean, "everyone knows."

She called back. "Well, can we meet so I can get my clothes?"

"Sure. Just have my money for the plane ticket," I said, explaining. "If you had fucked the hairdresser three months after we had gotten here, well, OK. But a week? Yeah. I figure you owe me for the plane ticket."

She grumbled and cursed but we agreed to meet at Steve's place. I could see they expected me to get violent. An option that felt crazy to me but she had spent the whole summer watching me beat people up so maybe not.

We met at Steve's place and she hadn't brought the money, hoping she could do something that no one's ever really managed to do and that's negotiate me *out* of money. I was resistant and standing up on a rise outside of Steve's apartment. She hurled invective and finally I had decided that if we were going to cross some lines it was my turn. It should be noted though, to her credit, she veered away from the racial, but it was her pointless attempt to be hurtful that made me pick up the truth.

"You're an under-educated piece of D.C. trash whose only apparent worth will be squandered by the time your worthless life skids into total meaninglessness. An event that, I believe, is about three years off."

She blushed a deep crimson and strode back toward me with her hand raised. Like in the movies. And it trembled there while I stared at her.

"If you're going to HIT me," she said, "go ahead and HIT me," she said a little too loud. I was sure Steve and his wife were listening but they didn't hear a Eugene out of control. They heard a Eugene very much in control.

"If you want me to hit you," I said, "all you have to do is hit me." I wasn't angry when I said it. But I said what I meant. "If you hit me, you have my 100 percent guarantee I will hit you back." And she trembled there for a minute before spinning on her heel and telling me I was an asshole.

"Get the money from your boyfriend" were my last words to her.

But she was not done with me. She managed to get back to New York where she told everyone that I had gotten her pregnant and thrown her out. While she was pregnant, it wasn't me who got her pregnant. There had always been this issue of birth control and supposedly she was taking "one" of Lisa's pills that you only had to take once a month.

But Lisa had gotten pregnant and now so was she and the New York scene, insofar as anyone gave a shit, was divided into two camps. The Eugene Is a Piece of Shit Camp and the No Eugene Couldn't Be a Piece of Shit Camp.

This was finally settled when the people who took her in woke up one morning to find all of their cash, drugs and clothes of some worth all gone. A fact that still makes me smile.

She went back to D.C. Skeeter from Scream told me that she had told the same story there. A story that would only be good until the kid was born since the hairdresser was Filipino and the kid looks nothing like me.

In any case, I was free and my last school year at Stanford had started with a bang.

Sadly, this was the only bang-worthy thing of the year, which passed by without much more significant incident. Excepting one event that was fairly noteworthy. I don't mean delving deep into religious philosophy and actually inviting in the Jehovah's Witnesses to try to chat up the women. I don't mean when a woman with very heavy gangster friends took umbrage at me telling another friend that she had been contemplating stripping for extra cash. She was about to dispatch some attitude adjusters to my little two-bedroom digs before cooler heads prevailed and it was explained that Eugene would shoot back. I don't even mean my stuttering and failed attempts at fucking, still largely a hit-and-miss proposition that could no longer be healthily just blamed on straight edge.

But . . . the breakdown.

Years of bodybuilding had given way to playing rugby as a tight head prop in the first line of the scrum. A role usually played by guys who weighed 250, I was jammed up in there because I was strong and apparently could take headshots. But I couldn't take headshots. Two separate concussions were the result.

Even bodybuilding had turned on me, and a back injury had laid to rest any hopes I had of competing again. So, like Captain Willard in *Apocalypse Now*, I just, sat, studied and got soft. This was one of those rare California years when it just rained through the entire winter. While I was no longer freezing living in the trailers and still marginally had a band (though Sam and Dave were well on their way to quitting), my days and nights were mired in reading, writing and nothing.

I did not feel bad so I can't explain how on one cold and rainy night, I decided to go out. I thought that it made no sense to wear much other than my shorts. I couldn't afford a dryer to dry my clothes. Or my shoes. So I left the apartment just for a . . . a change in perspective. And once outside I started running. First slow. Then faster.

I had on white rugby shorts and no shoes and now I was running faster. And further. I remember thinking that no matter how far I ran I'd have to run back. But running back seemed a quaint concept. I was running OUT and I ran until I ended up in the mud of the foothills, heaving, in the dark and the rain and the night of nothing.

I wasn't crying, or shouting, or evincing any sort of emotion at all, and when I started running again, it took a while before I started laughing. I had never felt more alone in my entire life and the thought of throwing myself in front of the wheels of a car rushing next to the road where I was now running had occurred to me. The "he came out of nowhere" exit.

But then, a strange thing. An erection. Stranger still because of the cold and the wet and the effort that it took to run. I had already

gone through the calculation that involved "I will get a vasectomy" and then canceling the appointment at the last minute and understanding that that was destiny talking to me. And here it was again, stiffening in my shorts.

And with it, an awareness of my present state being exceedingly hard to explain, all puns intended, if I was stopped by the campus cops, with whom I had already had nightstick-wielding run-ins. So I jogged until things settled down and reentered the campus confines where I ran into a friend who, not noticing my woeful state of appearance, asked me if I had heard.

"Heard?"

"Angie's dead. Stabbed to death. They haven't caught the guy." Angie had blessed me with a pseudo-macho sobriquet and we had an uneasy friendship, but stabbed to death? I jogged back to the apartments and popped up in the window of a first-floor friend that knew her as well.

Heading out on Whipping Boy tour number 2? 1983. First stop Camarillo. With Steve's sister and friend John. John's idea of funny was calling you a "faggot." Which did sort of amuse me. Far right is Whipping Boy manager Adrian Cavlan, later Mr. Friction from the Diesel Queens.

They screamed. I was covered with mud and scratches and I looked a sight but then, "Hey man," I said to the three guys in the room. "Angie's dead. They just found her stabbed." And even as I said this, I realized that along a cop nexus, this looked bad for me. Of course, their disbelief that I was telling the truth didn't help, even if their reaction did help me figure out that getting back to my room and getting cleaned up made a certain amount of sense.

The campus was tense for days afterward, and there was the unspoken belief that the killer had been Black, so it was with great relief that a diaper delivery service truck driver who had a pickup at the house where she was babysitting that day had been picked up trying to flee the country with his family. The fact that the killer was blond-haired and blue-eyed was an unspoken relief to every single Black cat on campus.

Ideas were being framed in my head about a possible future, no matter how unlikely that seemed, and as musical tastes were shifting. I started to listen to the Birthday Party. Rollins had given me a cassette tape with music by Swans, Diamanda Galas, and Einstürzende Neubauten. The Red Hot Chili Peppers and Jane's Addiction had just gotten signed by large record labels.

Whipping Boy had done two U.S. tours and was still playing a steady clip of shows whenever we could, and while it was clear to me that Sam and Dave wanted to relinquish their duties, Steve and I countered this by giving them greater creative input. Because? Because how long was hardcore going to hold us?

LSD: The Breakfast of Champions

I REMEMBER WHEN, having been a huge John Belushi fan, I had gone to see *Animal House*. I'd come home geeked out and told my stepfather, fired by all of the anarchic energy, that the first thing I had planned to do when I got to college was to join a fraternity. He snorted and set me straight: "Only the most conventional, boringly mediocre people do that shit. Followers. Of the worst kind."

Keep in mind this is also the man that told me, albeit jokingly, when I was 13 and learning how to drive that there were two types of drivers in the world: "Faggots. And speedsters."

I took it to heart and turned away the three fraternities that thought somehow I would improve their outlook. Omega Psi Phi, a Black fraternity that held their rush events in my trailer, since my roommate was a member. The Zetas, who were kicked off of campus for beating people up. And the Alpha Delts, also called Alpha Drugs, and typically where I'd go to buy my drugs from guys who always made sure to tell me that they were not drug dealers. Though I gave them cash and they gave me drugs.

While I declined all of their offers I was happy that the offers seemed to have been well considered given my extant character traits. However, before the tour, the summer in New York, and the short-lived experiment in having a crazy girlfriend, I had decided to become a boarder in a fraternity. If a boarder lived with a fraternity member they were less likely to get put out if there was a room crunch and it really did make sense for me to room with one of the guys I was getting drugs from but who wasn't a drug dealer.

LSD was cheap and that was never the problem. The problem was getting quality LSD and he had it, so we roomed together and coincidentally my intake of hallucinogens increased. We used to call it "The Dreaded" and Steve and I would go out "Magical Mystery Touring," which amounted to walkabouts at any hour of the night or day where we talked through the finer points of our lives as we understood them.

I scrawled a verse from a Birthday Party song on the wall. I answered the door one day to find Ian and Alec MacKaye standing there, which, considering how much space he had been occupying in my head, was like opening a door and finding the Pope standing there. I invited them in and Ian sat on my butterscotch couch that I had lifted from a dumpster and Alec shifted around uncomfortably.

I don't remember much of what we talked about—the element of surprise would do that to you—but he had explained how he had spent time with his professor parents at Stanford, was back visiting his sister who was on the faculty now too, and thought he'd come by and say hi. I enjoyed this, and was happy he had done so.

Before he had been beatified as Saint Ian, back when Biafra would heckle me about him—"Ehhh . . . why don't you ask what he does with all of his MONEY?!"—he was a good guy. Bright and curious, and not without some large measure of balls born of just fucking . . . character. While I always felt that Biafra was much less important than Biafra believed he was, Ian always seemed to me a man right on top of both his feet and his game. That he would later turn into a scene scold seemed to me to be a waste of his talents, as evidenced by the music he still makes.

But things are as they are. When I last saw him, like I said, it was in the body of a documentary on Midwest hardcore where he complained about me extorting $100 out of him after we had said we would play for free. He was right, we did, and he was even more right that that was fucked. Money makes a man funny, though. Seems like he should have understood that. But what I loved the most about Ian was that despite all of that Straight Edge hoopla he was not, musically speaking, doctrinaire at all.

"I'm singing my vocals now sitting next to the engineer," he had told me.

"What? You mean sitting in the control room? Why the fuck would you do that?"

"Well, when you sing them live there are people there, right?"

That he had thought this through impressed me. I still sing my vocals from a locked and blocked vocal booth but I liked his analysis.

Also, musically we were crafting the record that would be called *Muru Muru*. One of the reviewers noted that "this" is what happens when you take too much acid and they were probably right. But we were finding a compelling flexion point that would set the scene that would make sense later because the drive was to go beyond genre, because it was clear that genre was an imperfect vehicle for delivering vision.

Let me explain. For years I was bedeviled when going to other people's houses and wondering why any place that I had called home didn't have the coherence to look like other people's places. I figured it was a result of my mind, like a weird kind of color-blindness, but applied to everything. It took me years to figure out that things like homes must be designed and planned, but in this period, and in this phase, that was never clear.

That era was marked by the music. We didn't know what we were doing but we didn't want to do what we had been doing. And what was the essence of our musical expression anyway? We'd figure it out and maybe we'd have people who'd want to figure it out with us as well. For Steve, magical mystery touring with him had winnowed down to band-related stuff and practices.

Until I got a call one day. It was my roommate from the year before. He had become a Resident Assistant in a freshman dorm. Said there was some girl there whose sister was a Whipping Boy fan and did I want to come by to meet her? Her name was Josefine.

I begged off. For reasons unclear to me outside of me, categorically, I have never been into women younger than me, and a freshman felt like a high schooler. But one day I happened to be visiting him and she braced me in the hall outside of his room. Asking if I was me, and did I know her sister and some of their known associates in San Jose.

Some I knew, but as I tried to make my exit she and her friend invited me out that night. The two of them and me? "Well, bring someone!" I found her friend more attractive but her aggression was a net plus. Without an invite, I would have bumped back over the hill to where I lived and groused about not being able to get laid.

Muru Muru. *Very possibly my most favorite Whipping Boy record ever.*

Dragging my roommate from Alpha Delts with me, I was wearing a hastily donned costume of a dirty blue towel around my neck and my high school varsity letter for swimming, an S, pinned to my chest, while he wore a fedora with a press card in it. It was Halloween.

"Who the fuck are you all supposed to be?"

"I'm Superman," I said. "And he's Jimmy Olsen." It was as funny as it sounds and had the towel not been dirty and torn it would have had no genius about it at all.

A few things happened in the next few hours. I realized the amount of work I had to do to entertain her roommate, who was slightly more comely, was losing out to her very directed interest in letting it be known that she and I made much more sense. She was funny as fuck, hard to offend and manifestly interested in fucking, which made for a winning combination. There was still the whole 18-year-old thing, but she was a European 18-year-old, which was different from the 18-year-olds that had been making college a drag for me thus far.

By the time we had ended up together she had already been raped by a fraternity guy, though it took her years to come to that conclusion since no one had a name for what happened when you drugged your date back then, and she rolled with it. She took me to her family's in a nearby suburb for Thanksgiving.

What the family hadn't factored in were the massive amounts of LSD we had been consuming, and how, consequently, our relationship had deepened. This came during a period where I had become a "trips doctor" as I extolled the virtues of what they now call "therapy" and made believers out of folks who figured that if it hadn't made me any crazier(?), then maybe it had made me saner.

This was not without peril.

I had taken LSD one day with my former roommate who was Josefine's RA. When I invited him, mid-trip, to come back to my place just to hang, he demurred. Which I was fine with. But later when I was spread out on my bed something that had never happened before was happening. I was slipping into sleep. A very vivid sleep, but sleep nonetheless.

Until the phone rang.

"Hey man . . . " It was him.

"Yo . . . "

"Can you come over?"

"Nah, man. I just started falling asleep . . . I told you, you should have come over to hang and . . . "

"Please . . . "

He never said "please" and tonally it sounded like what it was. When I got to his place I climbed in through his window. I left instructions that he should leave it unlocked since I didn't want to be spotted by anyone who knew me and have to "talk." So, he did. Besides which, for whatever reason, I rarely used doors those days and have a steady memory of climbing in and out of windows, even on third floors, rather than either ride elevators up or be caught inside.

Jumping up into his window I heard a scream, a woman's scream, and my mind did a quick calculation that he had invited me to a threesome.

My First Threesome

THERE WAS ALL THIS STUFF I SAID I would never do when I went to California. Now I'm not offloading responsibility on a state and a state of mind, because the reality here is I'd been invited to threesomes before. But back in the '70s when *New York* magazine was extolling the virtues of bisexuality, I was certain that I didn't want to spend my threesome time fending off another man's advances.

Hot tubs were another one. I hated the idea of being in a bathtub with other humans. This changed as well. Besides which, bandmate Steve had had nothing but overwhelmingly positive things to say about threesomes even if one had resulted in him having to spend some time in a mental institution.

The idea here was like the orgy I attended after I overcame concerns of a sudden onset of homosexuality (a young man's concern), that there'd be none of that without me specifically requesting it.

So it was during one of our walkabouts we ran into a woman we knew named Betty. An ex of mine, and the daughter of a Nobel Prize winner of note. As she had nothing pressing happening and was secretly in love, or not-so-secretly in love, with the ex of Steve's that was a beauty and the one Steve went to the mental hospital for, she fell in step with our evening's plans, which had involved television, and the last tailings of some psilocybin.

Getting back to his room and not having any concerns about lurking homosexuality, we fell into his bed, and a threesome. I wish I could report that it was a drag, as that seems the socially responsible thing to do now, and then, maybe, when the world was aswirl with AIDS concerns, but I cannot.

I tried to communicate to Steve that I knew she was not on birth control but I had failed to do this in a coherent manner and while she mouthed me, he had sex with her, and though my memories of it might be inexact, I do remember with a certain amount of shock and interest that we all came at the same time. Hard enough to make happen when there are two people, but three?

I know she was hoping this would lead to further adventures with his ex, but this was a one-off that doesn't have her entering my life again in any noteworthy way until she accused me of raping her three years later. Not "rape" about the night I've just detailed, but three years later. Rashomon-like I also later, some 20 years after, interviewed her and everyone else involved after she admitted to fabricating said rape story. Her later explanation? "Hey . . . I was in analysis then." And then, an apology. Guess better late than never.

But it wasn't sex thrill. It was a scream of true panic. And a man's voice as well. A man that wasn't the man I had come to see.

"Turn the light on."

Someone did and I found him swaddled in bed. Blankets drawn tight around him. And washcloths on his face. The man and the woman were panicked.

"Please leave."

"But, well, he needs . . . should we call someone or . . . "

"No. Just leave." And they did.

"Thank you," he said.

"What the fuck, man?"

"I started freaking out," he rasped. "How do I know I'm not going to hurt myself?"

"How do you EVER know that?"

This made sense to him. He shook the blankets off. We talked about volition and as we talked, he sat at his desk and pulled out a book on circuits and devices. He was an engineer, after all. The pages turned and he was muttering. "It all . . . it all makes sense now . . . !"

He started talking to me about impedances and ohms.

"I got to go now."

"Yeah, yeah," he waved me out as I climbed out his window and scrambled back over the hill. When I climbed in bed, like trying to get back to a great dream, the moment was gone and I stared into the shifting purple night of meditations on service to mankind.

But Josefine and I were gobbling it and had reached an unholy accord. Her father, who initially had posited himself as the Swede with the groovy demeanor and enjoyed chopping it up with me about Miles Davis and '50s jazz, hadn't been savvy enough to figure out that she and I had fallen in love. And when she tearfully was sending me back East, where I would spend Christmas that year, he figured it out and the shit hit the fan.

Pre-Eddie Murphy, in a place that was provincial like California was, there was no means to understand Black folks as anything but bit players in the scenes of white folks' lives. Certainly not sex symbols, or simply, objects of romantic interest. Mothers always knew. One look at me and they knew. Also, me and the older woman thing. But fathers? Rarely.

In fact, when I got my first venereal disease, I went to the school doctor. I had been out of school about four months but could still fake going there.

"How many sex partners do you have?" he asked, not looking up from his clipboard.

"Five." This got his attention.

"STUDENTS?" I could see him thinking. Numbers like that, perhaps this unkempt Black cat is sleeping with professionals. "Concurrently?!?"

"Yes."

"WOMEN?" It amused me that he just didn't see it, even as it was there in front of him. I had to be sleeping with men, right?

"Yes: women."

I wondered if he had a wife and how he would tell her and what would happen in her head after he did. I also made sure we all went to the same doctor. I wanted him to feel it every time he gave one of us some antibiotics.

But her father went nuts. His best friend was an Indian guy who delighted in his discomfort and egged him on. He was threatening to no longer pay for her college since she wasn't "getting out of Stanford" what he hoped she would.

My plane landed after the holiday visit to New York and with her, we went straight there.

I laughed at him. "So . . . you wanna talk about Miles Davis some more?"

"Good you can laugh. This is not about racism, you know?"

"Really?"

"It's about, well, cultural differences . . . "

"She told me you asked if it had anything to do with the size of my cock . . . "

AND we were OFF to the races.

"It's CULTURE!"

"You're Swedish and your wife is Estonian. How different is that?"

"That's totally DIFFERENT!"

"Of course it is. You're both white. But that fails to be a singular culture, right?"

This went on for hours. I should have noted her silences but I was involved in what felt like a struggle for the soul of not so much America, but truth. What I didn't know, and wasn't revealed until decades later, was that he had fucked his daughter as a child. A state of affairs that was so regular as not to seem strange. He stopped when she was around four years old and could speak.

But he could never be sure of what she could remember and had always been very controlling of her dating life. So, as it happens, it may not have been about race, but more about control, but this made no difference to me then.

Especially insofar as she, her sister the punk rocker, and the enabler mother had now all turned against me, she hit me with the resulting discussion about seeing other people.

Which was how I ended up with five sex partners, and VD. It was also how she ended up getting engaged and subsequently married to her across-the-hall neighbor. Who, one day after a night I had spent over at her place, raped her as well. Something else I had not heard until she asked me to read her memoir that details her rise to being an internationally known Nietzsche scholar and professor of note, who then succumbed to a crack addiction that had her, the former Swedish royal and beauty contest winner, becoming a crack whore.

But you can't make the organic inorganic, and so we continued to see each other. Up to and including her spending the night before her wedding. This was an unmooring, and like Caligula and his dismasting at the death of his sister-lover Drusilla, I can safely say this experience changed me. Changed the music in my head, my outlook on the world.

I had started reading a lot about precognitive thought and thought transmission. One night when we were sleeping, I woke up and not moving so as not to disturb her, I closed my eyes and followed the purple behind my eyelids into what felt like a room. Once there I called her name. In my mind.

Her whole body flinched. I initially dismissed it as a coincidence. I waited an irregular period of time and did it again. Same reaction. I waited 15 minutes and did it once more. Same response.

The next day I asked her what she had dreamed, and she asked me, "What the hell were you screaming at me?" I told her what I just told you and we laughed and fell together. So, contemplating a future of nothing for no other reason than a withholding father seemed not only unjust but against universal law.

Though given all of what happened next, I now know that the father had served a much greater purpose that even I had not the perspective to see back then.

Dead Grass + The Eating of Dead Grass

I DISCOVERED A DISCREPANCY. Stanford had given me double credit for a class I had taken. Credits were like cash, and still needing a certain number to graduate, these would just about let me cross the line without me having to take another class. Unless the discrepancy was discovered. Then? Well, I wasn't going to take any chances, so instead of graduating in June of 1984 with my class I had one more summer quarter to go to. Which was fine.

Sam and Dave had already left Whipping Boy. Steve and I were left to fill the void. *Muru Muru*, as much of a creative "success" as it might have been, was a complete commercial failure, even by meager indie standards back then. It wasn't long before we added a second guitarist, a bass player and a drummer, but that's later so this summer there'd be none of that.

This summer, I rented a one-room shack back in the weeds of a house that was behind a place called the Grecian Health Spa. I went to class, dropped acid, listened to some Ronnie James Dio that Rollins had given me, in fact, listened to nothing but *Holy Diver* that summer, and finished taking classes.

There was a woman in the house who was continually trying to chat with me but her penchant for playing "Little Red Corvette" on repeat was a little red flag. She used to sunbathe in the backyard weeds, and I noticed her chaise lounge got closer and closer to my shack. Then she started sunbathing nude. Then she drew the chaise lounge across the only walkway out of my shack to the street.

I had class, was high and had to go. There was a wonderful kind of equanimity gifted to me by LSD that allowed me to see what I imagined was the essential nature of things. So, while I may have just vigorously masturbated, the lift of having to handle an actual human with a sexual agenda that veered toward the fanclubbing of men with Black penises, which is Black men, well, it was a lot to process.

"Excuse me," courtly manners style, I dipped, not too fast, and not too slow over her naked body as I made my way to my van. She was plenty attractive. But masks fell away on acid and her face told a story of sad that I thought I could healthily live my life without. Besides which I had a 76-year-old classmate I was hot for.

Stop laughing.

She and I were hanging out and she was funny as fuck, not too bad to look at and full of the kind of brio and comfortability with said brio that I imagined she'd be fun to have sex with. But . . . well: 76. I didn't know what that meant and couldn't imagine what it would mean. Back then things had to make sense since I was trying to make sense of things.

There was also the woman who singlehandedly made sure I could finish at Stanford. She worked in financial aid, and even though I got fucked by Reagan—if you were going to get federal student loans, you had to register for the draft, and I had refused—and had to borrow $10K in my last year, I got great terms because of her and we started visiting. She was divorced and in her late 50s and her daughter was older than me.

This made sense to me, and I had resolved one night to make my move. Which is how I thought of things back then. And after dinner as we sat on the couch and talked, I could see she had done the calculation as well. Like, this was the night. But she started to feel . . . uncomfortable. Not like I was making her uncomfortable. More like we were mired in the moment's discomfort and it dawned on me that just because she was older it didn't mean that she wasn't without weird-nesses and mores from her time in the sun that I had no idea about.

So, I left without making whatever move I had thought I was going to make and walked home, as I lived about 100 yards from her. But I wrote my ass off that summer. Made another edition of *The Birth of Tragedy* magazine. The rent was $300 a month, which I had to struggle to come up with, which often meant I had no food. The shack had no heat for the cold that California gets at night, and I couldn't afford a fan for the heat of the day.

Torpor-bound, I'd sit in the shack and slowly starve while writing. Steve came by every now and then to check to see if I was dead. Some-times he brought me food but Steve was like me, he framed me to a certain degree in this way: ask for NOTHING. So, I didn't. When he was upbraiding me for what he felt was lassitude I made the claim that I was hungry.

"Bullshit!" he good-naturedly announced. "You have a whole yard full of food!"

"I have a yard full of dead grass."

"It's edible!" And he jumped up and pulled large tufts of it out of the ground. Then he threshed it between his hands and the seeds dropped into a dog bowl he had pulled up out of the turf. When he had it half full, he presented it to me. "There!"

"I don't have any milk." I said this without affect. I wasn't angry about this turn of events. I still stole food when I could, breaking into the eating clubs on campus and filling garbage bags with whatever I could grab in the dark. Like 10-pound cans of sauerkraut. Or relish. Yet, I was resigned. Things would either get better, or I'd die.

"Here!" And he grabbed the garden hose and put some water in it.

"You eat it. First."

"Sure!" Steve chowed down with a plastic spoon I had and once he had, so did I. It wasn't the greatest but I could hear my stomach was happy. It was happy right up until the sunbather browbeat one of the main house dudes into mowing the lawn so she could sunbathe more effectively, a move that seemed totally emblematic of my time at Stanford.

I kept running into another woman on campus though. She was a year older than me but had delayed graduating for a year. She was relentlessly cheerful, a fact that I found fundamentally annoying, even if half of that was because she seemed happy to see me.

"HIIIII!!!"

"Yeah, yeah, hi. What's going on?"

"Today is my and Ralph's anniversary!" I didn't know who Ralph was but I did know that in some places and spaces this would mean she was announcing her lack of openness to the possibility of sex.

"Your anniversary, huh?" I sensed an opening. "So where are you going tonight to celebrate?"

"Well, he's not here. He works in Boston. I'm going to get a job there at WGBH soon and so . . . "

"And so . . . a lonely anniversary." My work largely being done, like the Johnny Appleseed of dour, I moved on. But not before "Well, if it gets too lonely come and find me."

She laughed, sort of. I finished my classes and then had to get out of the shack. A garage was opening up at a house in town and my non-drug-dealing drug provider was willing to rent it out to me for $50 a month.

But, "You gotta pay every month!" he said. "I mean, this is not The Eugene Robinson Welfare House!"

"Hey man . . . " He and I had already come to blows over something sensible like the telephone but given that he was ranked third in his state in wrestling, I lost that engagement. That didn't mean I was into that kind of fucking loose talk, though. " . . . What the fuck are you TALKING about? Have I ever not paid you for something?"

He apologized, I packed the van and moved into the garage. A half a block from a train that powered through there like Dan Aykroyd said in *The Blues Brothers* movie, "so often you won't even notice it." It was a garage. Stone floor stained with grease. I stole some plywood from a construction site, laid it on the floor, requisitioned some carpet and filled it with whatever passed for "my shit" then. I don't know why I never thought to insulate it, but I didn't and it was freezing in the winter, until I could afford a space heater. It was nice during the summer no matter how hot it got and after some minor mods it became a pretty cool hang.

The Death of My Budding Bromance with Rollins

"I CAN BULLSHIT YOU or I can tell you the truth. Which do you prefer?" The woman whose erstwhile anniversary it was, who I had spotted on one of my last few days as a student, had indeed come to find me. She came to find me by way of needing a "trips doctor" and I was willing. One day that fall we magical mystery toured it, out and about until the sun started setting and we had made a plan to go back to my house and watch television.

Which I am sure sounds like code but if I said television, I more often than not really meant television. But this was before. Also known as before I went crazy.

We laid on the bed and watched. I remember her asking if I minded when she placed her head on my shoulder. I said that I didn't. But in the chemically fueled mindset I had noted to myself, "I guess this is just what, on planet normal, friends do."

She then took her shirt off, and again I thought, "Well, it doesn't feel hot to me, but I guess the space heater is too hot."

Then she started kissing me and grabbing my cock. I had the sense to now figure out that we were moving outside of the place where things were merely friendly but then something else: LSD was such a mind thing for me that I had never actually managed to have very much significant sex on it. It just had never come up, and here it was, and it was noteworthy because of this and different and she stayed.

I'd always been mystified at the mechanics of friendship, and more often than not I had to be told "we are FRIENDS now," for me to make sense of why people kept calling or coming around. I didn't have any siblings until I was 10 and was used to being solitary, and feeling all right being so when I was alone. That is, it was rare for me to feel lonely.

But then she kept coming by and soon I figured out that this meant she was my girlfriend. I had no mechanism to understand what this meant by way of me fucking other women though, so I thought I needed to ask on the occasion of her asking me on Saturday what I had done on Friday night.

"I want you to tell me the truth." She looked confused and later it made sense to me. Who would opt for bullshit?

"I went to a movie and this woman picked me up there and I went back to her house and had sex with her." It wasn't an issue of being hurtful or not hurtful, but the difference between me now and the lifeguard I had been is that I had decided that opting for clarity was somehow going to save me, presuming I knew what clarity meant.

She shrugged though and thanked me for telling her the truth and then we went on like I hadn't said anything. But Josefine was still coming around, though she was now living with the man who raped her and who would become her first husband. They'd come by together but more often than not, she'd come alone. Ostensibly to not buy drugs from me, though I gave her drugs and she gave me cash for them. I was not trying to deceive, and so the occasion for asking me questions that would have had hurtful answers was infrequent. Though had I been asked, there would have been lots of hurtful answers.

A few months before the summer quarter, though, Black Flag played. The last time they had come through, Rollins and I had spent the day together in San Francisco. I had a tape recorder in tow and so we were marginally doing an interview but mostly we were hanging. We went to City Lights books. Shot the shit. Over the years people have asked me how I've found him, like he was a vacation destination of some sort. But I always found him to be like guys I went to high school with. Sort of Asperger-y about certain things and fairly engaging as long as you didn't wander too far from their wheelhouse.

The interview was good, he was candid, and if he didn't have an answer or couldn't analyze his way to one, he didn't try to bullshit, which was nice. Nice enough that when he came to town after that we'd find each other. He gave me *Black Spring* by Henry Miller to read. And when he told me he was getting into this idea of using language to destroy language, I stole and sent him a copy of Joyce's *Finnegan's Wake*. I was now deep into weightlifting and power lifting. Hadn't started taking steroids yet so we even approached this from a point of view of a certain adolescent purity.

He was the first one to give me Lydia Lunch's number, though he had no idea that I had stalked her when I was a teenager. He gave me Michael Gira's number because "you guys should really know each other." In the end that turned out to be amusingly prescient. Someone with an eagle eye spotted Gira and me at an SSD show at CBs, in 1981 or 1982. Even if the first time I called him he threatened to kick my ass after hanging up the phone on me, then he called me back to tell me I was a piece of shit for calling the first time. When he and I have met in person he's been unfailingly polite and I haven't had the heart to bring up the drunken Mr. Hyde he had been.

Rollins also, despite the public reputation for straight edge stuff, used to get acid from me. Or at least did so on a few occasions. That he never talked about this, until much later, I never viewed as prevarication or myth-making. I understood the straight edge thinking implicitly. I believed the idea was not to be a slave to much of anything outside of your own head. I was taking a lot of acid but I was not addicted to acid. I also still did not drink, smoke, or take any other drugs. I was frank with the press when asked but I wasn't having nearly the same number of press opportunities.

Earlier on, the friend who had originally introduced us called and said she wanted to catch a ride to the show with us. Black Flag was coming and she wanted a ride and wanted to bring a friend. I was driving the van, so I had room and said that was fine.

I was lazing around when my roommate comes barreling in wide-eyed. "Marianne is here."

Oh. Cool. Marianne was a year younger and as much as she reminded me of one of my sisters, she said that I reminded her of one of her brothers. So: no need to stand on ceremony. But my roommate's reaction had me confused. I get back to our room and I can see why. Her friend was . . . stunning.

"Eugene? This is Vivien."

Vivien and Henry had dated or some such thing, I was told. But in my time with Rollins, we had never fallen to talking about women the way that young men might and I remember arguing with him as we crossed the street going past the strip clubs in North Beach on the way to City Lights.

"It was a feeling like when you see a hot girl or something . . . "

In trying to pretend like I was better than I was, I begged off knowing what he meant.

"I'm not acting like that when I see a hot girl . . . " I demurred.

"It's the feeling I mean . . . " and of course I knew what he was talking about, the rush of the animal, but I was not copping to it. Like I wouldn't easily cop to digging Duran Duran, though I did.

Because it was precisely the kind of feeling I had driving to the city with Vivien sitting on the Econoline engine hump next to me. Black Flag came and went without incident but I understood that whatever crazy thoughts I was having, this wouldn't resolve itself in a "truth or bullshit" convo.

"Hey man. We're coming through again. Stay at your place?" I knew Black Flag was coming and had been expecting the call. The garage was big and at this point fixed up pretty nice.

"Sure." He found his way over. Told me Vivien was coming from Santa Cruz too. I said they could both stay. He was sitting on my couch and I was showing him something stupid—if memory serves, it was Dr. Fred Hatfield, a.k.a. Dr. Squat, his new patented weightlifting belt design. I had just got one. Mostly because I was now working. In the defense industry no less, as editor at *Defense Electronics* magazine.

It had taken me 17 months after graduating to get a real job. Until then I was moving furniture, painting houses, and bouncing. Money from whatever shows we were playing was usually plowed back into the band but my rent was still $50 so there was that. But there was a knock on my door and a friend asking if I was going to the show and when he yanked the door open and saw Rollins there, well, I might as well have had Mother Teresa on my couch. I had never seen someone star-struck, outside of the 15-year-old me at my first bodybuilding show, but this was that and the first sense I really had that Rollins' upside potential was probably well beyond whatever Black Flag was doing.

It was that very thing though that was causing friction. The show that night was great but Greg Ginn and Henry felt like they were in very different bands, and post-show Rollins corralled me and said, "Hey man . . . Greg is acting strange so we're not staying tonight. We're going to drive back to L.A. now."

There was no way to know this then but that was the last time I'd see Henry Rollins with Black Flag.

"But Vivien doesn't have a ride back to Santa Cruz. Can you take care of her?"

I agreed to do so, and we left the venue and drove back to my place chattering. I wasn't sure why she wasn't staying with Marianne. Or how she planned to get to Santa Cruz the next day or where my girlfriend was, but I was glad for the company and when back to the garage I got out some blankets and made up the couch for her before crawling into bed.

We talked in the dimmed light about 20 minutes more. I had dozed off when she called my name.

"Eugene?"

"Yeah?"

"It's kind of cold."

"Shit. Sorry. Let me turn up the space heater . . . "

"Or I could just climb in bed with you. I mean if you don't mind."

Yeah.

I had gotten myself into a philosophical cul-de-sac not too long before this where I had decided that decisions were killing me. The pressure to make them, abide by them, consider them. I decided I would make no more decisions. Like Devo sang, "freedom from choice" was what I was seeking. The next day I drove her back to Santa Cruz and we made plans to meet again. I was aware of the world being aware of things like moral frameworks, but I never considered that they had much to do with me. Which is to say: I felt great. Not riven with guilt and if anything, my attitude would have been marked by a big, fat "WHAT?"

I saw her only a few more times after that but, about a year later, I stopped hearing from Rollins completely. The universe is either causal or not causal but the patterns of my life as they have stood remain the same: people come and people go. If they go I don't try to make them stay, and if they stay I don't try to stop them from going.

I hadn't thought of him again until a friend called. He worked at a record label and was meeting a journalist and the journalist had just interviewed Rollins and then things got weird so she wanted to talk to someone who had interviewed him or knew him. He told her I had, and so the call.

"He stressed during the interview that he was not gay," she said. "And then he called me back the next day to make sure I had gotten that he wasn't gay."

And now I was remembering that not too long before this someone told me that Rollins was going to throw Jim Carroll a beating. Carroll *and* Lydia Lunch, apparently for telling people that he was gay. I called Lydia, due diligence, and by way of warning.

"Why the fuck would I say that?" she snorted. "If I was going to say anything it was that he had a small COCK, but that he was gay? He's crazy." At this point he had ceased all contact with her and sent her back everything she had ever given him in scorched-earth high school kid fashion. But it was clearly something that was bothering him and that he was having a problem with.

"What do you make of that?"

"That he's not gay?"

"Yeah."

"Well . . . he's never been gay with ME. So, there's that."

"You're a journalist. Would you put this in the piece?"

And I thought long and hard about it before finally offering, "Nah. If he is hiding, he's got to be miserable, and really, who cares? It's a total non-issue, it seems."

"In everybody's mind," she agreed.

"But his." We let the silence settle and she rang off and I've not thought about him again until I sat down to write this.

Undeniably Lydia Lunch + My Love Letter to the Same

"LYDIA'S IN LOVE." I'D ANNOUNCED IT within earshot of Steve Albini at one point. The reason why I said so wasn't entirely clear, outside of me explaining perhaps why she'd not be available to record with us.

"With someone other than herself?" I chuckled because it was clever and mean, but I was also totally incapable of being either clever or mean when it came to Lydia. Her totemic significance for me, branded as I was from early formative scene-crawling at CBs in the late '70s, made this impossible. So, I mumbled, grumbled really, and moved on.

After Rollins had given me her number, I sat on it for what felt like weeks, though. Some mixture of needing to get a hold of myself and dealing with what was totally and completely subrational. Like Dante and Beatrice, whatever it was she meant to me, in my head, was going to come face to face with the reality of whoever it is that she was.

The phone rang and when she answered I could hear her listening. She's talked about her father having been a grifter and if you grow up with grifter cant, you listen in a different way. Which means I got straight to the point. I wanted to interview her for *The Birth of Tragedy*

*The first night I met Lydia when I was not stalking Lydia. My profile on the left.
With my .38 in my waistband. Photographer: Adam Paal.*

magazine, still an ongoing concern after having survived the public upset over the "Sex & Depression" issue. When next she was in San Francisco this was a thing that needed to happen.

She agreed, and as luck would have it, she had a show coming up at the Oasis. I dragged along my photographer, a first- or second-generation Apple engineer for a weird fun fact if you care about such things. The club was crowded and she went to the stage, a binder and some papers clutched in her fist. I'd seen her do music before, had listened to all of her music, but listening to her speak, after the phone call, was rounding things out nicely.

Then everything got shot straight to hell.

Some wag from the audience started giving her some lip. She told him to shut the fuck up. A full bottle of beer came careening out of the club dark, hitting her on the head and breaking on the stage, a burst of broken glass and beer. The guy who I pegged as her bouncer shifted nervously by stage edge, while the wag scrambled up on the stage, presumably to get her. This launched the bodyguard into action who kicked the guy's feet out from under him and, as the guy tried to work his way back up, dragged a knife across the erstwhile heckler's forehead with blood bursting forth from the fresh cut.

As a Brooklyn kid, my tendency to overreactive Brooklyn shit had me moving forward to Deus ex machina a little peace and quiet into the proceedings. Courtesy of the .38 I now carried.

When I First Started Carrying a Gun. EVERYwhere

FOR MOST PEOPLE THE MANSON FAMILY and the murders are like some weird bit of California effluvia. A meme with the shimmying Manson, but in the mid-'80s Manson was still alive and well, and The Family, at his behest, had reached out to me. After having featured him in "The Fear Issue" of *The Birth of Tragedy* and having gotten photos of him from his lawyer and struck up correspondences with guys named Greyhound and Brother Icepick, it seemed a short step to selling The Family's musical endeavors through my store at the time.

CFY Records was the only tattoo parlor, tape, T-shirt, book, comic, video, poster and gun store in the history of suchlike stores. And in Palo Alto no less. Having a Federal Firearms License (FFL) made this possible, and while I didn't have display cases full of munitions because the store was all-ages, I was special-ordering assault rifles and Uzis that were then subsequently sold to a totally different clientele than the rest of the merch.

The Family though had some independently produced music, and I put it on consignment. Ninety-day consignment.

They called after six days asking for their money. The total amount, not even what was sold.

I explained what consignment was and what 90 days was. Then they made a killing error. They got heavy with me. Clearly trading on reputation, there were some noises made about coming to get it. A tonal shift that caused me to flip out.

I started screaming. Asked them to take out a pen so they could have my entire schedule which, given that I'm on the spectrum, varied not at all from day to day. I gave them times and addresses and told them if they wanted to go that road then they should.

Maybe it was the steroids I was using in the mid- to late '80s. Maybe it was just me. But I was already keyed up well beyond what was sane or helpful. The neighborhood I lived in, East Palo Alto, for a time was designated the Murder Capital of America. A sad fact driven by the CIA-fueled crack trade.

The upshot of which was I was lifting obscene amounts of weight, taking karate when I wasn't, and was also breeding pit bulls.

After I hung up the phone in a paroxysm of rage and trembling I realized what I had done was very stupid and was having a certain amount of buyer's remorse since when I was at the store I couldn't watch my house. Or my car. Or my motorcycle. I couldn't control who got into the gym. In short: killing me over $220 was crazy easy.

Having an FFL made the solution easy though, and so I started carrying a gun. I wish I could say "a" gun but I was carrying several. One on my ankle, one in my waistband and one in the small of my back.

At one point, on a date, I had draped my coat over the back of my chair in a tony restaurant where it slipped off of the chair and came to rest on the floor with a decidedly resonant THUMP. So loud and definitive that the entire restaurant noticed as I weakly exclaimed by way of explanation: "hehe . . . my KEYS . . . "

That would have been gun number four.

At 90 days I paid The Family what they were owed, in violation of the Victim's Compensation Laws, and shipped the unsold portion back.

I've never heard from any of them again.

I knew that gun-wielding activation would mean no interview, and since she seemed safe at this point and had already launched into a piece about being sexually molested by her father, the action-man shit could wait.

Her piece built to a screaming close and it was as heavy as heavy could be. I followed her, and her erstwhile bodyguard, out the back and up the stairs to the green room, not at all sure my voice would still work.

"Lydia?"

"Yes?" she spun on the stairs and fixed me with a wide smile.

"Hey. I'm Eugene. We talked on the phone . . . "

"Well, come the fuck up here, EUGENE!" She leaned into my first name in a way that had probably caused my father to use Stanley more often than he used Eugene. But I could hear her playing with it since we were both very certain that whatever stereotype existed for what a "Eugene" looked like, I wasn't it.

Back in the green room, the con had lit up the room. Turns out the "bodyguard" was Richard Kern. The audience wag was a plant. The bottle was very real, though, and really a happy accident. Jim Thirwell, a.k.a. Foetus, was there as well. I had danced to his music at the Mudd Club. I didn't make mention of this though I noted it in my head on meeting him.

We chatted and made a plan to meet the next day.

"Did your photographer get some good shots?" Kern took a special interest but my photographer had fled as soon as he could. The knives and the blood were a rougher pill than what he was used to swallowing.

"Yeah. He usually does."

The next day I drove the Ford Econoline Supervan up to meet Lydia and Jim at their hotel, some pensione on Market Street. I shifted on a side chair while they prepped for the outside world. I looked like a stevedore—not an affectation after a few years of hanging sheet rock, painting houses and moving furniture; though I was now healthily ensconced at *Defense Electronics* as an editor, old habits die hard. I wore a shirt and a tie to work, but Mr. Rogers-like, after work it was total prole. I'd not have thought to notice but for their finery.

Which in the end, well, they still had to squeeze into the dirty Econoline. Jim took shotgun. Lydia squeezed by him and sat on the engine next to me. We ended up by Union Square and at the bottom of each hill I had noticed the brake pedal getting closer and closer to the floor.

"Hey. This is a '65. So not so reliable," I tried to prepare them. "So, there's a chance the brakes are going to go out, so if I suddenly pull the car to the right I'm doing it so we don't all die."

Lydia laughed like hell. I got the sense not because she didn't believe but very specifically because she *did*.

We made it, I got them to where they were going, and the tape recorder that had been running the whole time got what I felt was a pretty great interview. I bid them farewell, and after they got out I drove a few blocks and pulled over. This was heady. This whole make-believe-person to the-person-sitting-in-my-van. Ineffable, this thrill, and while not sexual in nature, was damned near adjacent.

I transcribed and sat on my bed using glue sticks to lay out the new issue. Lydia was whip-smart and the interview was funny in all the right places, and it was almost like we were having fun because, I guess, we were having fun. You can never tell, though, and like the old Hollywood adage goes, "sincerity is everything and once you got that faked, you got it made." Maybe I was played. I didn't know and didn't much care and was perfectly OK to embrace the symbolic import of Lydia via the whole Horatio Alger aspect of her living by way of her wits after deciding at 13 that she had had it with whatever plans the world had for her.

I picked up the mail. Years of paranoia had me having a post box, and on a rotating schedule I checked it so as not to be predictable in my predictability. I had gotten a postcard. From Lydia. It had two characters entwined in ghostly embrace and said on the other side in her florid script "we shall dig no graves before our time."

Beyond that the upshot was that she'd be back, Kern wanted to take our photos and did I know a place? I knew the best of all places. A wealthy wizard had started to build this insane mansion in the woods, and on the suicide of his daughter stopped building and it fell into great disrepair and had become a focal point for all kinds of suburban Satanism. Also known as kids getting drunk and fucking shit up. We had used it for the back cover of Whipping Boy's *Third Secret of Fatima*, and Kern would use it for photos for a magazine article we were going to write together.

We called it "The Babydoll Murders." Later I would use it as a title for the OXBOW song "Babydoll." It was slated to be featured in a mag-

azine for thrillkillers and for my part it was based on a nightmare I had
wherein I was encouraged to rape and kill someone by the someone
that I raped and killed.

This story, I always preface in the telling, is a nightmare that has
caused me incalculable difficulties over the years. The great writer
Diane Middlebrook, who was married to Carl Djerassi, the inventor of
the birth control pill, had later been one of my reviewers for the Gug-
genheim Fellowship. She also hired me and a friend as movers initially,
but she had no idea who I was when she had done so.

Lydia Lunch and I at the wizard's castle. As hot as the photos were, it was freezing that
night. (Photo by Richard Kern)

She had just decided she wanted to bro down with the furniture movers by riding along in the moving van the first time we moved her stuff. She sat precisely where Lydia had sat and as we drove to her penthouse apartment, festooned with stuff from Henry Moore and maybe even Alexander Calder, stuff I recognized on sight from books, she figured out that the two movers who were arguing over Frantz Fanon were not the blue-collar types she had been hoping to rub elbows with.

"Are you guys movers?" She pushed her glasses up her nose. She may have added "really" before movers.

"We're moving your furniture, right?" I knew what she meant but I wasn't having it.

"What I mean is, what else are you?" I passed her an issue of *The Birth of Tragedy* Magazine and it wasn't but two days after that she called me. The ask was simple: would I speak to her Poetry and Poetics class? She could get me $350. Which was about what I had made for moving her furniture for eight hours.

I agreed readily and when I got there with all of those eager young faces, I knew that no other story but "Babydoll" would do.

"This is from a piece Lydia Lunch and I had written contrasting parts. My part was drawn from a nightmare I had."

At the story conclusion the sea of white faces were whiter yet. There was some applause, and the question-and-answer session that followed was . . . spirited. Days later Diane called to tell me that her graduate TAs were revolting and threatening to quit unless some cogent explanation was offered as to why I had done what I had done.

"So are you asking me if I raped and murdered Lydia?"

"No. Not really. I'd like you to explain it though."

"Other than reading it again and prefacing it like I did by explaining that it was a nightmare, I don't know how that would help."

Diane once asked me why I never took any English classes while I was at Stanford. I told her I had taken one before I figured out that I was wasting my time. I could learn something from journalists. But from collegiate writers and teachers of those writers? Feh.

"In fact, I'm offended that they asked and that you didn't push back, as I am quite sure if I wasn't a 210-pound, muscle-bound Black cat who, when they imagine such things, they imagine someone who looks like me doing it, they would have embraced the writing for what it was: masterful!" And then I laughed. But I laughed alone as this was the last conversation she and I had.

Lydia knew nightmares and even had some sort of sixth sense that the reason the piece worked was because material taken from real nightmares succeeds because it feels so real. Even if at story's end it takes a fantastical turn and the woman is revealed to be a young boy and then some demonic intersex creature.

But we took the photos. Lydia in her underwear. Me, shirtless. Jim didn't show this time and the taciturn Kern clicked away. To say that I didn't think of going for Method here would be a lie. But "trying" to fuck Lydia in the mud of the cold woods didn't appeal to me. Besides which, there was that whole "should I tell you the truth or bullshit you?" thing that me and the woman I was choosing not to bullshit were now living together.

Digging graves before our time was not what was happening though and so Lydia and I had plans to meet in New York.

Wising Up to How Beat the Beat Scene Was in Total

HITTING NEW YORK WITH a suitcase full of *The Birth of Tragedy* felt, well, sort of Player's Club. Like Travis Bickle's speech to Betsy in *Taxi Driver*, I'd not have felt I had the right to be there *but* for these issues. Because the whole time I was getting knocked out on stages seeing bands like Fear, I was also pursuing associations with the literary types that had somewhat framed my idea of what the West Coast was. Framed my multiple car trips across this country and created an urge to connect to those who had connected to the great machinery poised as it was to destroy the American mind.

Ferlinghetti was the first. I met him at the same time that I met Allen Ginsberg and corralled him and read him a poem and he grimaced like I had taken a shit. In front of him.

"You gotta write like you know you're going to read it out loud." Which, of course, was right.

But I interviewed him and then Allen Ginsberg. I could see Ginsberg had his schtick when I picked him up at the Ramada on Market Street and took him over to his friend Shig's place in North Beach. Gregory Corso would meet us there later but this would be after Ginsberg, in taking stock of me, decided he was going to play hard to get.

It's an old move, redolent of Dylan in *Don't Look Back*, or even the Sex Pistols on one of those interview shows that was supposed to show how *with it* the interviewee was versus the one doing the interviewing. If I had said poetry was a worthwhile venture, he'd undercut that premise. If I said it wasn't, he'd have undercut that too. His objective was to generate frustration and then the possibility of some satori around my role here and my place in his space.

Shig bumped around the place largely ignoring us as I glanced down at my notes and caught a gander at my "nuclear" question. This would be the question that I kept in my back pocket for the end of the interview. One that would, in all likelihood, make the continuation of the interview impossible because the person would be so enraged. If it happens at the end you still have an interview. But I was getting nowhere with Ginsberg so going nuclear now made sense.

"Today in the *New York Times*, James Dickey described you as," and here I looked down at my notes so I sure as fuck could say what Dickey had said, ". . . a . . . garbage man. Why would he say something like that, do you think?"

BOOM.

After showing him the quote and the clip, Ginsberg had given up fucking with the "cub reporter." He was bamboozled yet he answered my questions. And kept wandering back to Dickey.

"Well, it's probably because when I talk about ass fucking, I don't do it with the same horror that he does!" Ginsberg nodded. "It's traumatic for him . . . "

"Well, he describes rape as traumatic," I said. "And he wouldn't be wrong."

"But he thinks all ass fucking is traumatic. Especially between two men. Instead of it being a joyful expression of . . . " And he trailed off.

I had gotten what I needed and now we were just hanging. We went down to Balducci's where Corso already was and the hazing started again, but I wasn't gripping. Corso was just a bonus, and truthfully, if I opened with a question about the last book of his that I read and it was the very first book he had written I couldn't have expected much more. Either I hated his most recent stuff or I didn't know it. Either was a case for contempt.

Ginsberg had warmed to me, though, and as I gathered up my things to take my leave he gestured to me.

"Hey. Robinson." He waved at me with a hand motion that indicated that he wanted to whisper something to me. So, I bent down, turning my ear to him, only to have him kiss me on the cheek. A turn I found amusing, and laughed. "Get ahold of me when you get to New York. You know . . . dharma gates are . . . endless."

I did track him down when I got to New York, with a suitcase full of *The Birth of Tragedy*, but I had been gone from New York for long enough to forget an essential New Yorkism: fuck you. AND your magazine.

I tried to corral John Giorno, whose work I had admired, while I stood around with Ginsberg and caught shade at some shindig at the St. Marks Poetry Project. Peter Orlovsky, likewise. Karen Allen from the movie *Animal House* was there too, and it was the late '70s all over again. I might as well have had a squeegee in my hand.

I was once interviewed by a Black woman regarding the role and placement of Black artists in traditionally non-Black spaces; I waved her off. I didn't think this was an issue and, in fact, I didn't care what the issue was, as my MO was and would always continue to be the same. To borrow from De Niro in *Cape Fear* it was, and I paraphrase, "I will outfuck you, outfight you, outthink you."

But Kerouac had held such a place of prominence in my head I couldn't give up this obsession with the Beats that easily. I was lost in a swelter of "I'll show you." So, I persisted. Tracked down Amiri Baraka, formerly Leroi Jones. Called him at his house any number of times, though none of those times felt like there was anything going on but massive family discord, screaming and a phone that was eventually thrown back into the cradle. Ken Kesey was another try, and given that he was a wrestler, I imagined there would be common ground or at least some commonality, but we never got far beyond his obsession with hemp.

"You know how many things you can MAKE with HEMP?!?" I didn't. But he would tell me. And tell me.

I tracked down Joe Wolberg. He managed a writer/poet that I hadn't known until I left New York and wouldn't have grouped with the Beats proper, but I was a fan: Charles Bukowski.

"Buk doesn't see anybody," Wolberg told me. "But if you bring something to drink and some woman that's nice to look at, you probably got a chance." Finding any woman who actually wanted to meet Bukowski was not as easy as it sounds, though. Lydia would have been down, but she was off trying to track down Harry Crews. Naming a band after him was a smart way to go about it but I believe he avoided her just like he also avoided my requests for an audience.

Maybe it wasn't just the Beats. Maybe it was just . . . writers. Stories about writers. How they beat the Man yet succumbed to . . . what were they and I chasing? Kerouac dying in his mother's living room a wasted alcoholic, Cassady on the train tracks trying too hard with some pseudo-macho stunting. Maybe at least the myth would loom larger than the maker of the myth.

The friend who introduced me to Ferlinghetti also had hung with Jean Genet. Genet had stayed with him. I was overjoyed.

"When he left, a bunch of my stuff was missing," he said.

Which, in its own way, was pretty fucking perfect.

The Origin Story of My Hatred for the Red Hot Chili Peppers + Whipping Boy's Near-Final Stand

THE LATTER-DAY WHIPPING BOY, after six or seven years in, had gotten to a place that was even fundamentally more strange than where we had been with the acid-fueled *Muru Muru*. By the time we had gotten to the Klaus Flouride-produced *The Third Secret of Fatima*, music had changed enough to make having strange ideas about the business of music, not so strange at all.

By which I mean, as we got older, we also got to see people's Plan A's pan out. In wildly successful fashion. People who used to live in their cars were living in mansions, while Klaus was still, on occasion, working as a delivery driver to come up with the rent (a fact that irked him in light of Biafra having a custom-made elevator put into his own house). A disgusting careerism started to infest and infect even the most ardent contributors to whatever constituted musical art back then.

Whipping Boy was no different. With two guitarists—Bart Thurber, who had played with Chuck Berry, as well as the Mississippi Delta Blues Band, and guitar wunderkind Niko Wenner replacing the now-working orthopedic surgeon Steve Ballinger, it was probably inevitable. We could actually really play, so only playing hardcore seemed to make less sense than the metal-tinged direction we veered toward.

The record was mastered by Bernie Grundman. Who also mastered Prince and Michael Jackson. Now that some of us were actually working real jobs, this is where the money was going. And a potent reason why I still lived in the $50-a-month garage.

But like my confusion regarding why there was never anything very normal about places I was calling home, a gig with the Peppers played out similarly.

Witness: "Hey Eugene? Whipping Boy want to play with the Red Hot Chili Peppers for my birthday party?"

Karin Spies was doing the asking. She had had some history with the Peppers, intimated that it was intimate, but that made no difference to me. Despite the fact that I had been lukewarm on the band for almost

The penultimate version of Whipping Boy and our only version as a five-piece. Left to right, Steve Shaughnessy on drums, me, Ron Isa (later with Bl'ast) on bass, now-producer extraordinaire Bart Thurber on guitar, and Niko Wenner (previously with Grim Reality, later with OXBOW) on guitar.

ever, I understood an opportunity when it showed its face. Besides which it would give me a chance to see them for myself.

Past history had easily proved that my mind could be changed. Anti-Nowhere League wasn't that exciting on record but after having played with them, it was love all around. They were wonderful people despite publicly proclaiming a personal practice of fucking sheep and goats. ("So WOT?!?" they sang in response to the expected bestiality critique.)

The show was at the On Broadway in San Francisco and the load-in and meet-and-greet were without incident. Kiedis and Flea were both very L.A., in a way, and very small. Physically, I mean. Enough that I was surprised. They didn't seem especially weirded out by us spreading out in their dressing room, though I did note that after we left the room and as soon as possible after our exit, the door had been closed.

Karin sidled up to me, needing a favor: "Hey Eugene . . . do you mind if this couple comes out and gets married toward the end of your set? It'll only be a second . . . "

It was her ex, and in the spirit of comity she wanted to be a bigger person and give them space to tie the knot. Always ready for the weird, I say that I need to ask the rest of the band, but why not?

So, after collective agreement, we start playing, mindful of the fact that we're going to beat them. Them being the Peppers, which is to say, we're killing it, or at the very least, imagine we are. In the right spot, about a song from the end, the couple walks out, says their vows and are declared husband and wife.

They kiss and we tear into our last song when the power gets cut.

I say on the mic, "Oh. This last song is about two more minutes. Just let us finish it and we'll be gone."

A disembodied voice comes over the talkback mic: "No. You're done."

Which was, factually, incorrect. We weren't done. Far from it. Steve Shaughnessy, our cantankerous drummer, started drumming, while I started, in what felt like a reasonable way, to explain that we were nice enough to let the wedding happen, so they should be nice enough to let us finish the last song.

"No."

I could see the bouncers moving down the aisles to take Steve off of the drums. Kevin Conahan, a member in good standing of the L.A. Death Squad, or LADS, was our roadie and understood immediately that the best part of having control was losing it.

And we did. Kevin knocked the bouncers off the stage, the same stage I was now systematically destroying by yanking the PA stacks into the audience. Complete with monitor wedges and anything else I could get my hands on. Full bloodlust, as I stood in my dirty and now drenched underwear and did the math for them: we were NEVER leaving the stage.

I caught Kiedis' and Flea's eyes as they watched from the balcony. They were hardcore guys. With a word they could have delivered to us what was rightfully ours. They held my gaze for a second, their brows knit in some kind of consternation, before glancing away, making it more than clear that they were company men.

At this point I had screwed the mic stand loose from its base and was now light-sabering it at all and sundry who tried to stop us. Karin came on stage, unseen by guitarist Bart Thurber, who accidentally knocked her out when he went to swing his arm in some sort of rallying cry. Niko Wenner, usually a textbook definition "mellow" guy, was even activated, as was bass player Ron Isa. Fucking Shit Up was the order of the moment and was right up until I saw the cops heading toward me.

I instinctively understood that I was knee-deep in what could comfortably be called "a bad look." Nearly naked, shoeless, crazed and drenched in sweat. Having already bounced at places like the Mudd Club and raves, I intimately understood precisely what the cops were thinking and 'be nice to the crazy Negro' wasn't it.

Thirty yards away, I put my pants on. All while screaming my voice raw. Twenty yards away, then my shoes. Ten yards, my shirt and my jacket.

On stage now the cops surrounded me and the one standing closest, and in front of me, said, "You're finished."

What I hadn't known and later found out from a cop friend of mine in San Fran is that the call had gone out that the singer had lost his mind and was threatening to murder the rest of his band if they stopped playing. I would have been lucky to only get beaten like John Norman.

No, my lot would have been a mental hospital for observation for an indeterminate term. I didn't really have time for that.

"OK."

Total elapsed time 47 minutes.

When Whipping Boy next played we opened with the song they cut and so won some sort of moral victory. This is not what I held against the Peppers. No. That would come a few months later when I was in L.A., on Sunset Boulevard, going to some mastering session for the last Whipping Boy record before I had to threaten to sue Sony and the Irish band who, despite having been warned, decided that they also needed to name their band Whipping Boy.

The record was called *Crow*, a title I hated with artwork I hated, all conceived by Whipping Boy's last bassist. But while I stood there waiting to cross the street, I could see Flea driving toward me. It was an off-blue Mercedes-Benz, and while after the show I had apologized to them and got what I thought was some sympathetic understanding, there's a strong possibility that I was wrong.

But I stepped out into the street and waved at Flea who, surprisingly, to me at least, accelerated toward me. What is that they say happens in the face of the unbelievable? You tend to not believe, so I don't move and wave more as the car bears down on me. Then, like in the teenage moment when in the grips of a wash of testosterone I thought I could stop a subway train by jumping in front of it, I decided to *not* move.

If Flea was meant to murder me, then I would be murdered by Flea, so I just stood there. Waving. The car careened by me, inches by me, and I turned to see his Jimi Hendrix sticker disappearing off into the L.A. night.

That is what gave birth to the enduring Drax the Destroyer hatred for the band. This and Anthony Kiedis' ham-handed theatrics and a meeting I had with one of the founders of Autotune who explained to me why and how Kiedis could suddenly sing.

Sincerity is everything. And once you got that faked, you got it made.

When the Irish Whipping Boy Learned a Valuable Lesson About Cash

At first, I heard from someone at a label called Big Cat Records. Who knew if this was a real label, but their ask was simple: did we mind terribly if the Irish band Whipping Boy called themselves Whipping Boy?

Yes, we minded. We were about to put out a hardcore compilation called *Subcreature* and there are lots of letters in the alphabet. Choose others. If you have any interest in ever playing America.

Next time we hear from them, a similar request, a similar shutdown. The next time is when people start telling us that they heard us on the radio that day. I love Whipping Boy but the times we were played on any other radio than college radio? Few.

So I called their lawyer, a stooge at Sony whose name was on the back of the record.

"Yeah yeah . . . so look . . . what do you want?"

"I want you all to stop using our name."

"Sure, sure . . . how about we just cut you a check for, I don't know . . . $200?"

"Is that what you'd have to spend if I file this Temporary Restraining Order against you all and you have to pull every record, CD and cassette from every single store in America? You think that would cost $200?"

There was silence at the other end of the phone and then a sigh.

"Two thousand?"

"Try again. I mean this has caused 'reasonable market confusion' and has irrevocably damaged our brand. Also, to maintain our copyright you know as well as anyone that we have to vigorously defend it . . . "

I was irked. Maybe more so because of his assumption that I was some squat-dwelling Neanderthal for whom $200/$2000 would keep me steeped in meth and beer.

We settled for well more than that. More than I had made my entire time in Whipping Boy and more than enough to work my way out of the hole I had dug for myself when I went into credit card debt to pay guys like Bernie Grundman, lawyers to draft our letters of incorporation, pressing, printing, and mailing records that never sold more than 2,000 copies.

They had bought the right to sell what they had already printed. If they trammeled our rights again we could sue again for treble damages this time.

Footnote: years later while having a tea at the bar at Whelan's in Dublin during an OXBOW tour, a guy sidles up to me. Starts up a conversation. Makes some connections. Or had them already made.

"You're also the guy from Whipping Boy, right?"

Spider sense alight. "Yeah."

"Oh. I was friends with the Irish Whipping Boy . . . "

"They should have fucking changed the name. I gave them three chances."

"You ruined that band. They never bounced back from that."

"That was a completely avoidable mistake that they managed to not avoid." I sipped my tea; he finished his drink.

"Well . . . have a good show tonight."

"I most certainly will," and that night, before going on stage, I made sure I was armed.

Making it no different from absolutely any other night.

Death Was All Around Us

THE STINK OF IT. If you had gotten into punk rock in 1977, there was the first wave of deaths, kicked off by Sid, roughly speaking. But then over time, people who were not Sid were dying. Dave Insurgent from Reagan Youth, a friend and an unsung genius. His father was a Holocaust survivor, and father and son were constantly at loggerheads. His later junk use didn't help. Nor did his pimping his girlfriend out to the Long Island serial killer Joel Rifkin. Dave's subsequent death/suicide was added to the growing obit list, along with John Macias at the hands of Santa Monica cops. I'd seen John cold-cock an L.A. cop outside of a show in Hollywood and take off running only to return with a fake mohawk 10 minutes later.

Leon, Lazar, the cats from Flipper . . . the list goes on and sadly on, and while it was clear that the boat was leaving and some of us had driven Mercedes-Benzes to get there, it was not entirely certain what would happen to the rest of us. Yet at the end of 1985 the word had gone out that Van Halen had given David Lee Roth the boot and they were looking for a lead singer.

The skies parted and very possibly the least crazy of crazy ideas had made itself known: I was going to audition for Van Halen. Six degrees of separation style we all knew someone who knew someone, and why not? I had watched an endless array of cover bands do "Jump." I sang along as they did it. And "Hot for Teacher." It was this or a lifetime in a cubicle editing shit that people pretended to read while they stayed one step ahead of the Law who was chasing half the defense industry over the Iran-Contra deal.

I put together a tape. Me singing the above two songs and "Running With the Devil." It may sound ridiculous now but like Tina Turner once said, we could do things nice and easy but we NEVER do things nice and easy. "Hot for Teacher" sounded creepy as fuck. "Jump," less creepy, but no more "fun-loving," and "Running With the Devil" sounded like I totally meant it.

"We got your tape. We're going to pass it on."

My head was spinning. I told Bart, who was now a roommate, running his studio out of the upper bedroom while I still roosted in the garage.

"Really?"

"Yeah, man! They said they're going to pass it on!" I was impossible now. Counting chickens before they were hatched, oh, fuck . . . out of this garage finally and fuck, I could worry about the artistic ramifications later.

"Can I see the letter?"

I showed it to him. I strutted around the room. Laying out a revenge scenario. For? For everyone.

"Um. Hey man . . . it says that they're going to *pass on it*. Not pass it on."

"What? Lemme see that." Because, of course, that's exactly what it said. Which means: back to the death plan. Again.

The Death Plan

THE MINUTEMEN ONCE SANG a song about General George Custer who, they proclaimed, great Indian killer that he was, died with shit in his pants at the hands of those altogether worthy Indians who killed him. I liked the imagery, and more than that, I identified with the sensation of being both overmatched and having fucked around and found out.

In the grips of a sensation addiction that had stretched back to, yeah, 1977, at almost 10 years later, nothing was as I imagined it would be and discontent was mine. More than this, a resistance to going gently into that good night.

I've also been a merciless realist, and the reality was that everything in my life that constituted anything was nothing more than a lottery ticket. And like a three-card monte dealer once said when I asked him to explain the game to me, "No one who knows anything about life plays this game," I realized that lottery tickets suck.

Though I'd moved on from the defense industry to a gig at the Electric Power Research Institute and was living with my now-girlfriend (me being only occasionally unfaithful and being totally candid about those occasions), my magazine *The Birth of Tragedy* and the band had slowed to being only minor sensations.

"What's the difference between you and a scumbag?" This is what the girlfriend had asked me at the end of a broadside I had delivered regarding scumbags.

"The difference is I OWN my scumbaggery, while bona fide scumbags are permanently trying to conceal their scumbaggery." It was narrowly true but still I chuckled. She moved in. Then threatened to move out. She marshalled her family to help her do so and when they came by the garage, I sat them down and told them that the problem wasn't *me*, and she was welcome to leave any time she wanted. The problem was that her mother had been punishing her father by withholding *sex* for the last 20 years and this had caused a breakdown in communications that made her going back home with them part of the problem and not the solution.

Her father was the same professor who liberally used the term "wetback" until I explained that it was pejorative. I had some gender sympathy for him but being zigged upon was a cause for some upset when they expected a zag. So, while the current "romantic" situation was providing *some* sensation, I didn't think it was enough and I had routinely been torn between thinking I should force fate's hand and get married to their daughter or jump out into the great unknown.

Similarly, while things with Whipping Boy were moving along— tours with DC3, and shows with Social Distortion, UK Subs, the Damned, D.O.A., and Hüsker Dü—we were all mired in a liminal space between having done something seemingly significant and chasing that significance into total insignificance.

The third show of eight seeing D.O.A. play brought this home: how many times was I going to hear them sing about "Fucked Up Ronnie"?

I started to hang around the Survival Research Labs folks. Their "lab" was right next to where one of our record distributors maintained his shop, and both were next door to the Farm where we played our first show. Mark Pauline, in addition to having paid for his pleasure in blood when he blew his hand off, was a lifer. About 10 years older than me, it was clear he had embraced what Harry Crews, the writer and not the band, had called The Gypsy's Curse and in finding "a pussy that fit him" had no intention, need or interest in doing anything else for, just about, ever.

When I thought about working a Silicon Valley tech job at the Electric Power Research Institute—this was right after utilities in California had been deregulated so it was Wild West time—and though I had befriended the most degenerate guy there, I hated the job and refused to do a job I hated. I had no engineering skill, so I knew after talking to Pauline that outside of being a steady source of firearms and armaments I had no dog in their hunt, no matter how thrilled I was with the cult-y isolation and self-containment of both their aesthetic and their adherence to what felt to me like a newly created lifestyle.

I was lost.

The Birth of Tragedy still gave me avenues and glimpses of thrill. I interviewed sexploitation director Russ Meyer, his muse Kitten Natividad, Anton LaVey from the Church of Satan, and was communicating with mass murderer John Wayne Gacy for both an interview and an avenue via which he could sell his clown paintings. I was knee-deep, after having spent the last seven years taking karate, into Muay Thai, the deadly Thai boxing fight style.

I had picked up enough jack to get myself a 1967 Chevy Chevelle muscle car that I painted with a roller and steel paint in my driveway. A

The first time I met Anton LaVey, head of the Church of Satan. The lump under my bomber jacket was the interview tape recorder. It was raining outside and I didn't want to lose what we had spent two hours talking about. He praised me by interview end as being "satanic" and apparently I made a face that indicated I wasn't a mark so he explained, "I mean that in the good way." (Photo by James Rau)

flat matte gray, an Armageddon Enterprises sticker and a gun safe in the trunk, as well as a body that was fortified with steel sheets. Just in case.

But, yeah, I was lost. The girlfriend I hadn't been bullshitting didn't go back home. Josefine, my now-married lover, was asking me to murder her husband. First as a "joke" and then in that quiet space of "what if"s.

Of course now I was also, as a hedge against inflation, collecting debts for a bookie friend, while I worked my high-tech gig. I had stopped with the LSD, having grown bored of inner space exploration, and was deep into steroids, and a whole raft of questionable moral practices that flowed from having way too much testosterone inside of you.

On the surface, the film with Bill Cosby, the worst movie of 1987, the execrable *Leonard Part 6,* and the Miller Genuine Draft TV commercial with Gus Van Sant that would soon let me move out of the garage into a house, was a monetary boon, but money was never the balance around which my life swung.

Moreover, the storm that fueled all of this end-time ideation had started to congeal into a real plan. Like Caligula and his sister-lover Drusilla, I had concluded that a partner, a relationship, was the linch-pin that would make everything make all kinds of sense. Without it,

Me, disgraced America's Dad Bill Cosby, and George Abrams Junior on the set of the worst movie of 1987, Leonard Part 6.

continuing to live was a fool's errand. The professor's daughter wasn't it because, mostly, I couldn't see myself growing old with her parents. And Josefine wouldn't be because, well: murder.

Besides, if we were looking for signs, all of the college kids who used to live in our house had gone, replaced by guys who, we later figured out, had just gotten out of San Quentin. A house full of people starting and I had ended up with a houseful of people ending.

So, in my mind, there was really no other way. Since the truest love I had thought possible, that being Josefine, had fled, and the world had revealed itself to be irrevocably not right, I felt . . . make that FELT . . . the need to make a statement. I'd be cleaning my guns after having gone to the range. Alone, as I had asked my live-in to leave. I couldn't think with her always there.

Which, as it turned out, may have been a mistake. One of my main staff photographers from *The Birth of Tragedy* had been living in the house with me and the ex-cons. One day his alarm screamed to life. It was four in the afternoon. It kept screaming as I added my voice to the din while I knocked on his door.

"JAMES?"

Pushing it open, I yelled again. He didn't move. I threw his alarm clock to the floor. He didn't move. I made him for dead. Murdered? I wasn't sure. But I wasn't going to touch him with my hands. I pushed him with my foot. First a push, then a kick. Then I stuck a CD case under his nose to see if he was breathing. Condensation appeared.

I lifted his body up off the bed and dropped him back down. Nothing. Mystified, I left.

Later he explained to me that he had been shooting meth so he could work 72 hours in a row for a high-tech company and a boss he had explained the same thing to: his work rate was meth-fueled. And he believed he had a problem. His boss was classic Valley: "If *money* is a problem I can get you more of it!"

Him being a meth-head wasn't so much a problem for Valley bosses, as long as he was putting in those hours.

But he had started to slide. I noticed for real for the first time in the middle of an interview with Russ Meyer. He stared at a yellow legal pad the whole interview while taking notes. I happened to glance at the notes mid-interview and knew we were in trouble. Nothing said crazy like scribbled illos of eyes and knives and notes about the same.

And 40 minutes in he interrupted the interview to ask Meyer, "Do you have a bedroom?"

Meyer, confused, looked at me. "Well . . . yeah."

"Show it to me!"

We followed Meyer to his bedroom where the photographer instructed Meyer to get in bed where he took 11 photos of him before stalking out without a word.

I shrugged to Meyer and we finished the interview. Outside, when we took our leave, he was screaming by the car.

"YOU DIDN'T TELL ME HE WAS A PORNOGRAPHER!!!!!"

Meyer's soft, soft, ribald takes on tits and muscles had never approached anything that I would have jerked off to, so: not pornography. To me.

"Every woman I know has been raped. I was raped. By a woman, but still," he said. "I don't view heterosexual sex as anything BUT rape and he is the worst merchant of it."

We drove back home from Meyer's house near the Hollywood sign in silence.

Days later he woke me up screaming. Kicking at my door. I opened it and he stood in front of it, naked, screaming and making animal noises, then turning and fleeing into the rest of the house.

What had been something I was assiduously not dealing with was something I was going to have to deal with. He had purposefully dosed a friend with LSD as a "joke" and that friend lost his mind. As in: spent months in a mental institution. The weight of that result seemed to have caused a sympathetic reaction in him. Yet...

He came back, still naked.

"I NEED YOU TO CALL YOKO ONO!"

He had photographed Ono and Lennon on several occasions and had become a family friend. The thing that people always get wrong about "crazy" in the movies is that it's always played for laughs. Kramer on *Seinfeld* comes in, does something "wacky," cue laff track, cut to commercial. But in the wee hours of the morning a naked man making animal noises and waving around the phone receiver like a cudgel? About half as "funny."

He called and handed me the phone. It was probably early in New York but not strangely so. Yoko picked up the phone, right as he started wailing in the background.

"Yes?"

I hung up. The last thing she needed in her life was another crazy Hawaiian. So, I called his mother. She was sympathetic, understanding, and on it. Her plan? To send his father. I felt a certain amount of relief.

Two days later the father showed up. I had come home from work to find him cross-legged on my living room floor playing his acoustic guitar. Barefooted.

His son, still naked, ran around the house screaming. I asked the father what the plan was, and he burst into an improvised song that narrated precisely what we were living through right then. Like some kind of hippie Proust.

"Black guy . . . with a tie . . . wants to know whhhhyyyyy . . . ?"

The mom, the once-raped mom, had come up with a life solution to at least some of her problems: ship them both to California.

I kicked them both out of the house and in a moment of lucidity the drug-damaged and perpetually naked photographer told me, "Man, Eugene . . . that's kind of harsh."

"Listen," I said in what has now become an oft-repeated riposte, "If I'm the best friend you have? You're in big trouble."

But with them gone, a measure of peace and quiet returned to the house and I decided to kill myself. This was my death plan. You crest a hill and what comes into view is the total impossibility of any kind of future that makes sense until death makes sense.

The logistics were daunting. Who would find me, how would they find me, and what kind of explanation would I offer? I had figured out the rest of it, but the explanation seemed prosaic. Any idiot could leave a letter. Being a writer, this made a letter even more idiotic. No letter seemed excessively hostile. Or maybe not hostile enough.

I had accounts that needed to be leveled and finally figured out that a record would be the best method of explanation, and so started crafting the early strivings of what would later be OXBOW's *Fuckfest*. A tribute to a world where everyone was fucked over and fucked out of anything that made life worth living. Bart came in to record it, not knowing what he was recording. I played some basic drum tracks. Recorded some bass. And then had an awakening: bad music would obscure the message, in total, and I was no player.

I called Niko and asked him, who also had no idea what it was we were crafting, to help me craft my last message before exiting the planet. The record itself ended up being a dark tribute to what someone at *The Wire* magazine later called "an unspecified disaster." Disturbing and well beyond any theatrical angst, it was exactly the last message I wanted to send.

But if you've ever known anyone who speaks in tongues, you know that there is the speaker of tongues and the one gifted with prophecy who explains what all of the screaming is about. I had to designate someone who understood and so I picked our longtime roadie and friend Gabriel. Midnight drives through the hinterlands had led to a connection and I knew he'd know better than anyone that the death plan was the best plan.

I laid it out for him. At first cryptically and then a little more directly.

"Oh," he said. And then he stuck his chest out and launched into a pitch-perfect imitation of me: "KILL myself? You kill *YOURSELF*! I'm TOO HANDSOME TO KILL MYSELF!" He didn't laugh when he said this and it was a million times more effective than some "count your blessings" bullshit.

Beyond that, that night when I picked up the mail, there was a letter from England. A guy at a record label there had heard the record, thought it was phenomenal and wanted to bring the "band" I had decided to call OXBOW to England to do a few shows. I had never been to England before. Sort of thought this is something I should do before I died.

But I also decided not to die.

Now I realize what's more true than not is that there are a lot of people who deserve to die, a lot more than I do. This fact, alone, kept me going. Still keeps me going. Four daughters, two marriages, dozens of tours, records, TV shows, books, commercials, and films later, this realization still seems properly correct.

Or at the very least I'm happy enough to have ruled this out as an exit line. Thank fucking G-d.

For those about to OXBOW, we salute you. (Photo by Raffaele Pezzella)